CYBER CITIZENS

SAVING DEMOCRACY
WITH
DIGITAL LITERACY

HEIDI BOGHOSIAN

Beacon Press, Boston

Beacon Press
Boston, Massachusetts
www.beacon.org

Beacon Press books
are published under the auspices of
the Unitarian Universalist Association of Congregations.

28 27 26 25 | 8 7 6 5 4 3 2 1

This book is printed on acid-free paper that meets the uncoated paper ANSI/NISO specifications
for permanence as revised in 1992.

Text design by BookMatters

Library of Congress Cataloguing-in-Publication Data is available for this title.
Hardcover ISBN: 978-0-8070-1084-6
E-book ISBN: 978-0-8070-1085-3
Audiobook: 978-0-8070-2084-5

The authorized representative in the EU for product safety and compliance is Easy Access System
Europe 16879218, Mustamäe tee 50, 10621 Tallinn, Estonia: http://beacon.org/eu-contact

Dedicated to Andy Astor (1957–2000), dear friend, talented programmer and designer, with an offbeat sense of humor.

CONTENTS

INTRODUCTION   Our Internet Connectedness   *1*

PART ONE   **BACK TO BASICS**

CHAPTER 1   Flunking Civics 101   *9*

CHAPTER 2   Failing Digital Literacy   *20*

CHAPTER 3   Bad Digital Hygiene   *32*

PART TWO   **DEMOCRACY IN TILT**

CHAPTER 4   Mega Churches Meet Mega Think Tanks   *49*

CHAPTER 5   Hate Migrates Online   *63*

CHAPTER 6   Ad Tech   *79*

CHAPTER 7   Trillionaire Tech Overlords   *92*

CHAPTER 8   Surveillance: The New Critical Infrastructure   *109*

PART THREE   **PRACTICES FOR THE PEOPLE**

CHAPTER 9   Disrupters for Democracy: Open-Source, Blockchain, and More   *125*

CHAPTER 10   Bending to the GDPR   *138*

CHAPTER 11   Becoming Digitally Literate Citizens   *153*

CHAPTER 12   A Safer Digital World: Cyber Hygienists   *169*

CHAPTER 13   Correcting the Tilt   *185*

CHAPTER 14   Games for Democracy   *196*

CONCLUSION Cyber Sparks: Inspiring Informed Action *209*

A User's Guide for the Digital Age *215*

Organizations Supporting Digital Literacy, Privacy, Civics, and Activism *227*

Acknowledgments *233*

Notes *235*

Index *265*

Our Internet Connectedness

Humans have engineered and now inhabit a "smart" galaxy—a realm where being "offline" is rare. Our social fabric is intertwined with digital technology, forming a vast web of internet-connected devices and systems equipped with sensors and software. This network facilitates data exchange across a wide array of machines, from voice-controlled home speakers to complex systems like NATO's Integrated Air and Missile Defense. Powering this digital ecosystem are the arteries of the internet—cable, fiber-optic lines, and orbiting satellites—that have transformed yesterday's science fiction visions into today's reality.

We're a lot like our devices. Just as they regularly update with software to enhance their functionality, we humans continuously adapt to the ever-evolving digital landscape. We download new apps, navigate social media platforms, and stay informed through online news sources. Our desire for the latest updates and information drives us to stay plugged in, mirroring the way appliances connect to Wi-Fi networks for the most current data.

This interconnectedness raises questions about our autonomy and privacy. As smart gadgets are primed to scan, collect, and transmit information about our preferences and behaviors, we leave digital footprints that can be traced, analyzed, and manipulated, often without transparency or our consent. While internet-connected widgets send data back to their manufacturers or cloud servers for analysis and improvement, our online activities are relayed to and monitored by various entities, including platform owners, marketers, and government agencies. In the same way smart devices can inadvertently share our private information when not adequately secured, the way we handle our online presence can lead to unintentional data exposure or identity theft. By using the internet to navigate an infinite repository of knowledge and data, we ultimately create carefully curated digital personas of ourselves, blurring the boundaries not just between personal and public life, but between the physical "away-from-keyboard" world and a digital, global ecosystem of mutually accepted realities.

Just as internet-connected equipment experiences service interruptions and interoperability issues, we cyber citizens face disruptions that impede our daily routines and encroach on our freedoms. These disruptions, security gaps, and network reliability problems among humans arise from insidious forces such as aggregators, hate mongers, calculating corporations, and self-interested political actors. Their manipulation of information—from the highly intimate to the very public—to win political power erodes trust in democratic processes, from the electoral process to the peaceful transfer of power.

When we don't protect our data, we expose the broader digital ecosystem to cyberattacks. The commercialization of artificial intelligence (AI) amplifies existing threats: concentration of power in the hands of a few, perpetuation of algorithmic biases, surveillance and privacy invasion, and continued spread of mis- and disinformation. If that weren't enough, a history of AI misuse reveals its erosion of human decision-making, causing economic disruption and a fractured understanding of social reality spawned by domestic and international conflicts. Political parties become even more polarized in their echo chambers. The volleying course-correction and denial of mutually agreed-on facts incite either hateful action or withdrawal from civic duty. Among all the countries that host democratic elections, the United States consistently has the lowest turnout of civilian voters.

The electronic age compels us to balance the convenience of constant connectivity with the protection of personal privacy, security, and democracy. As cyber citizens, our best chance of thriving in the digital era lies in taking care of ourselves as diligently as we maintain our smart devices. This commitment begins with learning digital literacy and practicing sound cyber hygiene from the moment we first engage with technology. Mastering the fundamentals of civics—the rights and responsibilities of citizens—rounds out this democratic mission.

With AI and machine learning already transforming our twenty-first-century lives, we must embark on our own journey of learning and adapting. This new learning—our moral "charge" for the future—requires a different kind of cyber citizenship, one that is designed to save democracy.

All this to say, where do we begin to unlearn our ignorance about digital privacy and its relationship to democracy? What incited the shift to surveillance and rampant misinformation in the information age? How did we end up here? Where is digital democracy's ground zero?

Minutes after American Airlines Flight 11 crashed into the World Trade Center's North Tower at 8:46 a.m. on September 11, 2001, Americans flocked en masse to a newfound public space for information and collective mourning—the internet. News sites were inundated with visitors, experiencing three to ten times their normal traffic load. The surge in users caused much of the net to grind to a halt.

Fear and sadness mingled in a potent brew as a spectrum of feelings flooded online platforms, from condolences and grief (75 percent) to religious sentiments (61 percent); anger, hate, and fear (52 percent); and patriotism (46 percent).[1] In response, several websites emerged or were swiftly modified to provide updates and resources. These included missing persons registries and "I'm ok" message centers, along with internet billing systems for donating to relief centers like the American Red Cross.

Less constructive, however, was how the net relayed rumors and conspiracies. Hours after the attacks, claims spread that the attacks were an inside job, that the military fired missiles at the Pentagon and that explosives rather than passenger jets felled the towers. During the month of September 2001, the keyword with the greatest number of new searches on Google was *Nostradamus*, the sixteenth-century writer whom some theorized had predicted the attacks.[2] Even though the first-ranked site returned by Google—Nostradamus-repository.org—dispelled the rumor, it persisted.

Given the widespread popularity of early rumors, it was apparent that Americans had a hard time distinguishing online fact from fiction shared on the new borderland. This difficulty soon became an impediment to the thriving of democratic norms.

In the frenetic aftermath of the terror attacks, government agencies and corporate partners capitalized on the internet's potential as a mechanism for mass control.

The White House ramped up efforts to exploit the web for an ignoble purpose—mass surveillance. Swift enactment of the USA PATRIOT Act changed domestic surveillance laws, making it easier for government agencies to surveil and track citizens through their phones and electronic communications and activities. Federal authorities cast a wide net, amassing vast troves of online data about Americans. They often relied on major telecommunications companies to assist in collecting phone and other communications records.

World-transforming personal gadgets perfected this electronic surveillance apparatus. The iPhone 1 made its debut in June 2007, followed by Android 1.0 in September 2008. Smartphones offered direct portals into citizens' personal data and, consequently, their lives. In just a few short years, the internet shifted from World Wide Web creator Tim Berners-Lee's vision of "the decentralized, organic growth of ideas, technology, and society," into an electronic stakeout of epic proportions.[3]

Corporations capitalized on the emergence of new internet-based entertainment platforms, ushering in a digital renaissance that reshaped industries and captivated global audiences. Politicians benefited from these platforms. The first "internet election" took place in 2008 with candidates creating social media accounts and launching YouTube campaign videos. Silicon Valley— soon to be dubbed Big Tech, after economists predicted that if unregulated, they would consolidate market power—meticulously tracked users' digital footprints. Before long, data analytics companies would track user activity to influence politics.

Even as the full force of government and corporate interests descend on the internet, many individuals are oblivious to how their sites and postings divert attention from civic engagement. Users are overwhelmed by the deluge of misinformation circulated on social media platform posts, embedded and targeted advertisements, deepfakes, propaganda, and influencers. A note on terminology: *misinformation* refers to false or misleading information that is shared without the intent to deceive, often spread by individuals who believe it to be true. *Disinformation*, on the other hand, is deliberately fabricated and shared with the intention of misleading or manipulating others. *Fake news* refers to fabricated stories or news articles presented as legitimate news to mislead audiences or to serve particular agendas.

Information overload, also referred to as "data smog" and "information pollution," is both paralyzing and detrimental to individuals and society. In a 2024 letter published in *Nature Human Behaviour*, several scientists wrote: "With the internet at our fingertips with smartphones, we are exposed to an unprecedented amount of data far beyond our ability to process. The result is an inability to evaluate information and make decisions."[4]

Indeed, Americans seem to navigate through this deluge of information like automatons, lacking the cognitive capacity to distinguish fact from fiction. They've been slow to understand how influential actors exploit the internet to manipulate attitudes and behaviors. Each day, as 85 percent of Americans log on to the internet to spend an average of seven hours online, passive consumption erodes civic engagement and leaves us vulnerable to government and corporate forces seeking to exert control over us.[5]

Addressing data pollution requires applying critical-thinking skills to all online interactions. Since Phil Gilster coined the term *digital literacy* in his

1997 book of the same name, it has become widespread, and for good reason.[6] Public awareness of its essential nature is growing.

Strategies for the Digital Era

The reason many users fail to recognize online threats is their clever disguise in seemingly benign or even altruistic services. Take, for instance, web forms that promise convenience or safety but require our personal data to gain access to websites or to perform transactions. Algorithms further exacerbate this by serving tailored news tidbits, trapping users in opinion silos. Additionally, the incessant stream of notifications, with attention-grabbing sounds and visuals, effectively turns devices into miniature slot machines. This addiction to devices is fueled by surges of dopamine flooding users' brains. But the dopamine rush serves as a distraction tactic. While users revel in the momentary thrill, they unwittingly permit invisible adversaries—such as purveyors of fake news and hateful ideologies—to methodically erode their civic autonomy.

Our newest frontier, the internet, has sparked a raging battle to uphold online and real-world democracy.

The foremost hurdle in this battle lies within us, the users of technology. Psychologists attribute our susceptibility to misinformation to several factors, including our preference to take shortcuts in problem-solving rather than investing the necessary mental effort. We also tend to believe claims if endorsed by individuals we trust.

But digital naivete is not entirely our fault. Until recently, few educational and social institutions have taught the skills necessary to identify sources disseminating disinformation, fake news, and conspiracy theories. Caught up in the excitement of online connectivity, we tend to give equal weight to all purveyors of information and have been slow to build awareness of the inherent risks.

Internet-privacy activist and physicist Tim May, leader of the Cypherpunks—computer and cryptography experts advocating for cryptography- and privacy-enhancing technologies to bring about social and political change—wrote in his *Crypto Anarchist Manifesto* from 1988, "Just as the technology of printing altered and reduced the power of medieval guilds and the social power structure, so too will cryptologic methods fundamentally alter the nature of corporations and of government interference in economic transactions."[7]

In addition to early cryptologists' vision of encryption as a shield against corporate and governmental overreach, additional tools are necessary to identify and counter the forces threatening democracy on our digital frontier. These tools are the skills of digital literacy, digital hygiene, and a venerable discipline that has largely been abandoned in US classrooms: civics education.

Fortunately, these tools are well within our reach.

Cyber Citizens shows how democratic norms suffer when internet users can't distinguish online fact from falsehood, and how those who *can* tell the difference can help save democracy.

The following pages contain stories of Americans who demonstrate e-proficiency and confront populist threats to a pluralistic society. Digitally adept citizens can identify communications contributing to erosion of an independent judiciary, the separation of church and state, and the autonomy of executive and legislative branches. As responsible civic participants, they safeguard a free press, secular governance, and the independence of educational institutions and civil society institutions. Employing legal challenges, advocacy, education, and importantly, creative and fun online pursuits, they outmaneuver the tech titans seeking to dominate us.

A Note on Obsoletion and Sources

As technology evolves rapidly, some of the legal cases discussed here may be resolved by the time of publication, and certain apps, platforms, or businesses may become obsolete or have been absorbed by larger companies. Yet, the fundamental principles surrounding privacy, control, and accountability in our digital lives remain unchanged—and increasingly relevant.

I've relied extensively on the internet to access news articles, symposium recordings, social media posts, scholarly articles, and research studies. Many quotations are sourced from in-person interviews while others are from guests on *Law and Disorder*, a civil liberties radio show I've cohosted for two decades. I remain in awe of the vast resources at our fingertips. When used with care and diligence, the internet can be an unparalleled facilitator of social change, and a formidable ally of democracy. I have strived to use it responsibly, using trusted sources whenever possible, and double-checking less well-known sites. I take full responsibility for any errors I may have made.

PART ONE

BACK TO BASICS

A solid grounding in civics, digital literacy, and digital/cyber hygiene

CHAPTER 1

Flunking Civics 101

If American citizens were required to take a citizenship test, most would flunk.

In a twenty-question multiple-choice test modeled after practice tests for US citizenship, only residents of one state managed to pass—Vermont.[1] The survey by the Woodrow Wilson National Fellowship Foundation in 2019 assessed forty-one thousand Americans nationwide on fundamental US history facts.

The results aren't surprising.

Once integral to education, civics—the study of how the government works with an emphasis on the rights and obligations of citizens—is now a relic. According to the "Nation's Report Card," or the National Assessment of Educational Progress, as of 2022, only 22 percent of eighth- to twelfth-grade students achieved proficiency in civics.[2] In 2024, the US Chamber of Commerce Foundation released survey results showing that more than 70 percent of adults cannot name all three branches of government, the number of Supreme Court justices, or other fundamental democratic functions. Additionally, less than one-quarter of adults understand that freedom of religion is guaranteed by the First Amendment.[3]

For students going onto college, there's little chance to remediate this civics gap. A 2015 study by the American Council of Trustees and Alumni of one thousand United States universities revealed that only 18 percent require civics coursework or even one American history or government survey course.[4]

A lack of civics education has vast implications on societal vulnerability to propaganda and disinformation, potentially exposing many to social manipulation. The media and educational systems are key channels for information and decision-making. When citizens are uninformed about the balance of power among the three branches of government, and the media's role in accountability, they are less able to decipher political messaging. This vulnerability is being exploited by some on the far right, who push for politically influenced civics education agendas. Debates about school curricula in several states, for example, where discussions about how history and civics are taught, reflect larger political schisms. These debates often focus on how issues like racism, colonialism, and US history are represented, with significant implications for how young people understand their roles and power in society.

A cursory review of the history of civics education's demise shows it's been replaced with regimented thinking. As digital literacy becomes paramount on our new electronic frontier, and media coverage of political pundits demands critical thinking and nuanced evaluation, civics competency reemerges as an essential discipline.

Five Cents on Civics

Before the 1960s, it was common for high school students to have three separate courses in civics and government, according to the National Education Association.[5] Public classroom civics classes relied on textbooks, lectures, memorization, or recitation. These tools were designed to instill a strong sense of patriotism, national identity, and an understanding of the US political system to produce informed and responsible citizens.

School civics courses hit the chopping block after the 1960s, when federal policy shifted focus to math, science, and reading over social studies, history, and government. The 1965 Elementary and Secondary Education Act, amended several times, expanded federal involvement in education. The law's 2001 iteration, No Child Left Behind, ramped up state-mandated standardized testing. By the time the ink had dried on that bill, civics education dropped to the bottom rung of the ladder. The Obama administration's emphasis on STEM (science, technology, engineering, and math) further marginalized civics, neglecting crucial skills like news and mass media comprehension, vital for holistic cognitive development.

Harvard professor and political theorist Danielle Allen highlights the stark funding gap when it comes to civics: of the fifty-four dollars of federal funding allocated per student, a mere five cents is spent on civics.[6] This disparity is exacerbated by the booming global test preparation market, which bypasses critical-thinking valuation in favor of rote memorization, and is forecasted to reach $649 million by 2028, up from $489.8 million recorded in 2021.[7]

Students lacking an understanding of the importance of voting, how laws are made, or how to advocate for change may lead many to cede responsibility to a single leader to control their daily lives. In a concerning trend among young people regarding their attitudes toward democracy and autocracy, about one-third of young people aged eighteen to thirty-five support the idea of having a strong leader who bypasses elections and legislatures.[8] A Pew Research Center study backs this, finding that about 38 percent of Americans under thirty support nondemocratic governance models.[9] This shift in attitudes toward governance suggests that a significant portion of young people have become disillusioned with democracy's effectiveness to address their needs and concerns.

Standardized Testing as Social Control

Standardized testing, whether through IQ tests or College Board admissions exams, originated during World War I when the US military used tests like the Army Alpha and Beta to evaluate the emotional and intellectual functioning of recruits. Today's standardized school curricula—AP, SOL, SAT, and others—bear a striking resemblance to this military ethos. Both emphasize strict adherence to rules, disciplined execution of tasks, and a hierarchical structure that prioritizes performance metrics over individual creativity or critical thought.

Despite their prevalence, standardized tests fail to adequately measure crucial skills like news comprehension, critical evaluation of courses, and navigating the online news landscape. These abilities require a deeper level of thinking beyond rote memory preparation for multiple-choice tests.

Compounding the problem, some states attempt to address the civics education deficit by introducing even more—you guessed it—multiple-choice tests. For instance, in 2016, Arizona passed a law requiring high school students to pass a civics exam before graduating. The civics exam comprised multiple-choice questions that favored rote memorization over genuine understanding. It's a short-sighted approach. To pass, students cram to correctly answer sixty out of one hundred questions from the US citizenship test. As of 2023, seventeen states enforce similar citizenship test requirements for high school graduation.[10]

The Joe Foss Institute, based in Scottsdale, Arizona, has pushed nationally for the test, but tellingly, its Veterans Inspiring Patriotism program, in which military veterans visit schools so students can "interactively learn about the Constitution, patriotism, and the importance of being civically engaged," seems geared toward more regimented thinking.[11] Teaching patriotism is a dubious practice. It risks veering toward nationalism if it accompanies a sanitized history.

Amid America's standardized test–rich, civics-poor environment, a concern arises: what happens when a new teaching trend, branding itself as a civics initiative, emphasizes obedience to authority and conformity of thought, while stifling intellectual curiosity?

You Can't Teach Patriotism or the Will to Vote

The best place for kids to learn civics is at the dinner table or elsewhere at home, incorporated as one of life's important lessons along with basic social skills. Absent that, a next best approach is to integrate an appreciation for civics in all courses, and to do so in an engaging way that emphasizes critical thinking and not old-fashioned memorization.

It's just not happening.

A 2016 study conducted by the American Council of Trustees and Alumni (ACTA) of one thousand US universities, showed that only 18 percent of these institutions require students to complete any coursework in civics or take even one American history or government survey course.[12] This decline is attributed to a broader shift in priorities in which colleges have joined high schools in emphasizing STEM and business fields to align with job-market demands and to secure funding, leading to the marginalization of subjects like civics, humanities, and social sciences. Limited training for teachers is another factor that, combined with the others, can lead to uneven opportunities for college students to develop civic knowledge and skills, contributing to broader societal inequities in political participation.

This trend has sparked concerns that the diminishing focus on civics may have far-reaching effects on voter turnout. While many politicians and educators advocate for stronger civics education to increase turnout, research suggests that mandated civics tests fail to significantly boost the likelihood of voting among students, according to a 2023 study by researchers at Pennsylvania State University.[13]

Along with a push for stronger civics education come debates over the best methods to achieve it. Not everyone favors the citizenship-quiz approach. Some educators, like Joe Thomas from Mesa, Arizona, who teaches high school government, express concerns that a one-hundred-question test won't effectively engage students in civics education and will instead promote rote memorization over critical thinking. He emphasizes the importance of promoting civics education that genuinely engages students.[14]

Ongoing civics lessons in higher education that go beyond rote memorization could address the engagement concern. College-level programs often integrate interdisciplinary approaches, combining history, political science, and sociology to create a more holistic understanding of citizenship. For example, courses that incorporate service learning—a method that blends community service with classroom instruction—have shown promise in building a sense of civic responsibility and increasing active participation in democratic processes.

New ways of teaching are being introduced in some jurisdictions. Arizona's Board of Regents mandated university-level civics education in 2021. Given that high school students must already pass a citizenship test to graduate, mandatory college-level curricula can therefore take a deeper dive into civics. At the University of Arizona, Professor Suzanne Dovi and her colleagues are doing just that. They're developing the American Institutions and Civic Knowledge curriculum to include a survey course followed by an elective topic, such as American capitalism. Dovi will teach a survey course focusing on the theme of flawed democracies to equip students with tools to critically examine American institutions. Assignments include drafting a modern Declaration of Independence and conducting a "democratic audit" of the United States.[15] Other public four-year universities in the state are creating their own curricula to fulfill the requirement.

An International Lag

The decline in civics comprehension among teenagers is a global concern. Data from the International Civic and Citizenship Education (ICCE) study reveals a significant drop in the average civics knowledge of eighth graders in twenty-two countries from 2016 to 2022, with scores decreasing by 13 points out of 750. This decline pushed the average score from 517 to 504, effectively setting students' understanding of civic concepts and institutions back by more than a dozen years.[16]

The study encompassed approximately eighty-two thousand eighth graders from twenty-two industrialized countries spanning Europe, Asia, and South America. They represented a diverse range of political systems, from liberal democracies like Denmark to electoral autocracies like Serbia. While the United States did not participate in this study, the results closely align with those of the National Assessment of Educational Progress (NAEP) in civics, which also assessed eighth graders in 2022.

None of the countries included the ICCE study showed an improvement in civics knowledge, and six countries experienced a decline in performance. The remaining countries stagnated, a departure from the previous trend of widespread improvements and no country-level declines seen in the 2016 and 2009 assessments.

As for basic understandings related to voting? Slightly more than half of eighth graders across the twenty-two countries understood how voter privacy, voter identification, and the length of a voting period are interconnected with election fairness. Two-thirds of participating eighth graders demonstrated the ability to compare the concepts of direct and representative democratic governance.

Back in the United States, civics knowledge plummeted in 2022, with over 30 percent of eighth graders performing at a level *below* basic proficiency. ICCE and NAEP tests aren't directly comparable, but both assessments included questions on foundational civics concepts, the role of citizens, and the various forms and institutions of government.

The ICCE study measures eighth graders' civics knowledge, and assesses their behavior, intentions, and attitudes toward contemporary civic issues. These issues include environmental sustainability, digital technology, diversity, and equal rights. An encouraging finding from the study is that three-quarters of the participating students expressed their intention to vote in their respective country's elections once they become eligible. This is a notable increase from the 51 percent recorded in 2016. Students who achieved the highest two levels of proficiency in civics knowledge were likelier to express an intention to vote.

Military "Citizenship Programs" — Standardized Thinking

As civics education takes a backseat, Junior Reserve Officer Training Corps (JROTC) programs are making inroads into classrooms, armed with a mission, "To Motivate Young People to be Better Citizens."[17] Their reach spans over half a million students across roughly 3,400 high schools, military institutions, and correctional facilities.

These initiatives are redefining conventional notions of civic responsibility and civilian duties, such as voting, community involvement, and even engaging in discourse with those holding opposing ideologies. In JROTC programs, instructors prioritize hierarchy over fostering critical thinking and individual autonomy. And they tend to blur the lines between patriotism and militarism, equating the two in their teachings.

The JROTC program proudly touts itself as one of the "largest character development and citizenship programs" for youth globally.[18] Established under the National Defense Act of 1916, it operates in both public and private educational institutions. The expansion of JROTC in 1964, coinciding with the nationwide adoption of standardized testing, saw Congress broadening its scope to encompass all branches of the military. With approximately four thousand instructors, predominantly retired from active duty or serving in reserve duty or the National Guard Army, the program annually guides more than three hundred thousand JROTC Cadets through instruction and mentorship.

Many schools view JROTC or related programs as panacea for social and academic shortfalls, but without considering their downsides. As political rhetoric and violence grows in the United States, alongside a war-like ethos, it's not surprising that schools may look to a militarized structure for order. The Joe Foss Institute's Veterans Inspiring Patriotism program in Scottsdale, Arizona, for example, aims to teach students about the Constitution and patriotism, but risks—through having military veterans teach those topics—promoting narrow perspectives and sanitized versions of history. Despite the deficits of regimented, military training, an exposé by the *New York Times* in early 2022 revealed a concerning trend: thousands of high schools automatically enroll students in JROTC programs, often without offering viable op-out alternatives.[19]

While the military insists that JROTC isn't primarily a recruiting program, Rick Jahnkow, cofounder and board member of Project on Youth and Non-Military Opportunities (Project YANO) in San Diego, points out, "Testimony in Congress has labeled it as the military's most effective in-school recruiting program."[20] Around 30 and 40 percent of students who complete multiple years in the program eventually decide to enlist in the armed forces.

The JROTC curriculum's textbooks, steeped in military-based culture, contribute to recruitment efforts. Textbooks like *Leadership Education and Training* use a military model to emphasize "chain of command" as important to supporting the greater good.[21] *An Introduction to Global Awareness* omits the reality that military personnel are frequently deployed in non-defensive wars of choice, largely motivated by US economic and political interests.[22] Content related to Native Americans, Asians, and Latin Americans frequently perpetuate prejudicial stereotypes. In *Leadership and Ethics Naval Science 4 Selected Readings for NJROTC students*, Admiral Zumwalt recalls: "the most ruthless and cunning enemy I had ever had to face were the Vietcong women."[23] The phrase *ruthless and cunning* combines gender stereotypes and ethnic stereotypes. Textbook reviewers noted that all the cases and photographs in the book about leadership and ethics are military related; there are no examples or references to leadership in civilian organizations or in civil rights, peace, or feminist social movements.

According to Jahnkow, "JROTC educational materials are designed by branches of the armed forces to condition students to accept regimentation through military leadership and values."[24] Students are either rewarded or reprimanded, not only for their grades but for the military ranks they attain based on their ability to internalize military behaviors and perspectives.

Jahnkow advocates for a radically different approach to nurturing civic engagement among students, incorporating historical examples of when a lack of critical thinking, tolerance of diversity, and democratic processes resulted in significant societal problems.

We Want Civics!

Some students recognize the civics-deficiency problem. In one particular case, fourteen public school students in Rhode Island championed the virtues of a robust civics education. Their school, the students claimed, failed to teach them how to be good citizens. They wanted lessons on topics like the electoral process, political parties, and methods of civic engagement. Interactive exercises and debates, these students knew, could nurture problem-solving skills, and help them develop agency as they become eligible to vote.

In 2018, seventeen-year-old Aleita Cook, along with high school senior Musah Mohammed Sesay and twelve fellow students and their parents, sued Rhode Island's governor and education officials in federal court. They claimed that the events of the January 6, 2021, Capitol insurrection showed the potential consequences of inadequate education in government functioning and civic participation.

The legal brief to the court asserted that the Capitol attack was carried out by "a mob motivated by a fundamental misunderstanding of the Congressional role in counting electoral votes."[25]

Cook had never received instruction in government or civics during her four years at a technical school in Providence. Her experience was much like that of many other young people across the nation. However, she understood that without a solid grounding in civics, meaningful participation in a deliberative democracy suffers.

Musah Mohammed Sesay expressed his frustration. "I have attended the public schools in Rhode Island for my entire life and have not been exposed to how to engage sufficiently in critical thinking or even the basics of how to participate in democratic institutions."[26] He noted that his involvement with advocacy organizations had made him acutely aware of how school was failing to prepare him to be an active member of the community.

The lawsuit, filed by Michael Rebell from Columbia University Teachers College in New York and the Rhode Island Center for Justice, challenged a 1973 Supreme Court ruling that rejected the equalization of school funding between two Texas districts. The Court noted that "education…is not among the rights afforded explicit protection under our Federal Constitution."[27]

The Rhode Island students sought to establish a constitutional right to public education on par with freedom of speech and due process. But even initiating the legal challenge represented a significant step in exercising their rights as citizens.

Former Harvard Law School dean Martha Minow, in an amicus ("friend of the court") brief, highlighted the disproportionate impact of Rhode Island's failure to provide adequate civics education on low-income and racially minoritized students in comparison to more affluent peers in predominantly white districts. She noted that, "Disparities in civics educational opportunities leading to similar disparities in political involvement, disquietingly echo the de facto 'separate but equal' construct struck down in *Brown* [*v. Board of Education*.]"[28]

In June 2022, both sides in the lawsuit reached an agreement to strengthen civics education in Rhode Island. The *Cook v. McKee* agreement stipulates that the state's Department of Education will establish a civics education task force, including some of the student litigants and their attorneys. The task force will advise and assist the state in better preparing its students to be engaged, capable citizens. The Department of Education will also establish a diploma seal of civic readiness to high school graduates who complete a capstone civics project and achieve high proficiency in the subject.

"This agreement sets the stage for significant improvement in civic education in Rhode Island," said Rebell.[29] He hopes other states will follow suit.

Until then, one country demonstrates what it means to prioritize teaching civics and digital literacy on a national scale.

Finland's Exemplary Record

Finland consistently graduates high achievers in civic and citizenship education as well as resistance to disinformation.[30] Consistently topping international assessments of press freedom, transparency, education, and social justice, Finland sets a high standard even though the word *civics* doesn't appear in classroom curricula.

Finnish education prioritizes a clear vision of essential skills over a rigid, content-specific curriculum. It prioritizes thinking and learning to learn, participation and engagement, information and technology competence, multi-literacy, workplace skills, entrepreneurship, cultural competence, interaction, self-expression, self-care, and daily life management. Unlike the United States, Finland has no national testing.

Kari Kivinen, head teacher at a state-run college in Helsinki, recommends starting to teach critical thinking when children are young enough to read fairytales. "Take the wily fox who always cheats the other animals with his sly words. That's not a bad metaphor for a certain kind of politician, is it?"[31]

Secondary schools implement a multifaceted approach to information literacy and critical thinking, core components of Finland's national curriculum since 2016. In math, students learn how statistics can be manipulated. In art, they explore the manipulative potential of imagery. In history, they dissect historical propaganda campaigns. Language instructors demonstrate the many ways in which words can be weaponized to confuse, mislead, and deceive.

Kivinen emphasizes that fostering critical thinking, fact-checking, and information evaluation is integral across subjects to cultivate informed citizens and voters. That's because, as he says, "kids don't seek out news in papers or on the TV. Algorithms target them on WhatsApp, YouTube, Instagram, Snapchat...so they need the skills to approach it critically, not cynically."[32]

Finland launched its national strategy in 2014 after it was targeted with disinformation by Russia after invading and annexing the Crimean Peninsula.[33] Its media literacy campaign is overseen by a diverse thirty-member high-level committee representing twenty different bodies, including government ministries, welfare organizations, law enforcement, and intelligence and security services. The initiative has trained thousands of civil servants, journalists, teachers and librarians. Instead of the term *fake news*, the program uses three categories: misinformation, or "mistakes"; disinformation, or "lies" and "hoaxes," information that is false and spread deliberately to deceive; and malinformation. Malinformation, while not necessarily false, is taken out of context (i.e., time, space, or privacy) to convey a harmful message. Examples include phishing, catfishing, doxxing, swatting, and revenge porn.

"Even quite young children can grasp this," he said. "They love being detectives. If you also get them questioning real-life journalists and politicians about what matters to them, run mock debates and real school elections, ask them to write accurate and fake reports on them...democracy, and the threats to it, start to mean something."

Kivinen encourages students to delve into the origins of information: Who created it and why? What audience is it targeting? What evidence supports it? And is it purely opinion?

One student named Lila, sixteen, said she quizzed local politicians on the local radio station. Another, Alexander, seventeen, reported learning a lot from creating a fake news campaign. Priya, sixteen, described education as being "the best way to fight [disinformation]." Continuing education efforts are bolstered by non-governmental organizations. For instance, Faktabaari (Fact Bar), established ahead of the 2014 European elections and staffed by volunteer journalists and researchers, not only offers fact-checking services but also develops popular voter literacy kits for both schools and the general public. Each day, Finland's public broadcasting system releases news videos and media literacy tasks for students in first through twelfth grade. Approximately half of the country's teachers use the service. Its founder, Mikko Salo, a European Union independent expert on fake news, says Fact Bar provides tools so people can make their own decisions.[34]

In the run-up to Finland's 2019 parliamentary elections, the government launched an advertising campaign to raise awareness among voters about the potential influence of external actors. Its slogan was: "Finland has the best elections in the world. Think about why."[35]

America's national deficit in civics education compounds confusion from an information surfeit designed to manipulate the masses. If they lack a firm understanding of civic engagement, upcoming generations will struggle to exercise their rights. They won't be able, for example, to oppose restrictive voting laws, advocate for increased financial resources in disadvantaged communities, or hold their elected officials accountable, because they aren't encouraged from an early age to think more critically about how they receive information in their daily lives.

While citizenship education remains vital to the democratic process, the computer age has introduced additional imperatives: practicing good digital hygiene and honing critical media literacy skills. By mastering these disciplines, digitally literate citizens can collectively resist the undue influence of antidemocratic forces.

CHAPTER 2

Failing Digital Literacy

Humans have a complex relationship with information. Many readily embrace disinformation, conspiracy theories, and alternate realities. This struggle is underscored by a 2024 study indicated that Americans have a difficult time distinguishing statements of fact and opinion.[1] The RAND Corporation refers to this growing ambiguity as *truth decay*.[2] This phenomenon is marked by increased disagreement about facts, differing interpretations of data, an overreliance on personal experience over verified sources, and waning trust in once-respected sources of information.

A nation that lacks the skills to navigate the information overload of the twenty-first century is less resilient to challenge antidemocratic influences. The accuracy and authenticity of information can't be taken at face value, and "alternative facts," a phrase borrowed from former White House advisor Kellyanne Conway's notorious 2017 *Meet the Press* interview, aptly describes the circus-like ring in which anyone can present their version of the truth.[3]

Magical thinking plays a large role in this tendency, according to psychologists. This proclivity for irrational thought was a focal point in Edward Bernays's life work. The "father of public relations," and the nephew of Sigmund Freud, Bernays believed that humans are fundamentally irrational, conformist, and malleable.

Politicians and pundits exploit, with increasing sophistication and stealth, these quirks in our reasoning, and the fact that people tend to believe, and hence follow, what they're told. Demagogues manipulate human irrationality, funneling it into a perfect storm of anger, ignorance, and violence. They sow division to deter the populace from uniting.

Such deceptive maneuvers were a relative trickle in the analog world. With the advent of digital technology, they have become a flood of domestic dirty tricks.

When we can't agree on a shared reality, democratic discourse dies, as does all hope for an egalitarian society.

The Case for Digital Literacy: Compounded Technological Incompetence

The American Library Association defines digital literacy as "the ability to use information and communication technologies to find, evaluate, create, and communicate information, requiring both cognitive and technical skills."[4] It requires a holistic understanding of the online world.

In addition to the challenge Americans face in distinguishing between opinion and fact—a key indicator of digital literacy aptitude—many people have trouble with basic internet usage. According to the Pew Research Center's findings in 2018, 34 percent of non-internet users refrained from online activities because they had no interest, found it difficult, or perceived them as irrelevant to their lives. When it comes to specific skills like using a new tech device, 48 percent of adult respondents required assistance with setup and usage.[5] A mere 38 percent of adults demonstrated proficiency in navigating and comprehending complex digital tasks, according to a National Assessment of Adult Literacy study.[6] This disparity hampers their ability to navigate a world where tasks such as applying for jobs, accessing health information, booking travel, or scheduling appointments are more difficult to accomplish without a stable internet connection and digital savvy.

Furthermore, when it comes to navigating media online, citizens deserve to know how to find and consume content with an eye for biases, propaganda, and misinformation. That includes interacting with hyperlinks and related content such as videos, reader comments, pull quotes, and links to other articles. As they read, they can decide what to share with others and on what platforms to do that. E-literacy includes the process of finding articles: it involves knowing how to construct searches to obtain the best results. When presented with a list of sources, another layer involves discerning credibility and bias. These skills help prevent irresponsible sharing of material that is inaccurate or untrustworthy or is being used to confuse or manipulate others.

Digital literacy enables cyber citizens to engage effectively in online discussions about social, political, and economic matters. Adept users can share viewpoints and critically evaluate opposing ones, fostering a robust exchange of ideas essential for a dynamic society. They can navigate government

websites, participate in online forums, use digital tools to advocate, and petition to shape public policies and decisions.

A Case Study of Digital Illiteracy: "The Americans Believed"

The disinformation arena is made more madcap with troll farms, entities that
systematically interfere with political discourse. Troll farm operatives often use
fake profiles, automated bots, and deceptive tactics to amplify their impact.
They may masquerade as ordinary users or impersonate real individuals to
lend credibility to their messages. Often, they exploit algorithmic vulnerabilities on social media platforms to ensure their content reaches a wide audience.

During the 2020 presidential election, troll farm operations were highlighted by the activities of Turning Point USA and its affiliate, Turning Point
Action. These organizations engaged young conservatives in Phoenix, Arizona, to disseminate disinformation through social media about the electoral
process and the COVID-19 pandemic.[7] Some participants were minors acting
with parental approval and support. They were incentivized with payments,
including bonuses for posts that generated greater engagement.

But four years earlier, interference came from abroad. On September 13,
2017, Irina Viktorovna Kaverzina (also known as "Sasha") sent an email to a
family member saying: "We had a slight crisis here at work: the FBI busted
our activity (not a joke). So, I got preoccupied with covering tracks together
with the colleagues. I created all these pictures and posts, and the Americans
believed that it was written by their people."[8]

On February 16, 2018, the FBI issued a federal arrest warrant for Kaverzina's
alleged involvement in a conspiracy to defraud the United States. In late 2016, she
and twelve coconspirators from the Internet Research Agency (IRA), a Russian
propaganda organization, executed a campaign to sow discord among Americans. The operation placed targeted social media ads, often profane, threatening, and crude in nature. They inflamed tensions among various groups, including African Americans against police, Southern Caucasians against immigrants,
gun advocates against Obama supporters, and the LGBTQ+ community against
the conservative right. Ads encouraged minority groups not to vote in the 2016
presidential election or to vote for a third-party candidate.

The IRA relied on Americans' naivete and confusion, creating hundreds
of bogus accounts. A "Black Matters" campaign imitating Black Lives Matter
attracted more followers than the authentic one. Other IRA accounts mimicking popular social justice movements included "Blacktivist" and "United
Muslims for America." On the account "Woke Blacks," they posted: "[A]

particular hype and hatred for Trump is misleading the people and forcing Blacks to vote Killary. We cannot resort to the lesser of two devils. Then we'd surely be better off without voting AT ALL."[9]

Use of obscene language in these ads amplified feelings of anger and aggression. Yale University researchers found that when people read a message expressing moral outrage, they're more likely to be influenced by it.[10] Some go on to express more anger as a result of this design dynamic on social media. The IRA leveraged this psychological effect to enhance their messages' impact, making them more engaging and likely to provoke reactions. In turn, that led to high click-through rates. Their success in engaging users and spreading disinformation shows the potent influence of emotionally charged content in shaping public opinion and behavior.

The coconspirators maintained a stream of IRA disinformation—false information meant to mislead—for nearly four years. Central to their efforts were allegations of voter fraud by the Democratic Party. Between 2015 and 2018, Facebook linked eighty thousand posts from the IRA through nearly five hundred accounts. Meanwhile, more than fifty thousand Twitter accounts linked to Russian bots—fake accounts programmed to disseminate false information—further propagated their messages.[11] These bots were responsible for approximately 10 percent of all tweets related to the 2016 election, with 80 percent of them employing hashtags favorable to Trump. The IRA's objectives were clear: sow divisions within the US, undermine trust in democratic institutions, and target a significant portion of the American populace to disrupt their political processes, including the 2016 presidential election.

There's no evidence suggesting this interference campaign affected the election outcome. However, it did significantly damage public confidence in a fundamental aspect of democracy.

Faith in the electoral system sharply declined, a fact reflected in the events of January 6, 2021, when the US Capitol building incurred $2.7 billion in damages, accompanied by arrests and loss of life.[12] Polls consistently demonstrate that many Americans doubt whether election results accurately represent the will of the people.

A Case Study of Digital Illiteracy: Harm to Victims Deepens Fissures

Disinformation surrounding high-profile events has ushered in a decline in political civility. In cases of mass shootings, for example, it causes harm by distressing survivors and victims' families and fostering dangerous behavior.

The Sandy Hook Elementary School shooting in Newtown, Connecticut, resulted in twenty-six fatalities, twenty of whom were first graders. Some right-wing media outlets, including Clyde Lewis's *Ground Zero* radio show, propagated the false claim that the incident was staged with "crisis actors"—individuals trained to act out emergencies to help prepare responders, such as national guardsmen, firefighters, police, and EMTs.

On February 14, 2018, former student Nikolas Cruz opened fire at Marjory Stoneman Douglas High School in the Miami suburban town of Parkland, Florida, killing seventeen. Again, various actors stoked conspiracy narratives. Survivors Cameron Kasky and David Hogg, advocating for gun control, were wrongly accused of being "crisis actors."[13] News outlets like the Gateway Pundit, publishers of commentary and conspiracy theories, spread misinformation, while on *InfoWars*, Alex Jones called the Parkland shooting a "false flag" operation—a deceptive act designed to appear as if it was carried out by a different individual or group than the actual perpetrators—meant to push for stricter gun control laws, calling survivors crisis actors.[14] A National Rifle Association (NRA) program officer, Mark Richardson, contacted Wolfgang Halbig, expressing doubts about the shooting's official account and suggesting that the Parkland shooter was not acting alone, referencing uncertainties similar to those raised about Sandy Hook."[15]

The Parkland conspiracy intensified when Benjamin Kelly, an aide to Florida state representative Shawn Harrison (R-Tampa), was dismissed for emailing a photo and note to a *Tampa Bay Times* reporter claiming two students in a CNN interview, David Hogg and Emma Gonzalez, were crisis actors. Kelly supported his claim with another email and a video link sent from his official government account.

Response from the Parkland community was swift. Jaclyn Corin, the Parkland school's eleventh-grade class president, wrote, "We are KIDS—not actors. We are KIDS that have grown up in Parkland all of our lives. We are KIDS who feared for our lives while someone shot up our school. We are KIDS working to prevent this from happening again. WE ARE KIDS."[16]

Responsible journalism and factual reporting are essential in the wake of such national massacres to facilitate informed debates and meaningful change rather than to cement entrenched views. While the spread of fake news isn't unique to any political ideology, it is crucial for all media consumers to critically evaluate the sources they rely on for information and to demand accuracy and accountability in reporting.

Psych Out: The Rhetoric of Conspiracies

Conspiracy theories often contain language that plays on emotions, exploits uncertainties, and promotes distrust in official narratives. Some common linguistic features found in conspiracy theories and disinformation campaigns include the following:

- Sensationalism: Sensational language is designed to grab attention and evoke strong emotional responses from readers or listeners. This can include words like "shocking," "explosive," or "unbelievable."

- Exaggeration: Language often exaggerates the significance or impact of certain events or phenomena. Claims might be presented as "the truth they don't want you to know" or "the biggest cover-up in history."

- Fear and paranoia: Conspiracy theories frequently play on fears and paranoia, suggesting hidden dangers, secret plots, or impending catastrophes. This can create a sense of urgency and encourage individuals to take action or spread the theory to protect themselves and others.

- Demonization of opponents: Vilifying perceived opponents or those who disagree with the theory is a common tactic. This can involve labeling others as "part of the conspiracy," "puppets of the establishment," or "enemies of the truth."

- Pseudoscientific jargon: Some conspiracy theories incorporate pseudoscientific language or terminology to lend an air of legitimacy to their claims. This can include references to "quantum energy," "DNA activation," or "vibrational frequencies."

- Selective use of evidence: Conspiracy theories may selectively present evidence that supports their narrative while ignoring or dismissing contradictory evidence. This cherry-picking of information can create a distorted view of reality and reinforce belief in the conspiracy.

- Appeal to authority: Appeals to "alternative" or "hidden" sources of authority can include anonymous insiders, self-proclaimed experts, or whistleblowers with no verifiable credentials. This plays into individuals' desire for insider knowledge and can lend credibility to the theory in the eyes of believers.

- **Us vs. them mentality:** Conspiracy theories often divide the world into "awake" individuals who see the truth and "sheeple" who are blind to it. This fosters a sense of belonging and solidarity among believers while reinforcing distrust of outsiders.

Noticeably missing in conspiracy theories are credible sources, or conversely, the presence of claims that contradict established facts. An important part of digital literacy is reading with a healthy level of skepticism without falling into cynicism. Other red flags to look for are selective editing, out-of-context quotes, and misleading headlines.

New Challenges to Digital Literacy: Hallucinating and Deepfakes

Adding to the mix of twenty-first-century information confusion are generative artificial intelligence (AI) tools like ChatGPT, Bard, and Scribe, which produce text and assist in content creation. According to a 2023 Pew Research Center report, about one in five teenagers has used ChatGPT for schoolwork, and this usage increases to one-third among college students.[17]

These tools offer a valuable opportunity for teachers and students to explore the limitations of AI in the context of digital literacy. A relevant topic is the concept of "hallucinations" in AI, outputs that are inconsistent, incorrect, or lack context. Such responses may deviate from expected results based on training data, be decoded incorrectly by the AI's algorithms, or fail to follow a recognizable pattern.

AI hallucinations can lead to serious consequences if taken at face value. In healthcare, an AI system might wrongly classify a malignant skin lesion as benign, potentially leading to lack of medical intervention with serious or even fatal outcomes. In media, hallucinations from news-generating AI can contribute to spreading misinformation. These can be concerning for national security, especially in areas such as cybersecurity and autonomous vehicle technology.[18] To counter these threats, AI researchers are developing defensive measures, such as training models on a mix of normal and adversarial examples.

Adding to the arsenal of online deceptions are artificial intelligence–generated fake videos, commonly referred to as *deepfakes*. These sophisticated technologies manipulate audio and visual elements to create fabricated events. Social media platforms are fertile ground for such scams where they're increasingly used for malicious purposes, including political advantage, spreading disinformation, and disseminating "revenge porn."

One well-known example from 2019 involved a doctored video that falsely portrayed then House Speaker Nancy Pelosi as intoxicated, an alteration achieved by slowing down the video's speed to create a slurred speech effect.

In the same year, the AI firm Deeptrace identified fifteen thousand online deepfake videos.[19] A large majority, 96 percent, were pornographic, with 99 percent featuring the superimposition of female celebrities' faces onto explicit content, a practice known as "face-swapped pornography." Ordinary individuals, especially women, frequently become targets of deepfake abuse. Various AI tools and apps facilitate the digital modification of images, such as erasing clothing from photos or embedding faces into explicit videos. Typically, individuals featured in these deepfakes did not know about or consent to the use of their images.

Deepfakes have been misused in many ways, such as for grooming, harassment, extortion, identity theft, and bullying. While some might look convincing initially, discerning viewers can often spot irregularities in facial features, awkward positioning, or unnatural postures and body movements. Producing deepfakes is a labor-intensive process, resulting in most creations being fairly short in duration.

Between 2022 and early 2023, the number of deepfakes more than doubled, leading the FBI to warn about "sextortion schemes" in 2023.[20] In these schemes, criminals collect photos and videos from social media to create sexually explicit deepfakes. These manipulated images are often used to extort money from the victims.

Efforts to combat deepfakes have included introduction of the DEEPFAKES Accountability Act in 2018.[21] This law aims to require creators to disclose the use of deepfakes and prevent their distribution when they are intended to mislead during elections or damage someone's reputation. It would establish a task force within the Department of Homeland Security to analyze and mitigate the national-security impacts posed by these videos.

Despite its good intentions, the act's enforcement challenges are many, especially because bad actors can easily hide their identities and operate outside US jurisdiction, making it difficult to hold them accountable. The requirements for digital watermarks and disclosures may not be sufficient to deter actors with harmful intent, such as in cases of revenge porn or political manipulations. As well, the act's broad definition of deepfakes may burden legitimate users of the technology and lead to excessive litigation, potentially stifling innovation and creative uses of deepfake technology. It may be preferable to counter deepfake abuse through a combination of copyright, criminal, and state tort laws.

New Challenges to Digital Literacy: The New News

An essential bulwark against anger, misunderstanding, and confusion has long been the news media and a free press. Since the early 1920s, journalism has striven to uphold standards of impartiality, truth, and accuracy, as enshrined in the American Society of News Editors' Canons of Journalism.[22] Journalists were routinely fact-checked and held accountable for inaccuracies in their work. However, after the 9/11 attacks, a surge in nationalism influenced coverage of the government's response. Few journalists dared to question the official narrative regarding Saddam Hussein's weapons of mass destruction, fearing accusations of being unpatriotic.

While the rise of online platforms has democratized access to information, it has also undermined traditional journalistic standards, leading to a certain degree of recklessness among aspiring citizen journalists and others. Emerging technologies and social media platforms disrupt the traditional industry economics; they blur the distinction between journalism, opinion, propaganda, and disinformation. In an environment where sources, biases, and reliability aren't routinely scrutinized by discerning and computer-literate citizens, the negatives aspects of this new media landscape become self-perpetuating.

Mobile technology introduced a new era in sharing and consuming news. It has played key roles in political uprisings and live event coverage, with people moving from being passive consumers to actively participating in news creation and sharing. The demand for immediacy and sensational impact has, in part, replaced traditional editorial curation and oversight.

Exercising Digital Literacy: Watching the Watchdogs

According to *Axios*, a news site owned by Cox Enterprises, unreliable online news sites saw significant growth from 2019 to 2020.[23] Nearly one-fifth of engagement in the top one hundred social media news sources came from sources deemed unreliable by NewsGuard, a rating system for news and information websites. NewsGuard was founded by journalists Steven Brill and Gordon Crovitz; Brill founded Court TV and the Yale Journalism Initiative, and Crovitz was the publisher of *The Wall Street Journal*. As of 2024, its advisors include former homeland security secretary Tom Ridge, former CIA director and retired general Michael Hayden, and former NATO chief Anders Fogh Rasmussen.[24] Journalists rate a site's performance on nine apolitical criteria, each weighted differently with points for all adding up to one hundred, indicating the degree to which it adheres to the criteria. A site's score is displayed as an icon (green for sites that pass; red for sites with low scores) next to links on search engines and social media platforms.

But even NewsGuard has found its credibility impugned.

A Department of Defense Cyber Command contract for $749,387 directs NewsGuard to identify media organizations that publish known hoaxes, falsehoods, and misinformation narratives online. Consortium News (CN) argued that NewsGuard violated the First Amendment and defamed it by impugning the patriotism of its site and its writers with respect to content related to Russia and Ukraine.[25] The legal complaint asserts that NewsGuard issued warning labels to information the government disfavored, advising readers to exercise caution when reading CN and other news websites.

NewsGuard acknowledged its collaboration with Cyber Command, one of the DOD's eleven unified combatant commands. In a March 10, 2023, email, NewsGuard's cofounder Gordon Crovitz explained that:

> "[O]ur work for the Pentagon's Cyber Command is focused on the identification and analysis of information operations targeting the US and its allies conducted by hostile governments, including Russia and China. Our analysts alert officials in the US and in other democracies, including Ukraine, about new false narratives targeting America and its allies, and we provide an understanding of how this disinformation spreads online.[26]

The Consortium News complaint seeks a permanent injunction declaring the joint program unconstitutional and preventing the government and NewsGuard from continuing such practices. In its complaint, it notes that along with the United States, "NewsGuard... works to achieve a form of censorship designed to compel the removal of viewpoints that challenge policies of the United States and its allies. Labeling commentaries as "false content," "disinformation" or Russian propaganda, NewsGuard and the United States seek to silence or abridge debate and commentary."[27]

It Starts with You[th]: Introducing Digital Literacy Early

No longer is media literacy training the sole domain of specialized degrees, such as media studies, journalism, the law, and political science. After US

Surgeon General Vivek Murthy published an advisory about social media's impact on youth and mental health, emphasizing the need to incorporate media literacy into school curricula, prominent organizations have joined the call, including the American Psychological Association and the National Academies of Sciences, Engineering, and Medicine.[28]

As of 2023, eighteen states require the teaching of "media literacy" in public schools, with more bills pending. New Jersey became the first state to launch an "information literacy" mandate for K–12 education, with the state's education department creating a curriculum. Information literacy standards address topics such as the research process and how information is created and produced; critical thinking and using information resources; the difference between facts, points of view, and opinions; and the economic, legal, and social issues surrounding the use of information.

Parents can help their kids become digitally literate by actively engaging with their online activities. They can model fact-checking behaviors, such as examining the sources of shared media articles together and discussing the credibility of different websites. Openly expressing doubt and encouraging critical thinking about sensational headlines and opinionated statements can teach children to be skeptical of information they encounter online.

Just as we saw with a burgeoning effort to restore civics education in all levels of structured learning, efforts to expand media literacy to many ages and classes—not just in schools—are likely to follow.

In the years following Wikipedia's launch, skepticism was common among educators regarding its reliability. In 2007, six years after Wikipedia started, librarian Linda O'Connor took a stand; she created "Just Say No to Wikipedia" posters and displayed them prominently above the computers in the library of Great Meadows Middle School in New Jersey. Her initiative gained significant attention, leading to interviews with media outlets as distant as the *Inquirer* in London.

A year after creating the "Just Say No to Wikipedia" posters, O'Connor revised her approach, leveraging the opportunity to teach eighth graders a crucial digital literacy skill: how to validate sources. She changed the signage to "Wikipedia-Free Media Center" and began using Wikipedia as a teaching tool. She highlighted examples of inaccurate Wikipedia entries to teach students about the importance of evaluating the reliability of online information. Eventually, O'Connor removed the anti-Wikipedia posters altogether, shifting her focus toward teaching students how to critically assess websites in general. This change reflects a broader educational adaptation to the presence and use of online resources like Wikipedia.[29]

With more adaptive and creative teachers like Linda O'Connor, and with the many digital media literacy initiatives discussed later in this book, new generations of digitally literate citizens can remain resilient against antidemocratic influences.

CHAPTER 3

Bad Digital Hygiene

Residents of the scenic city of Oldsmar, Florida, population fifteen thousand, had no reason to suspect their water supply could be poisoned.

Yet on a Friday in February 2021, at 8 a.m. and again at 1:30 p.m., a hacker apparently used the remote-access software TeamViewer to breach the city's water treatment plant. The plant had set levels of sodium hydroxide, or lye, at a safe 100 parts per million—the standard practice designed to counteract acidity and forestall pipe corrosion. The attacker tried to elevate this level to 11,100 ppm. At that level, citizens could have experienced severe harm, from skin damage and hair loss to potentially fatal gastrointestinal distress. Fortunately, a vigilant system operator detected the breach and lowered the pH levels.[1]

Remote-access software is used for thousands of infrastructure sites, particularly in small communities like Oldsmar. TeamViewer is used on more than 2.5 billion devices globally.[2] Its ability to facilitate remote access potentially lets anyone with knowledge of its operation access users' data, files, and applications.

The FBI issued a report to operators of water systems, saying it was likely that hackers "accessed the system by exploiting cybersecurity weaknesses, including poor password security, and an outdated Windows 7 operating system."[3] But two years later, Oldsmar's former city manager Al Braithwaite clarified that, after further scrutiny, there had likely been *no* cyberattack.[4]

"After four months of investigation, a federal grand jury subpoena, and some interesting exchange from the general counsel of the EPA, the FBI conclusion was it didn't happen," he said. The incident, according to Braithwaite and the FBI, was likely caused by an employee of the water company.

And therein lies a big problem.

Internally caused incidents—whether from intentional sabotage or accidents—are as concerning as external attacks, if not more so. A joint study by Stanford University Professor Jeff Hancock and the security firm Tessian revealed that employee error accounts for 88 percent of data-breach incidents.[5] That's not surprising given that most employees undergo minimal training when hired and then only annual refreshers, which are inadequate due to rapidly changing cybersecurity practices. IBM's security research had a slightly higher number, 95 percent, noting that security teams are inundated with alerts and a growing number of tools to manage.[6]

Chris Krebs, former director of the Department of Homeland Security's Cybersecurity and Infrastructure Security Agency, highlighted the daunting task of safeguarding critical infrastructure. "Unfortunately, that water treatment facility is the rule rather than the exception. When an organization is struggling to make payroll and to keep systems on a generation of technology created in the last decade, even the basics in cybersecurity often are out of reach."[7]

Personnel responsible for operating critical infrastructure, spanning sectors such as finance, electricity, water, and nuclear energy, must uphold stringent standards of digital hygiene. The Oldsmar incident is a stark reminder of the consequences that can arise when individuals, corporations, and government agencies neglect basic cybersecurity practices, jeopardizing vital national services.

In 2022, the US Government Accountability Office (GAO) called for immediate action regarding cybersecurity measures for the "Internet of Things" (IoT)—products with sensors, processing ability, software, and related technologies that connect and share data with other devices and systems via the internet or other networks, including increasingly popular smart home devices—and other connected operational technology. Examples of the latter are industrial control systems used in power plants, manufacturing equipment, building management systems for HVAC (heating, ventilation, and air conditioning), and critical infrastructure like water treatment facilities. Emphasizing the urgent need for improved security measures across critical infrastructure, the GAO identified sixteen sectors as particularly vulnerable due to their reliance on internet-connected devices and systems.[8] These sectors are chemical production; commercial facilities; communications; critical manufacturing; dams; defense industrial bases; emergency services; energy; financial services; food and agriculture; government services and facilities; healthcare and public health safety; information technology; nuclear reactors, materials, and waste; transportation systems; and water and wastewater systems.[9]

Each sector was designated as "high risk" in the GAO's comprehensive report.

Digital Hygiene

Digital hygiene is a set of habits everyone should follow in the connected world to protect against exploitation of digital identity and associated sensitive data. Also called *cybersecurity hygiene*, it promotes a safer ecosystem. The term is recognized and used by various cybersecurity agencies, industry experts, and organizations, including the National Institute of Standards and Technology, the Cybersecurity and Infrastructure Security Agency, and several cybersecurity firms. Digital hygiene encompasses practices such as these:

- using strong, unique passwords or passphrases
- being aware of and cautious of suspicious links and emails
- regularly updating software
- installing antivirus software

Many consumers don't realize that the "smart" appliances in their homes—refrigerators, thermostats, light bulbs, security systems, and more—are potential entry points for cyber attackers unless properly secured. The "Internet of Things" has revolutionized how many people manage their homes and businesses, and good digital hygiene extends to these devices, as well as to phones and laptops. Without good digital hygiene, your house is wide open with a neon sign blinking "Welcome, malicious hackers!"

Let's begin with individuals.

Clicks and Consequences

In addition to holding the public and private sectors accountable for safeguarding our private data, every computer-using individual's knowledge of technology strengthens the health of the entire digital ecosystem. Even seemingly trivial data points can, when aggregated, reveal private details about an individual's identity, behavior, and preferences, making it crucial to treat all data with care and consider their potential implications for privacy and security.

One in ten Americans was a victim of identity theft in 2021, according to the Bureau of Justice Statistics, with one in five experiencing it in their lifetime. The financial losses from 2021's attacks totaled $16.4 billion.[10] The situation worsens as cybercriminals continue to refine their techniques. According to the Federal Trade Commission, there were approximately 2.8 million reports of identity theft and fraud that year—*an increase of 70 percent from the previous year.*[11]

Identity theft takes various forms, ranging from unauthorized access to a victim's financial accounts to the creation of fraudulent accounts in their name. It also includes impersonation for tax refunds or other benefits and using stolen identities for criminal activities. After such incidents, besides monetary losses, victims must deal with the headaches of replacing compromised Social Security numbers, bank accounts, driver's licenses, personal health information, and email accounts and passwords.

Soraida Morales was one such victim. She received an invoice for $399 for McAfee computer virus protection. Because she never enrolled in the service, she called the service number in the email. The technical support agent asked for remote access to her computer to reverse the charge. As trusting people do, Morales gave it to him and sat by watching the screen as the agent moved her mouse, downloaded apps, and entered code onto her device. With unfettered access, the agent then pilfered $3,000 of Morales's funds, money she was going to use for her wedding.[12]

Morales isn't alone. The FBI reports that in 2022, victims lost more than $31 million to tech support scammers.[13]

Mundane menaces confront ordinary Americans each time they log online.

Two grandmothers, one in Texas, the other in New York, learned this firsthand. Both were looking for love.

Yvonne Costales, a sixty-eight-year-old from the Houston area, decided to try the Tinder dating app. After swiping right, she connected with "Robert," who said he was fifty-seven years old and worked in Dallas. They texted and phoned daily. When she suggested they meet in person, he had several excuses. Even when she learned he didn't work in Dallas but was based in Turkey, Yvonne remained smitten—he was handsome and athletic—as he courted her for four weeks.

"In the beginning he asked me if I had any savings, and I said no, and he said, 'Oh, that's so unfortunate for you.'"[14]

"Robert" asked to borrow money several times to purchase work equipment or to help with family matters. He professed his love for Yvonne. "He said he wanted to make a life together and wanted to buy a house together and he said, 'Let me send you some money and you can buy the house that you want.'"

When Robert asked Yvonne for her Social Security number and other personal information, she did the digitally savvy thing that many older people fail to do.

She cut off the relationship.

Better still, she turned to Social Catfish, a California-based online investigation service. Named after the term for a person who creates a bogus online presence to trick others, Social Catfish helps users avoid internet fraud by running background checks, including social searches and reverse image searches. Yvonne learned that Robert's photos were stolen from a TV announcer in San Francisco. She filed a report with the FBI and stopped using dating websites and social media.

In New York, another grandmother also sought love online. We'll call her Louise.

Louise was seventy-two when "Thomas" asked to friend her on Facebook. Thomas presented as funny and worldly. They exchanged photos and communicated several times daily. Each time Louise posted something revealing an interest or passion in life, Thomas quickly replied saying he shared the same interest. He claimed success investing in cryptocurrency and offered to teach her how to do it. Louise sent $5,000 which he quickly "invested," doubling her money. Thrilled, Louise didn't think twice about wiring Thomas $250,000 from her retirement account to a different bank account in a small midwestern town. That's when Louise's sons spotted emails from Thomas on her open computer. But it was too late to stop payment on a third pending transaction. Louise's infatuation cost her more than a quarter of a million dollars, a sizable chunk of her life savings. And neither Thomas nor Robert was ever caught.

Yvonne and Louise's different outcomes show how even a basic understanding of online scams can protect one from financial and emotional distress.

David McClellan, founder of Social Catfish, notes that scammers are adept at pushing buttons to get what they want.

"Scammers have this playbook, they tweak it, they change the stories—they change the way they get money, and it's a constant work improvement."[15]

Confessing love quickly, along with poor grammar, not wanting to meet in person, and requests for financial assistance, are romance scam warning signs. Poor grammar is common, and surprisingly, it's an intentional feature and not a bug: by scaring off those with strong critical-thinking skills, it serves to help the scammer identify a promising mark.[16]

Elder romance scams in the US exact financial tolls estimated at $200 million each year. Apparently, only one in forty-four cases is reported, likely due to embarrassment. That suggests the problem is far greater than statistics indicate.

Older people aren't the only ones falling for online scams. The FTC reports that in 2023, 44 percent of people ages twenty to twenty-nine had a median loss of $408 to swindlers, contrasted with consumers in the seventy- to seventy-nine-year-old range, 22 percent of whom lost money to fraud.[17] When people aged seventy and older had a loss, however, it was significantly higher than that of other groups, at a median ranging from $803 (ages seventy to seventy-nine) and $1,450 (eighty and older). Younger users fall for online retail ploys, notably "pet and pet-supply scams" and bogus Amazon offers. Employment scams grew during the pandemic and saw an uptick in fake job offers that asked for users' Social Security numbers and birthdates. Phony check scams involve a con artist mailing a prize or refund "check," then following up with a request for some of the "accidental overpayment" to be returned.

Poor cybersecurity hygiene among Americans has profound repercussions on the nation's security, economy, and privacy. When individuals fail to adopt strong cybersecurity measures, either at home or in the workplace, their vulnerability to cyberattacks can lead to significant national financial losses through fraud or ransomware attacks, disruptions in critical infrastructure, and breaches of sensitive personal and governmental data. Such vulnerabilities jeopardize national security by potentially giving malicious actors access to government networks and critical systems. This collective oversight can undermine public trust in digital systems and stifle the economic advantages of a secure, reliable digital infrastructure.

The issue is not new; for years, experts have warned against using weak passwords, neglecting software updates, and falling for phishing schemes. Yet, people persist in using pet names for passwords, failing to update software, and opening attachments from unknown senders. They view their digital personas as detached from real-world repercussions. This disconnect fosters an environment where breaches, identity theft, and data loss are rampant. A critical challenge in cybersecurity emerges: how to bridge the gap between awareness and action to instill a deeper sense of responsibility and caution in users' online behaviors?

Corporate Carelessness

The corporate sector is a regular violator of digital hygiene. On July 19, 2024, a routine software update caused a record-breaking freeze across much of the world. CrowdStrike, a cybersecurity deployed by Microsoft systems, installed an update that analysts say probably skipped quality testing. The result disabled an estimated 8.5 million computers in perhaps the largest cyber event in history. Affected were Microsoft-powered systems critical to the online operations of banks, hospitals, police forces, major airlines, TV stations, and government agencies. Flights and surgeries were canceled, courts and government offices shut down, and new hacking vulnerabilities introduced, including for federal agencies.

Software-caused outages can be avoided in a few ways. Diversifying contractors and software options strengthens resilience and mitigates risks. By contrast, if everyone relies on just a couple providers, any single breakdown carries huge consequences. CrowdStrike, one of the nation's largest cybersecurity firms, exemplifies this issue; it counts more than half of the Fortune 500 companies as its customers.[18] Equally important is cybersecurity redundancy—multiple layers of security measures and backup systems that ensure continuous protection and functionality, even if one layer fails or is compromised. Although creating these redundancies may be initially expensive, they go a long way in maintaining trust between businesses and customers.

Around two-thirds of all known software vulnerabilities stem from memory-related security flaws, such as the misallocation or freeing up of memory spaces that can enable unauthorized access or the execution of malicious code. In early 2024, the White House urged the widespread adoption of "memory safe" programming languages such as Rust, Go, Python, and Java, which protect against certain kinds of bugs related to how memory is used.[19] Yet Microsoft and other Big Tech companies continue to use C/C++, which is not memory safe, alongside other languages because they are fast and used in developing firmware, programs embedded in hardware memory to help devices operate. It is worth sacrificing some convenience to avoid devastating security lapses.

We see disruptions daily as more consumers receive legal letters notifying them about data breaches that compromised their confidential information. Problems may stem from their rapid deployment of profitable new software to market without adequately testing for vulnerabilities. Other times, human error is to blame; companies may ignore stringent but onerous or costly security measures. Sloppy digital hygiene costs companies and their customers billions of dollars.

Cyber incidents divert a company's resources to remediation efforts. In 2024, the cost of a data breach in the US averaged $4.88 million *per breach*, according to IBM.[20] Costs can include legal and audit fees, ransom payments, lost revenues, remediation, and downtime. Customers and investors also bear part of the financial burden: 60 percent of breached organizations increased their prices shortly after the attacks.[21] And damage to their bottom line often ensues. Customers become wary. Credit ratings may drop, which in turn affects borrowing and credit rates. In 2018 Moody's Investors Service—one of the world's leading credit-rating agencies—announced that it would factor companies' cybersecurity practices into its credit-rating assignments.[22]

One of the most well-known industry breaches did, in fact, result in a 2019 credit-rating drop by Moody's. In 2018, Equifax experienced a breach, unprecedented in scope and severity. As one of the nation's three largest credit-reporting agencies, Equifax holds vast troves of Americans' sensitive personal data. Hackers exploited a known vulnerability, stealing sensitive data like Social Security numbers from the company's US online dispute portal, potentially exposing 143 million Americans, or more than 40 percent of the population, to identity theft and fraud.[23] Those who didn't change their passwords were especially vulnerable to their information being accessed and misused.

Equifax wasn't alone in the consumer reporting industry for subpar cybersecurity practices. From 2013 to 2016, Experian and TransUnion also experienced breaches, exposing millions of individuals' confidential and personally identifying information. The Equifax breach was largely due to a failure to patch a known software vulnerability, weak security practices, inadequate encryption, poor monitoring and detection, and organizational failures. Experian's breach involved a compromise through a third-party vendor, weak access controls, insufficient incident response preparedness, and inadequate security awareness among employees. Similarly, the TransUnion breach was characterized by vulnerabilities in their security infrastructure, insufficient monitoring, and delayed response to detected threats.

In addition to daily corporate breaches, government data breaches are frequent occurrences. The US Office of Personnel Management data breach in 2015 compromised the personal data of approximately twenty-one million current and former federal employees and their families. Attributed to a Chinese cyber espionage group, the stolen data included sensitive details such as Social Security numbers, fingerprints, and background investigation records.[24]

Breaches happen not just from malicious actors but also from third-party contractors that government agencies rely on. In a Department of Homeland Security data breach discovered in 2017, a contractor's compromised system led to the exposure of personally identifiable information of approximately 246,000 DHS employees.[25]

Outdated computers and software—another red flag for digital hygiene—also plague government systems, as one incident at a federal air force base revealed.

Aging Government Computers

Individuals and the corporate sector aren't the only poor hygienists. Government agencies are frequently hindered by legacy (old and outdated) software and hardware, bureaucratic inertia, and inadequate training and compliance systems. All those factors make them vulnerable to attacks.

Francis E. Warren Air Force Base, less than three miles west of downtown Cheyenne, Wyoming, is one of three strategic intercontinental ballistic missile (ICBM) bases in the United States. LGM-30G Minuteman III missiles are stored and deployed from silos in missile alert facilities, and each has a buried and hardened launch control center and an aboveground launch control support building.

The more than six-thousand-acre facility at Warren AFB is toxic. It is listed as a Superfund site because the land is contaminated from prior operations and disposal of hazardous chemicals. Nearby residents exposed to decades of toxic groundwater contamination and vapor plumes face serious health issues.

Posing another kind of risk are the 90th Missile Wing's computers: the mainframe dates to the John F. Kennedy administration. *It uses eight-inch floppy disks.*

At 1:30 a.m. on October 23, 2010, launch officers at Warren AFB lost contact with fifty Minuteman III missiles, as LFDN (for "Launch Facility Down") popped up on their monitors. Officers couldn't communicate with their missiles for one hour.[26]

When communication was restored remotely by computer, they found the missiles safe in their silos. An improperly installed circuit card, dislodged by vibration and heat, was responsible for sending the faulty messages to the missiles.

The missile system had jammed.

The air force publicly ruled out a cyberattack on the nuclear command-and-control system. But a 2013 Defense Science Board report found that the Pentagon's computer networks were "built on inherently insecure architectures that are composed of, and increasingly using, foreign parts."[27] The board had deployed "red teams"—security experts who simulate attacker techniques to evaluate an organization's security posture—to disrupt the systems to identify critical vulnerabilities. The report recommended that more red team simulations and other proactive measures be implemented to continually assess and enhance the security posture of military networks.

Former missile officers contacted the television show *60 Minutes* about old computer systems at the base, and the program aired a segment on it in 2014.[28]

Many other federal agencies use IT systems running decades-old COBOL and Fortran programming languages, or even computers from the 1970s. Despite spending more than $80 billion annually on IT, agencies devote about 75 percent of their IT budgets to maintain existing or legacy systems. Replacement parts are difficult to find. This is part of a long-term crisis of national infrastructure underdevelopment.

Former US Chief Information Officer Tony Scott oversaw the federal government's computing infrastructure under the Obama administration. Trying to make current computers safe from hacking, says Scott, is like trying to put airbags in an old car.[29]

A Government Accountability Office (GAO) report noted that it would be better to upgrade systems rather than pour funds into maintaining old equipment. Even though the White House has pushed to modernize systems, the budget for doing so dropped to $7 billion less in 2017 than in 2010.[30] Problems pervade federal agencies, such as the Treasury Department, which has the oldest system, dating back to 1960, whose outdated computer language is difficult to write and maintain. The GAO estimates that the government spent at least $80 billion on information technology in 2015.[31] But the total could be higher. Not counted in the report are certain Pentagon systems and independent agencies such as the CIA. In government jargon, major federal IT systems are called "IT investments."[32] And these investments are becoming obsolete, according to the GAO report. "The federal government runs the risk of continuing to maintain investments that have outlived their effectiveness and are consuming resources that outweigh their benefits."[33] These legacy systems, both hardware and software, were purchased with the expectation that they would last a long time. In the age of planned obsolescence, however, the concept of relying on legacy technology as IT investments has also passed its prime.

In late 2018, Congress announced an investment of $90 billion to modernize the 1950s ICBMs.[34] Regulators rely on information in the US Department of Transportation's Hazardous Materials Information Center to track incidents. In 2023, the system was about fifty-three years old, and some of its software was no longer supported by vendors. The Department of Defense's system that coordinates nuclear force using eight-inch floppies was sixty years old in 2023.

Microsoft's Grip on Government IT Systems

While legacy problems put the nation at risk, equally concerning is industry's grip on government contracting. This affects both the private and public sectors' hygiene lapses.

A leaked memo dated August 16, 2023, from White House national security adviser Jake Sullivan to US Cabinet secretaries highlighted the failure of several government agencies to comply with the Biden administration's 2021 cybersecurity executive order, which mandates agencies to modernize and strengthen their cybersecurity practices.[35] The memo outlines the government's persistent challenges in upgrading its IT infrastructure to defend against cyber threats. The predicament is exacerbated by uncompetitive technology contracts and procurement processes that hinder innovation, choice, and ultimately, national security.

From 2014 to 2022, a spate of cyberattacks has cost nearly $26 billion to local, state, and federal agencies.[36] One of the most notable breaches was discovered in 2020 with the hack of Solar Winds, an IT management software company compromising the data of more than thirty thousand organizations. The blame for these vulnerabilities lies with entrenched, interdependent legacy IT companies and the dynamics that perpetuate their dominance.

Among these legacy providers, Microsoft holds 85 percent of the federal government productivity software market.[37] Microsoft's software failures and unwillingness to improve product security are responsible for the lion's share of the vulnerabilities cataloged by the Cybersecurity and Infrastructure Security Agency in its *Known Exploited Vulnerabilities Catalog*.[38]

And yet, many agencies lack the ability or incentive to switch. A research report by the trade association NetChoice revealed that government software providers use a practice called "vendor lock."[39] They use restrictive licensing and punitive audits to thwart competition among comparable software providers and force government customers into a cycle of renewals and upcharges. For years, legacy IT providers have leveraged these anticompetitive business tactics to create an IT monoculture across federal government agencies. They have blocked competitors, hindered innovation, and prevented the government from accessing cutting-edge cybersecurity technology.

Regulators, government agencies, and public officials are finally responding to these practices. US and EU regulators have initiated investigations into issues like vendor lock, restrictive licensing, and related anticompetitive practices.[40] It also appears that the latest major cyberattacks to hit the US government—in which Chinese hackers infiltrated dozens of government email accounts—was the tipping point for congressional leaders, including Senator Ron Wyden. After the hack, he wrote to the Justice Department, FTC chair Lina Khan, Cybersecurity and Infrastructure Security Agency (CISA) director Jen Easterly, and others, arguing that "negligent cybersecurity practices... enabled a successful Chinese espionage campaign against the United States government."[41]

In December 2022, the 90th Missile Wing continued modernization efforts on the Minuteman III ICBM system with the start of launch control center block upgrades at the Kilo-01 missile alert facility near Dix, Nebraska. The block upgrade program will replace antiquated or obsolete equipment and support the weapon system with newer technology. Floppy disc drives will finally be replaced with flash data drives.

School Districts: The New Bullseye for Attacks

School districts, considered a part of local government, are prime targets for cyberattacks. They hold sensitive data on students, teachers, and staff, including information on allergies, suspensions, household income, and court orders.

After being hit with a cyberattack in November 2017, Stillman College in Tuscaloosa, Alabama, had to shut down its campus and manage its finance accounting, registration, and financial aid manually for nearly nine months.[42] Support arrived from the West Virginia Independent Enterprise Consortium, a collaboration of higher-education institutions that share servers, software licenses, and technical personnel, while maintaining exclusive access to their own data. Following this support, Stillman launched its own cybersecurity clinic as part of the Consortium of Cybersecurity Clinics.

Most public school administrators don't practice sound digital hygiene, risking exposing approximately fifty-three million K–12 students to costly disruptions.[43] Until recently, few used two-factor authentication, and many relied on outdated "legacy" equipment, third-party contracts, and inexperienced staff. From January 2023 through June 2024, at least eighty-three potential ransomware attacks on school districts were reported, according to CBS News.[44]

Compounding these problems, the very IT professionals contracted to protect computer systems cause at least 75 percent of data-breach incidents in public K–12 school districts.[45] According to Rotem Iram, CEO and cofounder of At-Bay, a cybersecurity insurance provider in California, the reliance on different tech vendors means that something, somewhere, is always broken.[46]

More help is needed, such as incentives for obtaining insurance policies; it's difficult for schools to qualify for cyber insurance without sound security systems in place. Even when they do, the cost of remediation may be prohibitive.

Myth of the Digital Native

Speaking of school districts, we all know how parents and grandparents ask their children and grandkids for help with technology. But how much do kids really know? We don't have national standards for cyber-hygiene education. We're stumbling along in trying to find effective ways to teach it.

The term *digital native* is often used when describing a young person who has grown up surrounded by digital technology. It suggests that because these individuals have never known a world without the internet, smartphones, or social media, they innately possess a deeper understanding of digital landscapes and proficiency in using these tools. But the idea that age alone confers digital literacy is misleading. The myth oversimplifies the complexities of digital literacy and falsely assumes that exposure to technology equates to understanding.

This misconception masks the genuine vulnerabilities that young people face online, from cyberbullying to misinformation. They may assume that their tech proficiency makes them immune. As a result, many young people may underestimate the threats posed by malware, phishing, and data breaches. This lack of critical thinking in the digital realm, combined with naivete about safety and ethics, is even more reason they need a solid grounding in online media literacy and cybersecurity best practices.

Many teenagers can fluidly navigate social media platforms like TikTok, Snapchat, or Instagram, uploading and editing videos or photos with ease. Yet, when faced with evaluating the credibility of an online news article or understanding the nuances of online privacy settings, they may struggle. A study from Stanford Graduate School of Education in 2016 found that students, from middle school to college, often had difficulty distinguishing between credible information and fake news or advertisements online.[47] Just because they were comfortable using digital platforms didn't mean they had the critical thinking skills to discern trustworthy sources from unreliable ones.

On the hardware side, while many young people can intuitively operate laptops and smartphones, this doesn't necessarily translate to broader technical competencies. An educator might assume that students, as "digital natives," would know how to use word processing software or a spreadsheet. Yet, many educators must teach these basics. Just as one wouldn't assume that someone who can play a video game can automatically code a website, proficiency in one digital domain doesn't guarantee proficiency in another.

The digital-native myth can also marginalize those who don't fit the stereotype. Many young people, particularly in underserved communities, have limited access to the latest technology or high-speed internet, putting them at a disadvantage. The assumption that they should "naturally" understand these tools can lead to further disparities in digital hygiene training.

While younger generations may be more adaptable or comfortable in digital environments because of early exposure, this doesn't guarantee that they will fully understand all aspects of the digital world. The digital-native concept overly simplifies the complexities of digital literacy and hygiene, while deflecting the onus of systemic inaction onto young individuals. It's essential for parents and educators to recognize the importance of teaching cyber hygiene at the same time they provide kids with a computer, a tablet, or another digital device yet to be realized.

Equally important, people of all ages need to be aware of the different online threats to democracy. Part 2 explores several of these powerful forces: ad tech, white radical nationalism, trillionaire tech monopolies, and widespread mass surveillance.

PART TWO

DEMOCRACY IN TILT

Absent a foundational understanding of civics and digital literacy and hygiene, individuals are ill prepared to recognize online threats, advocate for their rights, and engage in informed decision-making. Over time, this inability undermines the health of our democratic society and personal freedoms.

Prominent threats to our democracy include tech monopolies, online hate-mongering, advertising technology (ad tech), and mass surveillance. Tech monopolies can stifle innovation, limit consumer choices, and wield excessive influence over public discourse and policy. Online hate proliferates in digital spaces, imperiling social cohesion and individual well-being. Ad-tech practices often exploit user data without informed consent, leading to privacy invasions and manipulation. Mass surveillance by governments and corporations erodes civil liberties and creates a climate of constant monitoring and control.

Let's explore the extent of these threats and how to recognize them.

CHAPTER 4

Mega Churches Meet Mega Think Tanks

The term *think tank*, originally used during World War I to describe secure venues for discussing military strategies, began to be associated with non-profit policy research organizations by the 1960s. These early think tanks were established to professionalize government and advance the public interest through impartial advice. Notable examples include the Carnegie Endowment for International Peace, founded in 1910, and the RAND Corporation, founded in 1948.

By the 1970s, however, conservative think tanks began shifting their focus toward promoting their pro-business, small-government ideology to policymakers, exemplified by organizations like the Heritage Foundation, founded in 1973. In 1981, Heritage published *Mandate for Leadership: Policy Management in a Conservative Administration*, a guide for the incoming Reagan administration designed to reduce the size of government and encourage renewed interest in capitalism and free-market principles.[1] According to Jason Stahl, author of *Right Moves: The Conservative Think Tank in American Political Culture Since 1945*, these think tanks were instrumental in breaking away from policies of New Deal liberalism.[2] They also differed from their predecessors by actively engaging in shaping public opinion and directly influencing policy, especially through media and lobbying.

As political divisions intensified, beginning in the 1970s and escalating in the 2000s, a wave of "pseudo" think tanks emerged. Divisions stemmed from a realignment of party loyalties, particularly in the South, and the rise of cultural and social issues as key political battlegrounds. Partisan media arrived, coupled with more polarized rhetoric and campaign strategies. Political affiliation become central to one's identity, making differences feel personal, which exacerbated societal polarization. The American Enterprise Institute grew from a staff of 24 and a budget of $1 million in 1969 to a staff of 125 and a budget of $7 million in 1978.[3]

Yet many of these institutions over the decades have shifted from altruistic purposes to self-serving ones. Rather than offering research-based information for policy making, they seek to sway public opinion to serve the interests of a privileged few. By 2020, with more than two thousand think tanks in the United States, right-leaning ones gained momentum, outnumbering their liberal and nonpartisan counterparts by a ratio of two to one.[4] Staunch conservative supporters with deep pockets recognized the potential influence these organizations can wield.

The latest iteration of think tanks is banding together to form large and powerful networks that can be identified as conservative mega think tanks. A unified voice affords them a competitive edge in shaping public policy. Associations such as the Atlas Network, the State Policy Network, and the American Legislative Exchange Council (ALEC), wield significantly more power than many smaller, independent think tanks by pooling resources, experts, and networks, creating a formidable force in public advocacy. Substantial funding from corporations, wealthy donors, and foundations aligned with their pro-business, small-government ideologies has allowed conservative mega think tanks to maintain a robust presence in Washington, DC, with the ability to fund extensive research, lobbying efforts, and media campaigns.

Conservative think tanks have traditionally had more cohesive funding, better coordination, and greater historical influence. Liberal think tanks, on the other hand, got a later start. Their work is often remedial in nature, with a focus on social justice and equality issues, in direct opposition to the pro-business, deregulation-focused agendas championed by their rightist counterparts. Groups seeking to restore economic fairness, like the Economic Policy Institute, founded in 1986, and groups supporting democratic governance, such as the Brennan Center for Justice, founded in 1995, have allies in the Center for American Progress, founded in 2003, and the Century Foundation (founded in 1919, but with its status elevated in the nineties and early aughts after gaining attention for its influential research on welfare reform, healthcare, and educational equity).

The growth of mega think tanks mirrors the rise of mega churches in the United States, which, according to the Council for Secular Humanism's former executive director Tom Flynn, have more than quadrupled since the late 1990s.[5] Mega churches are defined by a membership of 2,000 people or more; in 2024, there were approximately 1,800 such institutions.[6] Examples include Lakewood Church in Houston, Texas, with 45,000 weekly attendees, and Saddleback Church in California, with 30,000 weekly attendees across multiple campuses. These large congregations largely align with conservative values promoting prosperity theology: the belief that God's blessings,

particularly through financial contributions to the church, can increase individual wealth. Emerging as they did around the same time, these large think
tanks and church conglomerations offer a broader strategy for influencing
the public square.

Mega think tanks adopt church-like methods to build their support base
by appealing on social media to individuals seeking a larger community of
like-minded thinkers. Tailored messages appeal to online users searching
for meaning, identity, and purpose, mirroring the approaches used by white
nationalists. These think tank associations also publish opinion pieces, issue
policy recommendations, hold conferences, and organize public speaking
events. As a result, they have become what some researchers call "digital advocators."[8] They forge close relationships online with the public, media, and
government leadership in a way that is extremely cost-effective compared to
methods used in previous eras of recruitment.

Hiding Behind Tax Status

Think tanks typically register as nonprofit organizations under section 501(c)
(3) of the IRS tax code, which imposes restrictions on political activities. To
bypass these limits, many groups often shift some operations to 501(c)(4) status. This allows them to engage directly in lobbying and advocacy activities
without disclosing the names of their donors, a practice that uses what is
commonly known as *dark money*. Legal issues arise if a (c)(4) engages in
activities that require public disclosure, such as hiring a lobbyist, yet fails to
do so. Lobbyists typically must disclose the nonprofits as their client, and
nonprofits may need to file client reports. Fraud can occur if a 501(c)(4) do-
nates to an entity like a super PAC that should disclose its donors but does
not. Major contributors, such as Americans for Prosperity and the Super PAC
Crossroads GPS, often leave most voters in the dark about their true sources
of funding and their influence of political campaigns and advocacy efforts.[7]

An example of a white-leaning think tank is the National Policy Institute (NPI), which gained attention for espousing white power ideals under
the guise of academic research. It has been credited with expanding the alt-
right: NPI's founder, Richard Spencer, advocated for a white ethnostate and
openly promoted the notion of a "peaceful ethnic cleansing"—including gov-
ernment-forced sterilization of Black women—to achieve his vision.[9] Despite
condemnation from mainstream conservatives, Spencer and NPI found a
platform in certain conservative circles, blurring the lines between conserva-
tism and white nationalism. In 2017, the IRS revoked the group's tax-exempt

status due to a failure to file tax returns for three consecutive years. As of 2024, its status remains listed as revoked.[10]

Some antidemocratic think tanks also adopt the mantle of "church" to benefit from church tax-exempt status. This means that they not only behave like mega churches but also purport to operate as such. In 2022, forty members of Congress urged the IRS and the Treasury Department to review the pattern of conservative advocacy groups registering as "association of churches" to abuse tax-exempt status. By operating under the guise of religious organizations, these groups evade audits and face fewer stringent reporting requirements. Like churches, they are exempt from filing Form 990s, which disclose annual information such as grants received, board member identities, staff salaries, and significant payments to contractors. However, such audits are rare and typically ineffectual. In 2023, no churches lost their tax-exempt status because of IRS disciplinary actions.[11]

Consumers of digital information require newfound vigilance about the threats to democratic values posed by the combination of professed expertise and new technologies. Because the most popular posts from think tanks appear supported by more people, think tanks can more easily attract the attention of decision-makers. There's a risk that think tanks may help foster populism by pushing their views online to enlist more people into their camp.

For computer users, the challenge lies in identifying the influence of white nationalist ideologies and their threat to the principles of pluralism, equality, and democracy. This is sometimes difficult because many organizations claim to espouse altruistic values while simultaneously working to undermine them.

From Policy to Propaganda

With vast memberships and resources, well-funded mega think tanks divert many politicians from serving democracy's collective decision-making process. Their support for authoritarian policies and laws undermines constitutional protections, notably affecting the welfare of non-white communities.

The American Conservative Union, founded in 2002, and its affiliate, Conservative Political Action Conference (CPAC), have centered their focus on the Make America Great Again mantra, with Trump dominating its 2024 annual event. The slogan's adoption in political discourse and its implications raise concerns about democratic principles, especially when advocating for democracy's overthrow. On February 22, 2024, more than fifteen thousand followers on X (formerly Twitter) "liked" a post by Jack Posobiec, a CPAC attendee, Pizzagate proponent, and white supremacist collaborator: "Welcome to the end of democracy. We are here to overthrow it completely. We didn't get all the way there on Jan. 6, but we will endeavor to get rid of it."[12]

Such rhetoric popularizes and gives a platform to white supremacist and antidemocratic values. Katherine Stewart, author of the 2022 book *The Power Worshippers: Inside the Dangerous Rise of Religious Nationalism*, describes self-professed think tanks as "represent[ing] something new in modern American politics: a group of people, not internet conspiracy freaks but credentialed and influential leaders, who are openly contemptuous of democracy."[13] Stewart highlights the Claremont Institute. On January 5, 2021, Claremont's president emeritus Brian Kennedy tweeted from Capitol Hill using the hashtag #HoldTheLine: "We are in a constitutional crisis and also in a revolutionary moment.... We must embrace the spirit of the American Revolution to stop this communist revolution."[14] In 2016, the Claremont Institute published conservative writer Michael Anton's "The Flight 93 Election," a title referring to United Airlines Flight 93, whose hijacked flight path to Washington, DC, on 9/11 was intervened by passengers and crew on board. Anton's essay urged conservatives to metaphorically charge the electoral cockpit by voting for Donald Trump or face death. While Charles Kesler, editor of the *Claremont Review of Books*, would not publish "Flight 93" in its print edition, the essay appeared on the *Review*'s website. After Rush Limbaugh read excerpts on his radio show, hundreds of thousands of listeners flocked to the *Review*'s site, causing it to crash.[15]

An exercise in digital and media literacy is to ask ourselves what these democracy critics are afraid of, and who they are targeting with narratives promoting authoritarianism, discrediting electoral processes, and demonizing any opposition as unpatriotic. Such rhetoric often appeals to individuals seeking a sense of belonging to something larger than themselves, tapping into the human desire for community and purpose. Criticizing others—and depicting them as "others" or unlike "us"—provides a sense of righteousness and moral superiority that reinforces group identity. Divisive terms like *traitor*, *enemy*, and *un-American*, and calls to "take back" or "defend" the nation against perceived threats, soon reveal existential fears on the part of the communicators and their audience.

Values long associated with democracy—like inclusion and diversity—become threatening to those without a foundation in civics education and an understanding of the political dimensions of digital literacy. This helps explain why so many self-proclaimed patriotic Americans are embracing an authoritarian state. As Donald Trump promised an audience of Christian conservatives in July 2024: "I love you. You got to get out and vote. In four years, you don't have to vote again. We'll have it fixed so good, you're not going to have to vote."[16]

Online Pulpits for Democratic Disdain

It's no surprise that mega think tanks invest in social media experts, influencers, and communications experts.

By harnessing the power of digital technology, these super-sized networks stand at the forefront of shaping discourse and societal change.

Calling itself a think tank, the Acton Institute for the Study of Religion and Liberty espouses the values of both mega church preachers and conservative think tank CEOs. It touts the benefits of integrating Judeo-Christian truths with limited government and free-market principles. Events, several publications, and a podcast emphasize the connection between individual liberty and religious principles. The Acton Institute saw a 61 percent traffic increase on its platforms and websites in 2023.[17]

The avowedly conservative Turning Point USA (TPUSA) witnessed a 65 percent increase in social media subscriptions in 2023.[18] In her eye-opening 2022 book, *Raising Them Right: The Untold Story of America's Ultraconservative Youth Movement and Its Plot for Power*, Kyle Spencer describes how Jake Hoffman, founder of an online marketing firm that worked to get Trump elected in 2016, was hired to oversee digital campaigns for Turning Point Action, the group's political arm:

> But the most excitement at Turning Point's new headquarters was inside its growing multimedia wing, which now buzzed with activity, as analytics experts, social media specialists, and producers tested the click-ability and share-ability of edited videos and brainstormed ideas for a roster of online shows to be released that winter. It was all part of a costly and pointed effort to produce conservative messaging that targeted Millennials and Gen Zs on TikTok, Instagram, Twitter, YouTube, and Facebook.... The messaging would be a boost to Trump, indeed. But the real end goal was much more ambitious: to reach further and further into the American mainstream, influencing not just conservatives but the politically searching as well.[19]

Conservative think tanks' insinuation of white nationalist, antidemocratic, and misogynist values, aided by social media, challenge democratic norms and undermine public trust in the electoral process. The Claremont Institute and the American Principles Project pushed "Stop the Steal" rhetoric, falsely claiming that the 2020 election was stolen, and the Heritage Foundation hosted events promoting election-fraud narratives—all of which contributed to the massive antidemocratic intent behind the January 6 Capitol insurrection. Support has grown for policies that perpetuate racial and gender inequalities and restrict voting rights under the guise of preserving traditional American values—patriotism, freedom, and the Constitution. As the election-denier movement continued, the Brennan Center reported that in 2023, state legislators passed a near-record number of restrictive voting laws (2021 holds the record, most likely in response to "Stop the Steal" rhetoric). Part of practicing digital literacy involves being able to discern when language is hypocritical, as terms like *freedom* are too often used to mask exclusionary or regressive agendas.

"The Uptown Klan" — The Language of the Right

By assuming a semblance of respectability, groups supporting white nationalism create a veneer of legitimacy for their racist perspectives. Massimo Pigliucci, professor of philosophy at the City College of New York, describes this facade in an interview with *Wired* as "a mix of selected truths, half-truths, and downright fabricated stuff in order to manipulate people."[20]

Unapologetically nationalist think tanks include the New Century Foundation, run by Jared Taylor, founder of *American Renaissance* magazine, which is known for publishing articles by eugenics proponents and anti-Black and anti-Latino racists. After adding a daily feature of articles catering to racist readers, the foundation's website—amren.com, which features the banner "American Renaissance"—rose to one of the world's top twenty thousand sites, according to the Southern Poverty Law Center. In June 2020, YouTube banned the American Renaissance channel for violating the platform's hate-speech policies.[21]

Another white-dominant think tank is the Council of Conservative Citizens (CofCC), formerly the Citizens' Councils of America (CCA). This coalition of white supremacist groups formed in the 1950s, committed to whites-only schooling after the Supreme Court's 1954 *Brown v. Board of Education* decision outlawed racial segregation in public schools. Outwardly, it projected respectability, earning the nickname "the Uptown Klan" after journalist Hodding Carter denounced the CCA before the Memphis Public Affairs Forum in 1955 as "a kind of uptown Ku Klux Klan."[22]

The content on the CofCC's website, conservative-headlines.org, is overtly pejorative. In February 2024, its top story about critical race theory and Black academics, titled "Monkeys and Typewriters," featured a photograph of monkeys sitting at computer monitors. One sentence read: "There's no small element of irony in black 'academics' redefining words in the English Lexicon, especially since blacks have never, themselves, invented a written language in the hundreds-of-thousands of years they've managed to walk upright."[23]

Groups like the California-based Goyim Defense League and others avoid terms like *white power*. Instead, they opt for symbols like Christian cross emojis or words like *anglo* to exploit social media platforms, online forums, and websites to reach a global audience.[24] Under the guise of offering a platform for "academic discussion" or "free speech," their online spaces provide a sense of belonging for individuals feeling isolated. These sites use code words, dog whistles, and subtle messaging to avoid direct violations of platform rules.

From Mega to Mother: Atlas and ALEC Conglomerates

As if the influence of individual, white-leaning think tanks weren't already a significant threat to public welfare, many are now forming alliances to create even mightier networks. These coalitions amplify their reach by pooling resources and coordinating strategies to exert greater influence on public discourse and policymaking.

The Atlas Network is fast becoming the motherlode of think tanks, asserting that "only by protecting the civil rights of all can the institutions of liberal democracy truly flourish."[25] Founded in 1981, as of 2020, it consists of 506 conservative think tank members globally, including corporations, nonprofits, and wealthy individuals. The network shapes public opinion, influences elections, and impacts government policies to favor its members' interests by giving grants to new think tanks, hosting global networking events, and creating resources such as videos. One video, *Freedom Worldwide with Tom G. Palmer: Helping Americans Free Themselves from Welfare*, criticizes local government regulation of housing and what they call restrictions on and abuse of property rights. Host Dr. Tom G. Palmer, described as "a renowned advocate of freedom," spoke with Daniel Erspamer, CEO of the Pelican Institute for Public Policy; Christina Sandefur, executive vice president of the Goldwater Institute; and Eric Cochling, chief program officer and general counsel of the Georgia Center for Opportunity—all organizations that advocate for free-market principles.[26]

The Atlas Network's organizations, located in approximately one hundred nations, advance free-market and neoliberal ideologies such as refuting climate change, defending the tobacco industry, and advocating for oil and gas development on Indigenous lands. Notable funders have included oil billionaires like Charles Koch and Richard Scaife, as well as ExxonMobil, Google, and MasterCard. One prominent member of the Atlas Network is the American Legislative Exchange Council (ALEC). Just as the mission of Atlas is to "litter the world with free-market think-tanks," ALEC is itself a "big boss" in pro-corporate and free-market state-level policy influence.

ALEC was significantly involved in 2020 election denial and connected to events leading up to the January 2021 insurrection. Several ALEC-associated politicians actively promoted the "Stop the Steal" movement. Notably, Arizona state representative Mark Finchem and former Arizona state representative Anthony Kern, both with ties to ALEC, were listed as speakers at the rally preceding the insurrection. Additionally, thirty ALEC state politicians signed a letter to then vice president Mike Pence on January 5, urging him not to certify the election results. ALEC's CEO, Lisa Nelson, indicated that the organization had been working on efforts to question the validity of the election results. And ALEC has a partnership with right-wing groups like Turning Point USA, which played a role in organizing transportation to the January 6 events.

ALEC's Anatomy and the Push for Nationalist Policies

Established in 1973, ALEC is a self-described nonpartisan, voluntary membership organization of state legislators committed to principles of federalism, free markets, and limited government. "Limited government" is coded language for states' rights, reflecting the politics of the white supremacist, slave-owning South; the Confederacy; and those Americans who rejected the outcomes of the Civil War, Reconstruction, and the Civil Rights Amendments.

As Dominic Renfrey from the Center for Constitutional Rights (CCR) in New York points out, comprehending ALEC's role requires understanding the influence of evangelical Christian conservative activists in the late 1960s and 1970s.[27] Around that time, ALEC's founder Paul Weyrich cofounded the Heritage Foundation and other right-wing entities like the Moral Majority political action committee to bring evangelical Christians into politics.

As new social movements of activists and lawyers emerged in the 1960s, evangelicals and corporate CEOs saw their hold on power slipping. One funder of newly forming conservative groups like ALEC was the Carthage Foundation. It was established in 1964 by Richard Mellon Scaife, dubbed the "funding father of the right" by the *Washington Post*, and an heir to the Mellon banking, oil, and aluminum fortune.[28] Carthage also gave millions of dollars in funding to the American Enterprise Institute and the Heritage Foundation. And it donated nearly $2 million to fund an investigation by the conservative magazine *American Spectator* for its "Arkansas Project," which, in the mid-1990s, aimed to uncover and publicize scandals involving then president Bill Clinton. The foundation merged with and into the Sarah Scaife Foundation in 2014.[29]

"In the late 1980s, ALEC saw corporations seeking more access at the political level. ALEC realized they were helpful to the tobacco industry to push back against the attacks the industry was facing," notes Renfrey. Around this time, the professional lobbying industry came into full force. From 1971 to 1982, the number of registered lobbyists in the nation's capital burgeoned from 175 to 2,445.[30]

ALEC generates substantial income by selling memberships to corporations, trade associations, and conservative advocacy groups, with private sector membership costs ranging from $7,000 to $25,000, as of 2023.[31] Task force membership costs an additional $5,000, and provides members with the opportunity to draft, debate, and vote on model legislation aligning with their interests. These task forces cover policy areas such as education, healthcare, and environmental regulation. Once a task force approves a model bill, it is distributed to state legislators who are also ALEC members, with the goal of having it introduced and passed in states across the country. This process allows corporate and special interest groups to directly influence state policy.

Among ALEC's members are hundreds of corporations, corporate lobbying institutions, nonprofit organizations, right-wing activists, and a significant number of state lawmakers, estimated to comprise one-third of all lawmakers. Renfrey calls membership a quid pro quo arrangement. Corporations seeking access to legislators' private rooms are required to pay tens of thousands of dollars. "Companies with a particular regulation they want passed, such as privatization of prisons, go to ALEC with a law in mind. They pay for access to politicians to draft laws, then farm out that model legislation."

ALEC's model laws are provided to lawmakers "off the rack," a fashion term for ready-to-wear clothing, allowing replication or adaption for use at the state level. Model bills have been introduced more than ten thousand times over eight years.[32] According to a joint investigation by *USA Today*, the Center for Public Integrity, and the *Arizona Republic*, from 2010 to 2018, more than six hundred ALEC-model based bills became law. ALEC-driven laws have had a disproportionate impact on communities of color. In North

Carolina, ALEC-supported voter-ID bills have made it more difficult for BIPOC communities to access the ballot by imposing stricter identification requirements that many in these communities find difficult to meet. "Stand Your Ground" laws—allowing the use of deadly force in self-defense if a person reasonably believes they are in immediate danger—in more than half the states, as of 2024, have been shown to disproportionately affect Black individuals. Data suggests that these laws are likelier to be used successfully as a defense when the victim is Black and the shooter is white. Similarly, ALEC-backed "three strikes" laws and mandatory minimum policies contribute to higher incarceration rates in Black communities, exacerbating racial disparities in the criminal justice system by imposing harsher penalties that do not account for socioeconomic factors or systemic biases.

In the oil and gas sector, ALEC has been a key player perpetuating doubts about climate change. It lobbies against regulations aimed at reducing carbon emissions, such as the Clean Power Plan under the Obama administration. Instead, ALEC supports fossil fuel interests, advocating for the continued use of coal, oil, and natural gas while opposing subsidies and incentives for renewable energy development. Beginning in 2016, ALEC's involvement intensified during the passage of laws in response to peaceful Standing Rock protests at the Dakota Access Pipeline (DAPL). As a result, as of early 2025, up to twenty-one states passed versions of the critical infrastructure law, which imposed severe penalties on protesters, showcasing ALEC's influence in shaping legislation that supports corporate interests and curtails environmental activism.[33]

ALEC and Christian Nationalism

ALEC's leadership has included individuals steeped in Christian nationalist views and insurrectionist tendencies. In 2018, ALEC's former Washington state chair, Republican representative Matt Shea, was found by the Washington House of Representatives to have planned, promoted, and participated in three armed conflicts against the government between 2014 and 2016. In 2018, he was referred to the FBI Joint Terrorism Task Force for distributing *Biblical Basis for War*, a manifesto advocating for a Christian holy war to halt abortion, abolish same-sex marriage, and replace the American justice system with biblical law.[34] In addition, *The Guardian* reported in April 2019 that Shea took part in conversations related to "carrying out surveillance, 'psyops' and even violent attacks against his perceived political enemies."[35]

After this became public, it took nearly a year for ALEC to remove Shea as its state chair, even after his chairmanship of the Republican Caucus was rescinded. With no criticism of the extremist firebrand's violent viewpoints, ALEC quietly took Shea off its state chair list while also increasing its collaboration with extremist groups and funders. The delay in dismissing Shea is likely due to ALEC's reluctance to alienate a segment of its base that shares similar views, or perhaps a strategic decision to avoid a public controversy that could have exposed deeper ties between ALEC and extremist elements. The hesitation suggests an underlying alignment or tolerance to such viewpoints by the organization.

In 2021, the Center for Media Democracy and the Southern Poverty Law Center revealed that ALEC was partnering with two designated anti-LGBTQ+ hate groups, the Alliance Defending Freedom and the Family Research Council, in a "Back to Neutral" coalition.[36] The coalition aims to encourage American corporations to discontinue "radical political activism," a misnomer for diversity, equity, and inclusion programs. "Back to neutral" is a nod to the Supreme Court case *Plessy v. Ferguson*, upholding "separate but equal" facilities and explaining Jim Crow laws as neutrally enforcing the separation of races.[37]

Renfrey summarizes the organization's role: "ALEC vacuums up the most radical [fringe right-wing] ideas in a particular state then broadcasts them nationally." In a 2019 report titled *ALEC Attacks*, the Center for Constitutional Rights and other groups bluntly describe ALEC's role in advancing white nationalism, asserting that "conservative and corporate interests have captured our political process to harness profit, further entrench white supremacy in the law, and target the safety, human rights and self-governance of marginalized communities."[38]

ALEC and the State Policy Network

Closely aligned with ALEC is the State Policy Network (SPN), another umbrella of conservative think tanks and tax-exempt organizations that operate in fifty states, Washington, DC, Canada, and the United Kingdom. Founded in 1991, the State Policy Network operates as the policy, communications, and litigation arm of ALEC, providing them with a veneer of academic legitimacy and state-based support. A self-described network and service organization for the "state-based free market think tank movement," its mission is to give strategic assistance to independent research organizations aimed at developing market-oriented solutions to public-policy issues.[39] SPN groups write and disseminate "studies" to support ALEC legislation, tailoring model laws to be specific to different states. As of 2022, SPN reported having ninety national partners, sixty-three independent think tanks, and more than sixty-six state partners in key capacities like litigation, advocacy, and investigative journalism.[40]

Other groups, like the Goldwater Institute in Arizona, have launched litigation centers to advance the joint SPN/ALEC agenda. Many SPN entities present themselves as independent and nonpartisan, while promoting union busting, attacks on the tort bar, and voter-suppression efforts. By directly challenging laws and regulations in courtrooms across the country, Goldwater's advocacy initiatives allow it to shape legal precedents, influence judicial interpretations, and shift the legal landscape in favor of its ideological objectives. Litigation also generates media attention and public discourse around specific issues. High-profile court cases can attract widespread attention, drawing focus to underlying policy debates and rallying support for conservative causes.

In one such high-profile case, *Janus v. AFSCME*, decided in 2018, the plaintiff, Mark Janus, was represented by Goldwater, alongside the National Right to Work Legal Defense Foundation and the Liberty Justice Center, the litigation partner of the SPN affiliate, Illinois Policy Institute.[41] The case reached the US Supreme Court, where it challenged the practice of public-sector unions charging "agency fees" to nonunion members. The court ruled in favor of Janus, effectively making it illegal for public-sector unions to charge agency fees, significantly weakening unions' financial power. The case received extensive media coverage and had a substantial impact on labor law in the United States.

This amplification through legal channels helps conservative mega think tanks to galvanize their base, mobilize activists, and pressure lawmakers to align with their priorities.

Tricks of the Trade

The nonprofit status of conservative mega think tanks provides a convenient veil for engaging in extensive lobbying and political activities without the transparency and accountability required of traditional political entities. This allows them to wield significant influence behind the scenes, shaping public discourse and policymaking in ways that serve their ideological agenda while evading scrutiny. These outsized advocacy groups, networks, and now legal entities exploit the guise of patriotism and the cover of nonprofit status to pursue antidemocratic aims, and they exert undue influence on the political landscape.

The evasive tactics used by these think tanks mirror the clandestine operations of online, violent white extremist groups. By posing as legitimate or benign, they make it difficult for users to detect and counter their activities. Addressing the proliferation of extremist ideologies online requires a combination of technology, vigilant content moderation, and crucially, user education.

CHAPTER 5

Hate Migrates Online

In 2020, Amazon removed all copies of *The Turner Diaries*, a neo-Nazi novel by William Luther Pierce, written in 1978 under the pseudonym Andrew Macdonald.[1] The book, detailing a violent overthrow of the United States government by white supremacist terrorists, is credited with inspiring events like the 1994 Oklahoma City bombing and the 2021 Capitol attack.[2] It is considered a key text for violent far-right extremists. Although banned from Amazon, copies remain available online through some bookstores and public libraries.[3]

Another title revered by white nationalists is Jean Raspail's best-selling 1973 anti-immigration novel, *The Camp of the Saints*, which depicts the demise of Western civilization though third-world mass immigration to France and the Western world.[4] *Kirkus Reviews* likened the book to *Mein Kampf*. As Seyward Darby, author of *Sisters in Hate*, a book about white nationalist women, told the *New York Times*, many of these books have seen a resurgence of interest online.[5]

These books are not just controversial literature; they're potent tools for extremist recruitment and incitement to violence. However, they're only a small part of a growing and increasingly powerful white nationalist ecosystem.

"Many of the ideas that are central to *The Turner Diaries* have [been] turned into memes and proliferated online in right-wing media," explains Cassie Miller, from the Southern Poverty Law Center. After the January 6 riot, users on militant websites and chat platforms such as Stormfront, Telegram, and 4chan rejoiced and compared the lethal attack to *The Turner Diaries'* "Day of the Rope." One user posted on Telegram, referring to the insurrection, "The turner diaries [sic] mentioned this. Keep reading."[6]

Since its publication, the novel has been linked to more than two hundred murders, according to J. M. Berger, a fellow with George Washington University's Program on Extremism. Timothy McVeigh used the same type of bomb described in the book in Oklahoma City—a mixture of heating oil and ammonium nitrate fertilizer. Berger says the *Diaries* was McVeigh's "constant companion"; he carried it with him while traveling and sold copies at gun shows.[7] In the United Kingdom, terrorist David Copeland, responsible for nail-bomb attacks in 1999 targeting London's Black, Bangladeshi, and gay communities, resulting in 3 deaths and 139 injuries, told police the *Diaries* had inspired him. Before the 2020 presidential election, extremists like the Proud Boys circulated online references to it. That November 8, after news media projections of the election result, Staten Island resident Brian Maiorana was arrested for a call to bring *The Turner Diaries* to life and to "blow up the FBI building for real."[8]

The terms *extremists, far-right extremists, violent extremists, white power, white nationalists,* and *white supremacists* are used interchangeably in the following pages because of their shared antidemocratic ethos, implicit and explicit references to violence in their discourse, and the real-life violence ensuing from it.

White nationalism perpetuates systemic inequality and undermines equal representation and justice. White Christian nationalism conflates religious identity with national identity, often leading to exclusionary policies and rhetoric that marginalize non-Christian and secular communities. Its messaging can incite violence and intimidation against minority groups, discouraging their participation in democratic processes.

Before Barack Obama's presidency, former Ku Klux Klan leader David Duke predicted that Obama's election would serve as a "visual aid" for what he perceived as the loss of control by white Americans over their country.[9] This sentiment, aided by the rapid expansion of internet platforms, has evolved into a significant threat to national security and the stability of democracy.

Online platforms are the new breeding grounds for extremist ideologies, enabling the rapid spread of hate speech, radicalization, and coordinated attacks. This contemporary digital imprint amplifies the danger posed by white supremacist groups, making it a complex and urgent challenge for law enforcement and society. According to Evangelicals for Democracy, a Virginia-based nonprofit of evangelicals seeking to preserve democracy, harms from Christian nationalism include "voting restrictions on a massive scale; more aggressive police tactics targeting Black and brown communities; prohibiting interracial marriage and transracial adoption; ending protections for the religious liberty of Jews, Muslims, and other non-Christian faiths; and enacting policies that are hostile to immigrants and refugees."[10] The nonprofit cautions: "Now add to this the belief that women should be subservient to men and you have a dystopian society straight out of *The Handmaid's Tale*." Christian nationalism, it notes, has influenced policies such as book bans and the reinterpreting of US history in schools. Less well known are efforts to require "In God We Trust" to be displayed widely in public places, and laws favoring intimate sexual relationships only between married, heterosexual couples.

White supremacist and Christian nationalist thinking have significantly influenced Supreme Court decisions, reflecting their growing impact on the American legal and political landscapes. In the 2022 case of *Dobbs v. Jackson Women's Health Organization*, which overturned *Roe v. Wade*'s legal right to abortion, Christian nationalist proponents were instrumental in shaping the antiabortion movement and elevating restrictive religious doctrine over public health, women's autonomy, and public opinion favoring a woman's right to choose. During the same week, the court held in *Carson v. Makin* that the state of Maine must allocate public funds to pay private tuition for religious schools. That marked the first time the Supreme Court mandated taxpayer support for a religious activity, signaling the beginning of the end to the constitutional separation of church and state.[11] The ruling could affect communities of color and low-income households, particularly in states with less educational funding.

Grand Tech Wizards

Looks can be deceiving, both in real life and online. As white nationalism spreads into mainstream society, its appearance isn't relegated to neo-Nazi fashion tropes. Hate, often conspicuously clothed in khakis or business suits, can be surprisingly banal, especially online.

Extremists' mundane appearances mirror much of their online communications, which can seem innocuous, humorous, or patriotic. Anonymous, instant mass distribution of online threats makes it difficult to assess their seriousness and their potential physical-world impact. Without a grounding in digital literacy that emphasizes the importance of context awareness, these identifying elements can easily slip by casual internet users.

Technical sophistication among the far right makes it difficult to discern when humor rises to the level of real threats, when discourse is satiric, hyperbolic, or genuine, or when efforts are directed at recruiting newcomers or amplifying inciteful speech. Through intentional tactics like "Leaderless Resistance," which eschews hierarchical structures and operates in a decentralized fashion, the white power movement remains more resilient and adaptable. This is true even in nations with stricter laws against racist content than the

US, as individuals there can still communicate online without fear of government reprisal.[12]

Technology has accelerated the spread of extremism, according to Pete Simi, a sociologist at Chapman University and the author of *American Swastika: Inside the White Power Movement's Hidden Spaces of Hate*. Simi notes that in the 1980s, radical white extremists (RWEs) used electronic bulletin boards to disseminate news and directives to followers. These computer networks allowed RWEs to post messages that remained visible for extended periods, coordinating activities and facilitating discussions, advice-seeking, and responses. Bulletin boards were organized into segmented chat areas known as "echoes," catering to various interests.[13]

The White Aryan Resistance, led by influential white supremacist Tom Metzger, was a trailblazer in using an online bulletin board to share news and instructions, leading in one case to the 1988 murder of Mulugeta Seraw, an Ethiopian immigrant and college student in Portland, Oregon, who was targeted because of his race.

In the 1990s, extremists transitioned from electronic bulletin boards to websites, then later adopted podcasts, social media, and semi-encrypted platforms. By the early 2000s, they had developed a cultural infrastructure across various media, encompassing videos, memes, and more traditional formats like books and speeches. Offline, this influence extended into settings such as house parties and Bible study groups, appearing benign while spreading extremist ideologies. More modern platforms like Stormfront and 4chan, which launched in 2003, have since become prominent spaces where white radical extremists can freely share their extremist views without interference.

Individuals with anti-government or white nationalist leanings are often indoctrinated through a tactic called *subversive exposure*. This involves using disinformation and deceit and normalizing extremist beliefs to attract vulnerable people, notably young online gamers, into right-wing groups without knowing their real nature.[14]

Into the Mainstream

Some extremist messages are communicated through coded language or "dog whistles"—nuanced messages understood primarily by a specific audience. Others use a more overt approach to normalize their ideologies, such as militant rhetoric about Latin American immigrants as invaders which began around 2016.[15] Pete Simi provided expert testimony in the trial of the white nationalist organizers of the deadly 2017 Unite the Right rally in

Charlottesville, in which the organizers were found liable for conspiracy. Research conducted by Simi and his colleague Kathleen Blee of the University of Pittsburgh revealed how the defendants used coded messages on the platform Discord to orchestrate the rally while concealing their true intentions.[16]

According to Simi, a key example of this normalization is how critical race theory—an examination of how systemic racism and inequalities are embedded in laws, politics, and culture—has been framed over several years as fundamentally anti-American. Extremists brought this once obscure, academic topic into the mainstream, turning it into a rallying point. In December 2017, a leaked copy of *The Daily Stormer's* style guide sent to *HuffPost* journalist Ashley Feinberg revealed strategies for influencing readers. A section titled "No Such Thing as Too Much Hyperbole" promotes exaggerated language and advises appealing to primal instincts, for example glorifying the arrest of teenagers for their racist Twitter posts as "eternally noble warriors bravely fighting for divine war to protect the blood heritage of our sacred ancestors."[17] Feinberg writes that the style guide advises using caution with racial slurs to avoid "raging vitriol and provides a list of 18 acceptable racial terms and four prohibited ones, consolidating all enemies into a singular target: Jews."[18]

Yet *The Daily Stormer* acknowledges that overt hate can hinder recruitment efforts. It recommends using patriotic themes to amplify threats identified by conservative media. That attracts followers and promotes "accelerationism," a belief that societal collapse and chaos should be hastened to create opportunities for radical change. Accelerationism is linked to several violent attacks, including the mass shootings in Christchurch, New Zealand; Buffalo, New York; and El Paso, Texas; and the synagogue shooting in Pittsburgh, Pennsylvania. Accelerationists use various internet platforms, including encrypted chats and social media, to spread their ideology and incite chaos to further extremist views.

As social media has become more decentralized, and white power activists are less wary of being deplatformed, animated calls for violence proliferate online. Some extremists have even called for an all-out race war as a means to create a racially pure society. For example, the Terrorgram Collective, a white supremacist network, used Telegram to promote racially motivated violence; members shared instructions on constructing bombs, aiming to destabilize US society and to provoke a "race war." In September 2024, the Department of Justice indicted two alleged Terrorgram leaders, Dallas Humber of Elk Grove, California, and Matthew Allison of Boise, Idaho, on fifteen counts including soliciting hate crimes and conspiring to provide material support to terrorism. They allegedly used Telegram to solicit attacks on Black, Jewish, and LGBTQ communities and on immigrants.[19]

Tech companies play an important role in stemming the spread of extremism, but equally important is digital literacy. A vital step in counteracting white supremacism is educating users about extremists' use of language and symbols to cloak their ideologies. A list is included in the User's Guide.

Complicating matters, researchers explain that by modifying language, extremists can outsmart AI hate-speech detection models. They can remove spaces, change vowels to numbers, and alter words in other ways, for example, by replacing S with $. One detection model, Google's Perspective API, rated "IHateYou" very low when compared with "I hate you," which scored high in "toxicity."[20]

Still, the more that e-citizens learn to spot hate in benign contexts, the more they can exert pressure on elected officials, tech superpowers, and advocacy groups to develop and enact effective solutions, including more sophisticated and effective hate-detection models.

So, let's go over some identifiable white nationalist tactics.

Extremist Recruiting Through Memes and Games

According to Heidi Beirich, founder and executive vice president of the Global Project Against Hate and Extremism, since 2015 there has been a notable increase in the number of individuals exposed solely to online, rather than real-life, violent extremism.[21] Online platforms serve as the primary tools for recruiting new members, fundraising, and planning activities. These groups target young people by weaving humor and inside jokes into multiplayer online video games and other entertainment platforms. Users seeking community—especially young audiences—are often attracted to engaging memes, songs, videos, and other content created by extremists.

However, unlike the routine deplatforming of Islamic extremist activity, Beirich notes, white extremist propaganda is often tolerated by government agencies and technology companies. This discrepancy has helped allow violent white extremists to thrive unchecked in the online realm.

Crafted to be subversively suggestive, memes with racist undertones often encourage viewers to question established truths and explore alternative perspectives.[22] Memes often incorporate familiar visuals, pop culture references, and elements from major political events to provoke laughter (lols) and engagement, serving as a gateway to gradual radicalization.

Memes also foster interaction and normalize hate by presenting as countercultural opinions. A notable example is the internet meme "Pepe the Frog," originally a harmless cartoon character that far-right circles co-opted. Catalogued by the Anti-Defamation League (ADL) are versions of Pepe depicted as Hitler, a Klansman, and various racist caricatures. While many Pepe memes are benign, the ADL points out that a significant number on platforms like 4chan, 8chan, and Reddit are racist or bigoted, reflecting the darker side of meme culture.[23]

Researchers at the Geneva Center for Security Policy find parallels between the normalization of hate through memes and psychologist John Horgan's six-stage theory of how child terrorists are socialized: seduction, schooling, selection, subjugation, specialization, and stationing. Extremists use similar methods to draw individuals into their circles, gradually imparting ideologies, identifying suitable candidates, and sharing information on planning attacks.[24] Unlike traditional methods that might involve physical subjugation, such interactions primarily occur online, using psychological subjugation and bullying to weaken potential recruits' mental states. Anonymity in online forums often emboldens users, making them more receptive to exploring extremist ideologies without the immediate social repercussions they might face in real life.

For example, Super Chats are a YouTube feature that allows viewers to pay to have their messages highlighted during live streams. Messages appear prominently in the chat feed and can be pinned to the top for a set period, depending on the amount paid. Super Chats have been used to highlight and amplify hateful messages, making them more visible to a larger audience. Extremist content creators can receive financial support through Super Chats, incentivizing them to continue producing and sharing hateful content. Funding can help sustain and grow their platforms while prominent display of hate messages can help normalize extremist views. When viewers see these messages highlighted and seemingly endorsed by the content creator, it can legitimize them. Super Chats can be used to recruit new members to extremist groups, directing viewers to join private groups, websites, or forums where more radical content and direct recruitment occur.

Former white supremacists, commonly referred to as "formers," have recounted their experiences of being groomed in online groups. Former neo-Nazi Christian Picciolini was recruited into the white nationalist movement at fourteen years of age through various means, including online forums and chat rooms. Picciolini now runs a nonprofit to help extremists leave hate groups.[25] In another case, Megan Phelps-Roper was groomed into the Westboro Baptist Church's extremist ideology and was ultimately de-radicalized through Twitter interactions.[26]

Historically, integration of new members has often stemmed not only from the allure of friendship but also from specific skills they could offer, such as military training or software engineering expertise. Women are frequently targeted for recruitment due to a belief that they possess superior persuasive skills to attract new recruits.

Over time, exposure to increasingly extreme content erodes both decency and moderation, while also desensitizing audiences to violent language, images, and ideas. To maintain their presence on various tech platforms, extremist groups regularly engage in rebranding.

Rebranding Hate

The term *white nationalist* is a more sanitized version of *white supremacist*. Don Black, a former KKK grand wizard—a national leader of several different KKK organizations—and founder of Stormfront in 1996, the largest white nationalist site on the internet, helped popularize this rebranding. His child, J. Derek Black, who founded the Kids' Stormfront website as a teenager, renounced their views in 2013 at the age of twenty-two. J. Derek explains that the difference in terminology reflects a desire for forcible racial segregation, but for the good of everyone and without a desire to cause harm.[27]

However, the rebranding of white supremacist as white nationalist has not eradicated the violence associated with white supremacy. The Department of Homeland Security defines violent white supremacist extremists as people "who seek, wholly or in part, through unlawful acts of force or violence, to support their belief in the intellectual and moral superiority of the white race over other races."[28]

Related believers, white Christian nationalists, hold that the United States was founded as, and should remain, a Christian nation. Amanda Tyler of the Baptist Joint Committee—a group founded in 1936 to protect religious liberty for all and defend the separation of church and state—suggests this belief centers on cultural identity rather than religious faith, incorporating antidemocratic ideals such as white supremacy, patriarchy, militarism, nativism, and authoritarianism.[29]

With awareness of the online tactics and rhetoric of white nationalists, users can better navigate the complexities of modern information landscapes, recognize threats to social cohesion, and uphold the values of an inclusive and informed democracy.

Encouraging people to scrutinize the underlying messages and intentions of organizations and movements fosters informed decision-making about which groups and ideologies to support or oppose. It also helps prevent manipulation and the spread of misinformation. When hate groups successfully rebrand, their ideologies can become normalized and accepted within mainstream society. Increased division, discrimination, and violence often ensue. Understanding and identifying rebranded hate groups enables communities, law enforcement, and policymakers to take proactive measures to protect vulnerable populations and maintain public safety.

Victimization and "The Other"

An overarching theme to look for in white supremacist messaging is victimization. Christian nationalists believe *their* rights are being violated and that they're subjected to greater discrimination and marginalization than other groups.[30] Victimization is usually rooted in fear of losing power, status, or cultural dominance in an evolving social landscape.

Language touting equality, freedom, and rights is common in both white supremacist and white Christian rhetoric. Discerning the differences between white supremacist and liberal and libertarian rhetoric involves understanding their core ideologies and motivations. In contrast to the white supremacist belief in the superiority of whites—driven by racial hatred, fear of demographic change, and a desire for dominance—liberal rhetoric favors individual freedoms, equality, and social justice. Libertarian rhetoric emphasizes individual liberty, free-market capitalism, and minimal government intervention, driven by a belief in personal responsibility, economic freedom, and limited government.

Hateful rhetoric often uses religious quotes in secular settings, with language vilifying "the other." Secular diversity, equity, and inclusivity efforts to remedy historical injustices or systemic inequalities are portrayed as undermining nationalists' religious and cultural identities.

Words suggesting threats to the white Christian nationalist identity include *culture wars, oppression,* and *persecution.* Perceived enemies are presented as *groomers, sheeple, snowflakes, woke, liberal elites,* and *RINOs* (Republicans in name only). Terms historically used to seek equality for marginalized citizens, such as *election integrity,* are reengineered to invent or invoke voter-suppression laws.

Language may imply that the US is superior to other nations. Phrases like *true patriots, decent Americans, our America, respecting the flag,* and *Americanism* are common. Good and evil may be depicted as *patriots* versus *communists*. The Appeal to Heaven flag, popularized by the New Apostolic Reformation (NAR) leader Dutch Sheets, relays a call for Christian revolution in the United States. NAR is a movement within Pentecostal and Charismatic Christianity emphasizing modern-day apostles and prophets believed to receive direct revelations from God. Historical inaccuracies may venerate the past while ignoring prior crimes against humanity.

Christian nationalist politicians regularly invoke religious rhetoric in speeches and policy proposals, presenting their agendas as divinely ordained. They may advocate for legislation based on conservative principles, including restrictions on abortion or LGBTQ+ rights, framing policies as essential to preserving the nation's moral foundation.

Younger generations, with increasingly limited knowledge of history and civics, are especially susceptible to narratives blending religious agendas with secular governance.

Hyperbole, Conspiracy Theories, and Violence

Hyperbole and metaphors are used liberally in white nationalist communications, as in the January 2024 viral campaign video "God Made Trump," which Trump shared on Truth Social: "God had to have somebody willing to go into the den of vipers, call out the fake news for their tongues as sharp as a serpent's, the poison of vipers is on their lips."[31]

Conspiracy research supports a link between religion, conspiratorial thinking, and political violence.[32] Conspiracy theories advance nationalist agendas by tapping into preexisting fears and grievances, feeding self-perceived victimization. The "Great Replacement" theory, coined by French white nationalist writer Renaud Camus, suggests that white Christians are being systematically replaced by immigrants and minority groups, orchestrated by a shadowy elite seeking to undermine Western civilization.[33]

The QAnon theory envisions a secret cabal of Satan-worshipping pedophiles within the "deep state." White supremacists often refer to the theory using coded language, such as the term *The Storm,* referring to a prophesized event in QAnon beliefs when elites will be arrested and brought to justice. Another common phrase is WWG1WGA ("Where We Go One, We Go All"), signifying unity among QAnon followers and used to indicate allegiance to the movement.

Fearful that their existence is imperiled, Christian nationalists see violence as a necessity. Many insurrectionists who stormed the Capitol on January 6 believed that perceived election transgressions justified nothing short of spiritual warfare.

To justify violence, statements demonize marginalized groups and frame political opponents as existential threats. Traditional images such as flags, crosses, iconography, language, and even prayer are weaponized to invoke violence cloaked in the mantle of divine authority. Christian nationalists proselytize across television, print and social media, right-wing talk radio, religious podcasts, and advertisements intertwining religion with secular institutions, patriotism, and politics.

Hate on Gaming Platforms

"Entryism" is another strategy white supremacists use; they infiltrate and exert influence in existing online communities or forums that aren't inherently extremist, such as gaming platforms, which have text or voice chat functions in the games, and "gaming-adjacent" social media platforms and third-party applications that host video game content and discussions about gaming. Online game platforms like Roblox and games including *World of Warcraft*, *Fortnite*, *Apex Legends*, *League of Legends*, *Madden NFL*, *Overwatch*, and *Call of Duty* have seen instances of white supremacist ideologies and themes spread among players. Initially discussing unrelated topics, online groomers gradually introduce newcomers to extremist views. Capitalizing on the anonymity and accessibility of the internet, acolytes are often emboldened to participate in vitriolic discourse. Unchecked bias can escalate, leading to exposure of increasingly extremist ideologies. In 2022, the ADL's Center on Technology and Society's annual survey of hate and harassment in games found that adult exposure to white supremacy in online games has risen to 20 percent of gamers from 8 percent in 2021. And 15 percent of young gamers between ten and seventeen years of age have been exposed to white nationalist views and themes in online games. Gaming platform communities, according to the ADL, are filled with so much hate that they rival spaces like 4chan.[34] As this hate surges, in 2021 an international Extremism and Gaming Research Network was founded by researchers and practitioners to study the relationship between online gaming and radicalization.

Such normalization is evident in the popular game *Call of Duty: Warzone*, which boasts more than 85 million players worldwide. In the game, extremists use the battle cry RAHOWA, for "racial holy war," in usernames on the game's headboards. Notably, neo-Nazi Mark Collett, leader of Patriotic Alternative, has leveraged the platform by hosting public tournaments and actively promoting racist conspiracy theories through his group's online channels. In one tournament, participants' account names referred to hate figures such as Adolf Hitler and Oswald Mosley, who headed the British Union of Fascists from 1932 to 1940; players also posted coded graphic racist messages. One account featured an anti-Semitic username, while other accounts used the term *joggers*, a veiled reference to the N-word, in referring to the 2020 shooting murder of Ahmaud Arbery, who was jogging in Georgia.[35]

Members of the Patriot Front engage in activities on Roblox, a platform featuring recreations of mass murders and games depicting slavery, while former leaders of the neo-Nazi group Feuerkrieg Division have been active on gaming platforms such as Steam, which is owned by Valve Corporation. In 2022, Senator Margaret Wood Hassan (D-NH) urged Valve's CEO, Gabe Newell, to take measures to prevent harmful content given the nexus between online remarks and real-life violence. With her request for information about how Valve moderates the Steam community, she noted its "significant presence of users displaying and espousing neo-Nazi, extremist, racial supremacist, misogynistic, and other hateful sentiments."[36] While there is no record of Newell responding to Senator Hassan's request, in 2024 Valve updated its guidelines for online conduct, notably prohibiting encouraging real-world violence.[37]

After the mass killing of Black shoppers at a Tops Friendly Markets supermarket in Buffalo, New York, on May 14, 2022, the eighteen-year-old shooter Payton Gendron posted on Discord logs: "I probably wouldn't be as nationalistic if it weren't for Blood and Iron on Roblox," referencing the game centered around the Napoleonic Wars.[38] This incident underscores the emerging recognition of the role of racist ideologies in online gaming as a matter of national security concern.

Recognizing this concern, in 2021, the United Nations Office of Counter-Terrorism launched a three-phase initiative to address exploitation in gaming. This initiative began with expert consultations to review existing research on the nexus between video games and violent extremism. Focus groups then aimed to bridge knowledge gaps by incorporating diverse viewpoints on gaming culture. The initiative concluded with an expert roundtable in December 2021.[39] As well, the Department of Homeland Security's Office for Targeted Violence and Terrorism Prevention is actively engaged in addressing the risks of radicalization to violence through online gaming platforms. Since 2015, it has held several digital forums to explore and mitigate these risks, underscoring the importance of proactive measures to safeguard against the potential consequences of extremist ideologies in virtual spaces.

Alt-Tech Social Networks

White nationalist propaganda dissemination has also experienced a notable uptick on college campuses, according to the Anti-Defamation League.[40] Organizations such as Identity Evropa, Turning Point USA, and the American Identity Movement have been prominent in this surge. Of these, the American Identity Movement stands out for its adeptness at toning down extremist rhetoric in favor of immigration-control advocacy, targeting young Republicans via platforms like Gab and Telegram. This strategy has yielded results, with documented hate incidents on five college campuses in the final week of November 2019, coupled with a staggering 120 percent surge in the distribution of white nationalist material across the US throughout 2019.[41]

To evade detection on mainstream platforms, from which many have been expelled, white extremists have forged a parallel tech ecosystem for recruiting under the radar. This online milieu, the "alt-tech ecosystem," champions absolute free speech and self-governance, fostering and enabling hate activities. These spaces often lack hierarchical structure by design, allowing for decentralized control among diverse subgroups.

Following Facebook's November 2020 decision to ban the Stop the Steal Group, comprising more than three hundred thousand members, far-right groups shifted to smaller, alternative social media platforms. Many conservatives, feeling marginalized on Facebook and Twitter, sought refuge on platforms embracing an "anything goes" ethos and positioning themselves as champions of free speech.

Platforms such as the European social network VK, the Dubai-headquartered Telegram, and Chinese-owned TikTok, all outside US jurisdiction, are often used by hate groups for propaganda dissemination, recruitment, and fundraising. American-owned alternative sites, such as Gab, Parler, Bitchute, Odysee, and the now-defunct Voat, tolerate unmoderated extremist discourse, serving as entry points for recruitment. Their content and visuals are highly shareable, meaning that their entertainment, utility, or inspirational content motivates people to share it with their networks, facilitating the spread of extremist ideologies.

Closed-community communication apps, including messaging apps and platforms that support gaming like Telegram, facilitate private group discussions of racist speech shielded from detection. Hate actors seeking swift responses or concerned about privacy favor these apps because they offer end-to-end encryption and coordination features, including audio, video, and multi-person channels. By blending social networking with private messaging, hate-mongering communities erect barriers against removal by mainstream platforms that have anti-hate-speech policies.

In response to the November 2020 presidential election, Parler quickly gained popularity by attracting a new account, called Stop the Steal, which swiftly amassed more than one hundred thousand followers.[42] (Parler was shut down in April 2023.) Gab experienced an influx of far-right individuals, QAnon conspiracy theorists, and Trump adherents, claiming 1.7 million new users in just one week.[43] The Rumble app, positioned as a conservative counterpart to YouTube, witnessed a surge in users. MeWe, a self-proclaimed Facebook alternative that eschews targeted ads, jumped in popularity on Apple's App Store and Google Play. However, MeWe's CEO, Mark Weinstein, cautioned against becoming an unregulated "anything goes" platform and pledged increased vigilance in content moderation to prevent such an outcome.[44]

Repackaging Racism

Daryle Lamont Jenkins is dedicated to raising awareness about white hate groups, successfully assisting some extremists, such as Bryon Widner, subject of the 2018 film *Skin*, in renouncing their hateful ideologies. Hailing from New Jersey, Jenkins began documenting and writing about white supremacy in 1988, while serving as a police officer in the US Air Force. The son of a drug treatment counselor and a Pentecostal missionary, he has actively confronted clandestine Ku Klux Klan rallies, and rock bands with neo-Nazi connections. Through his organization, One People's Project, Jenkins researches and publicly exposes individuals and organizations identified as right-wing, far-right, or racist.

The Project's website features a "Rogues Gallery," an alphabetical list containing photos and biographies of individuals identified as white nationalists. Clicking on a name allows users to access a biography that includes aliases, place of residence, social media accounts, employment histories, and group affiliations. PBS has referred to this practice, known as doxxing—publishing an individual's personal information without their consent—as "an attempt at vigilante justice" against hate groups, domestic terrorists, and extremists.[45]

Jenkins underscores the fact that what he calls "fine-sounding words" of extremists, such as *race realist, cultural Marxism, love your race,* and *cultural enrichment*, pose a greater threat than open expression of hateful ideologies. White radical organizations with seemingly respectable names, he notes, often receive support from mainstream politicians.

Just as the term *white supremacy* has been rebranded to *white nationalism*, rebranding in general is a key tactic used by groups like the Patriot Front, which purports to further patriotic values. Instead of displaying swastikas or Black Sun imagery, the group uses symbols like the upside-down American flag or Betsy Ross's 1777 flag representing the thirteen original colonies.

Jenkins warns that the next significant threat to democracy will likely not identify themselves overtly as the Ku Klux Klan. "They're going to call themselves names like the Council of Conservative Citizens, or the National Policy Institute. They'll have websites called American Renaissance."[46] Their tactics are steeped in deception, including astroturfing—a method wherein fake grassroots activity is created to conceal the true sponsors of a political or public relations message, presenting as an authentic grassroots movement. "In truth, they are created and funded by larger well-funded interests, like corporations and PACs [political action committees]. They're pawns of larger political interests."

In addition to adopting patriotic-sounding identities, Jenkins says that groups like the Conservative Political Action Conference (CPAC) prefer sponsoring conferences over street rallies to network and promote propaganda. Turning Point USA (TPUSA), the Leadership Institute, and Young America's Foundation (YAF) actively groom right-wing activists on college campuses. In 2023, Turning Point reported a record number of student attendees who launched nearly 50 new high school and college chapters in one weekend, growing TPUSA's presence on more than 3,500 campuses.[47] The Leadership Institute website claims it has a college network exceeding 2,300 conservative campus groups and newspapers. YAF is anemic in comparison, with 250 high school and college campus chapters. Investigative journalist Alex Kotch wrote in a 2017 article of YAF president Ron Robinson's "white nationalist leanings."[48] Along with YAF board member James B. Taylor, Robinson operated a political action committee, America's PAC. In 2004, it gave $5,000 to the white nationalist Charles Martel Society. Taylor served as president of the National Policy Institute, run by white nationalist Richard Spencer.[49]

Recognizing gradations of online hate becomes a cultural necessity as extremism permeates digital spaces. As hate is normalized in society, the boundaries between casual discourse and violent rhetoric blur.

Many white nationalists prefer autocracy over democracy, as authoritarian systems align more closely with their goals of enforcing strict racial and cultural hierarchies and centralizing power to control or exclude certain groups. Autocratic governance offers a level of control and conformity that democratic systems, with their inherent diversity and pluralism, do not support. White nationalists view democracy's commitment to equality and civil rights as a threat to their ideals of racial superiority, often perceiving inclusivity as a dilution of "traditional" or "pure" societal values.

CHAPTER 6

Ad Tech

Have you ever clicked your mouse right HERE? YOU WILL.
—AT&T's banner ad on hotwired.com

On October 27, 1994, a small graphic with these words in a rainbow font appeared on *Wired* magazine's web portal, www.hotwired.com. AT&T paid $30,000 to display the banner ad for three months. It achieved a remarkable click-through rate of 44 percent, a figure that would astonish modern-day marketers, given that the current average click-through rate is about 1 percent (for every thousand times an ad is shown, one person clicks on it).[1]

AT&T's integrated marketing campaign, centered around "futurist technological wonders," included features like phone video calls and remote library book borrowing, according to Joe McCambley, the author of the banner.[2]

Advertising would never be the same.

Targeted Ads: "This is a terrible idea"

A year later, the company WebConnect introduced CustomView, a tool that helped advertisers place online ads where potential customers were most likely to see them. This heralded the start of the targeted ad era. To combat "banner fatigue," CustomView limited the number of times a specific user saw the same ad.

Ad servers—software hosted on servers specifically for advertising—transformed the digital landscape by making the web more appealing to media buyers. This technology revolutionized ad delivery, content storage, and search optimization. It allowed publishers to place ads without hard coding, where data is directly embedded into an application's source code. Additionally, revenue models evolved from selling time-based slots to charging based on the cost of one thousand ad impressions (CPM, or cost per *mille*, meaning "thousand" in Latin).

Advertising technology (ad tech, for short) companies like DoubleClick, founded in 1996 and acquired by Google in 2008 for $3.1 billion, were pivotal in transforming digital marketing. Their model relied on creating "cookie"-based profiles of web surfers by tracking their activities across various domains. Cookies (also referred to as browser, web, or internet cookies) are small text files that a website places on a user's device through their web browser, which can later be retrieved to recognize the user. (The name comes from the programming term *magic cookies*, pieces of data passed from one program to another, then returned for authentication.) The process, known as cookie profiling, compiles detailed user profiles based on behavior, interests, and preferences.

Cookies are like name tags at a conference. When you arrive on site, you're given a tag telling everyone your name and other details like your company or title. As you move around different rooms and meet various people, they quickly glance at your name tag and learn something about you without having to ask every time.

Similarly, when you visit a website, it gives your browser a cookie, like a digital name tag. The cookie stores information about your visit, preferences, or login status. Each time you return to the site, your browser shows the cookie to the website, helping it remember your prior activities and preferences, or to keep you logged in. This way, the website can personalize your experience based on the information stored in your cookie, just as people at the conference can tailor their interactions with you based on the information on your name tag.

Cookie-based ads are privacy pirates, tracking users' online activities across multiple sites without explicit consent. Personalized ads can feel intrusive or unsettling, particularly when they reflect private or sensitive interests. Online footprints become more accessible to advertisers, often without users' understanding or control.

Jay Schwedelson, founder of WebConnect, expressed skepticism in 1995 about this approach: "I was like, wait a minute. So you're telling me we're gonna drop something on somebody's computer, and then we're gonna follow them around the internet and we're gonna see what they're doing? And then we're gonna target based on that?—that's horrible! This is a terrible idea. They're gonna get into a lot of trouble...but there was no trouble to get into."[3]

It would take years until the privacy concerns Schwedelson found so distasteful were recognized by the public and addressed by policymakers.

Google: The King Kong of Online Ads

In their early days, companies like Google, Facebook, LinkedIn, and Netflix resisted incorporating advertising on their platforms. Google founders Larry Page and Sergey Brin wrote in a 1998 paper that from the consumer perspective, "the better the search engine is, the fewer advertisements will be needed for the consumer to find what they want. This of course erodes the advertising supported business model of the existing search engines."[4]

Page and Brin, both of whom had parents who were professors, based their search engine on the citation ranking systems academics used to evaluate and rank the quality of academic journal articles.

"We believe a well-functioning society should have abundant, free and unbiased access to high-quality information," the two mavericks wrote in their 2004 initial public offering letter. One of the tenets listed was "Don't be evil."[5]

Two years after Google's 1998 launch, VISA approached Page and Brin with a $3 million offer to display an ad for the credit card company on Google's home page. The two former Stanford University graduate students turned it down. But they quickly changed their stance. On October 23, 2000, Google introduced the groundbreaking online advertising platform Google AdWords (now Google Ads). It initially operated on a pay-per-impression model and displayed ads exclusively on the right-hand side of search results. Advertisers could specify how much they were willing to pay per thousand impressions, with higher bids securing better placements, such as first-page or top-of-the-page results. In its first year, Google AdWords generated more than $70 million in revenue.[6]

Google is now one of the largest purveyors of online ads. The company developed and acquired various advertising technologies and platforms. In addition to acquiring DoubleClick, some of its acquisitions include the demand-site platform Invite Media in 2010 for approximately $81 million, allowing advertisers to purchase display ads in real time. That same year it purchased AdMob for $750 million, expanding its reach to mobile advertising. In 2011, it bought AdMeld for $400 million, providing ad optimization solutions for publishers.[7]

In 2015, Google changed its publicly traded name to Alphabet. As of 2024,

Alphabet boasted a market capitalization exceeding $2.093 trillion, making it one of the world's most valuable publicly traded companies. Despite Google's self-identification as a tech company, it's the largest media company globally with online advertising being its primary source of revenue. In 2023, Alphabet raked in nearly $237.86 billion in revenue, with over 80 percent—totaling $147 billion—coming from Google advertising.[8]

That's beneficial for Google shareholders but problematic for its end users. Google has been an accelerant of propaganda, and it has harmed smaller businesses through anticompetitive practices.

Giving Hate an Edge

Over the years, Google has faced criticism for its ad platform's role in spreading hate and prejudice. Due to its automated placement system, which matches ads with content based on keywords and viewer demographics, Google Ads have sometimes appeared on websites or alongside YouTube videos promoting extremist views. In 2017, this issue led major companies, like AT&T and Johnson & Johnson, to pull their ads from YouTube after they were shown next to videos promoting hate speech and extremist content, highlighting the need for more careful scrutiny.[9]

Google's search engine can be manipulated to spread vitriol and extremism online. On the heels of the 2016 presidential election, Jonathan Albright, a communications professor at Elon University in North Carolina, conducted research on right-wing websites, uncovering a complex web of sites that share thousands of links to other sites, forming what he describes as a right-wing propaganda apparatus. He describes this network as an ecosystem that surrounds the mainstream news.[10]

In this context, Google helps breathe life into extremist ideologies and helps them gain a broader audience. This highly linked, self-referential network of hate creates a vortex that distorts search results. It's also a journalistic strategy, as a result of competing for readers' attention (and wallets, if sites are monetizing their links). Extremist "news sites" have developed methods to manipulate or outsmart Google's PageRank algorithms, boosting their rankings.

Albright found that conservative ideologues have effectively occupied digital spaces concerning topics like women, Jews, Black people, and Muslims more so than their liberal counterparts. As users search for information on these topics, they are often directed by algorithms to hate sites. Each click not only increases traffic but also falsely enhances these sites' perceived authority and credibility, further boosting their rankings. Albright describes this as a "circular knowledge economy" that consistently reinforces harmful messages, including portraying Jews as evil, glorifying Hitler, advocating the destruction of Islam, and demonizing women.[11]

According to a 2023 report by the research firm Adalytics, Google's Search Partner Network—intended to "extend the reach of Google Search ads to hundreds of non-Google sites, as well as YouTube and other Google site"—includes thousands of websites that breach Google's publisher policies.[12] These violations include ads appearing on hardcore pornography sites, disinformation platforms, and even sites in Iran, breaching international sanctions. Specific instances include an FBI application/career ad on an Italian pornography site and on the website of the Iranian Alloy Steel Company in Tehran. BMW's ads were displayed on Breitbart, despite BMW's request to avoid the site known for disseminating disinformation. Ads for alcohol brands were even found on children's websites.

Google responded to the Adalytics report by criticizing the methods used to reach its conclusions. They publicly discredited the report, citing issues such as leading questions, confirmation bias, sampling errors, and a disregard for billing and safety protocols, which they argued resulted in erroneous data. Google also pointed to several third-party data platforms that contradicted Adalytics' findings, indicating that advertisers weren't necessarily charged for all ads in question.[13]

In response to ongoing concerns, in 2024, the watchdog group Check My Ads called for a dismantling of Google's ad-tech monopoly. Its website urges consumers and advertisers to pressure Google to make participation in its Global Search Partner Network opt-in rather than the default opt-out.[14]

In Kong's Shadow

Google's dominance in the advertising industry has negative consequences for segments of the economy, particularly small businesses. Yet Google portrays itself as a champion of American small businesses, especially in the early days of the COVID-19 pandemic.

The reality is quite different. Despite facing antitrust lawsuits and the potential for government actions to break up its monopoly, Google has become a feudal lord in cyberspace. In 2021, the American Economic Liberties Project pointed out that Google profits from content stolen from small businesses and publishers by displaying it in its search results. It permits competitors to buy ads using other businesses' trademarks, essentially forcing these companies to pay to regain their own customers. The ad giant's platform also enables the proliferation of fraudulent listings for small businesses, harming legitimate businesses and customers. The sheer size of Google makes it difficult for small businesses to receive adequate customer support and correct inaccurate listings.[15]

Preferential treatment on Google's search and advertising platforms hinders small businesses' ability to compete effectively. Google also makes arbitrary decisions to ban entire industries from advertising on its platform, which leads to substantial revenue loss for businesses like independent tech repair shops. To boost ad sales, the ad-tech giant steers customers searching for local vendors to Google Maps or Shopping, even when services like TripAdvisor or Yelp offer superior listings and information. Because Google's advertising markets are complex and costly, small advertisers have limited transparency and high expenses.

Google's dominance creates what is often referred to as a "kill zone," discouraging investment in startups that could potentially compete with or be acquired by the tech giant. And it undermines local news outlets by monopolizing the digital advertising market and monetizing news content without fairly sharing revenue.

In 2023, the Justice Department and several states filed a lawsuit against Google alleging that the advertising giant unlawfully monopolized the more than $250 billion online ad market through years of self-dealing, anticompetitive acquisitions, and pressuring businesses to use its suite of products."[16]

The Ad Industry's Lobbyist

Policymakers face formidable opposition from lobbyists when they seek to enforce antitrust laws and promote legislation aimed at mitigating the negative impact of Google and similar companies on small businesses.

The Interactive Advertising Bureau, or IAB, is one such influential body. Formed in 1996, the IAB is a membership nonprofit organization representing more than seven hundred media companies and technology firms, including Google and Meta. It conducts research, creates industry standards, and provides legal support for the online advertising industry. It enforces legal and conformity guidelines in display ads, such as pop-up and banner ads on websites and social media.

The IAB also lobbies. Its influence was evident in spring 2022 during a congressional hearing on the Banning Surveillance Advertising Act, introduced on January 19, 2022, by Representatives Anna Eshoo (D-CA) and Jan

Schakowsky (D-IL), and Senators Ron Wyden (D-OR) and Cory Booker (D-NJ). The act aimed to prohibit advertisers and ad facilitators, such as Google and Facebook, from using personal data for targeted ads. It also sought to prevent targeted ads based on sensitive information such as race, gender, religion, and personal data acquired from data brokers.

Senator Booker emphasized the exploitative and invasive nature of surveillance advertising, saying, "We should not have to choose between using the internet and sacrificing our most personal and sensitive data."[17]

The IAB, representing its more than seven hundred members, submitted a letter to House Energy and Commerce Committee leaders opposing the legislation. It argued that the proposed law would result in the loss of millions of jobs and have a detrimental impact on the data-driven advertising economy. IAB CEO David Cohen had a dramatic prediction for bill passage: "Everything from online retail to the new 'creator' economy could cease to exist. This terrible bill would disenfranchise businesses that advertise on the internet, and hundreds of millions of Americans who use it every day to find exactly what they need, quickly. It could eliminate the commercial internet almost entirely."[18] IAB chairperson Randall Rothenberg tweeted that the act was "a sexy-named bill that would eliminate 140 years of direct-marketing practice, destroy the US Postal Service, kill American retailing, and stop all DTC (direct to consumer) development dead in its tracks."[19]

The Banning the Surveillance Advertising Act died in 2022 after opposition from the IAB and the Network Advertising Initiative. Representatives Eshoo and Schakowsky and Senators Wyden and Booker reintroduced the Act on September 18, 2023. The nonprofit group Accountable Tech's executive director, Nicole Gill, said the act will "not only protect consumers from this exploitative business practice" of data collection and retention in pursuit of surveillance advertising, but will also "mitigate Big Tech's unchecked harms as we face a growing environment of online manipulation and disinformation."[20]

It's Launch Time!

Every September, Apple releases a new iPhone. Strategically timed, it capitalizes on the year-end holiday shopping season and the back-to-school period, attracting students eager for the latest model.

Similarly, the government often launches significant military campaigns with strategies akin to those used in commercial product launches, carefully crafting messages to shape public perception and gain widespread support.

Criminologist and TV analyst Scott Bonn recounts how during a 2002 press corps event near Labor Day, Andy Card, the White House chief of staff, likened the marketing of the Iraq invasion to product promotion. When asked if the nation was going to war, Card responded, "Timing is everything from a marketing point of view. You don't introduce new products over the summer."[21]

The Bush administration's approach to invading Iraq was marked by a well-orchestrated media campaign highlighting specific narratives, such as the search for weapons of mass destruction and the promotion of democracy. These messages were repeatedly broadcast across various media platforms, creating a sense of urgency and suggesting that intervention was a moral imperative.

This marketing push, focused and repetitive, helped align public opinion with government policy; many Americans accepted official statements and rationales without question. Like a product launch, the "product" was a strategic military action, packaged and presented to ensure public buy-in and minimal initial resistance.

The internet has helped in the marketing of government propaganda. Two years after the 2001 launch of the Global War on Terror and within the first week of the US invasion of Iraq, a Pew study reported that 77 percent of Americans used the internet for news about the conflict.[22] During this pre-iPhone era, the internet's popularity surged as people sought real-time news and platforms for connectivity and personal expression.

For five weeks, the Bush administration marketed the war. The day after Card's comment, a *New York Times* front-page story by Judith Miller and Michael R. Gordon reported that Saddam Hussein was intensifying his search for A-bomb parts, citing Bush administration officials as sources.[23] Vice President Dick Cheney referenced the article in a speech and on *Meet the Press* the same day it was published. Saying he couldn't mention specific intelligence sources, he reiterated that Saddam Hussein had sought to acquire tubes needed to build a centrifuge. "The White House scheduled five A-list administration officials on each of the Sunday TV talk shows," commented Bonn on the administration's post-summer full-court press.

Following the 9/11 attacks, phrases such as "axis of evil," "evil doers," "mad men," and "mad dogs" began to characterize public discourse, painting Iraq as a significant threat. Leaders evoked imagery of smoking guns and mushroom clouds, implying that inaction could lead to another disaster like 9/11 or worse.

"As the volume cranked up higher and higher," Bonn observed, "public opinion mirrored the rhetoric." Bonn noted from Gallup polls conducted before the war that rhetoric about Iraq grew increasingly inflammatory and punitive. Just before the invasion began, on March 19, 2003, 70 percent of the public supported going to war, and an almost identical 70 percent believed that Iraq was involved in 9/11.[24]

Bonn notes that politicians often use sound bites and persuasive information to craft appealing narratives, using repetition and emotional manipulation in effective propaganda. Reflecting on Secretary of State Colin Powell's presentation to the United Nations on February 5, 2004, just before the war began, Bonn said, "It was a beautiful multimedia presentation, and we now know that it was a complete falsehood."

Case Study: Cambridge Analytica and Ad Tech's Threat to Democracy

The ad-tech industry has contributed to an erosion of democracy. Extensive tracking of user behaviors not only undermines privacy; it infringes on individual freedoms. Users are fed constant streams of material aimed at influencing their decisions. Ad algorithms designed to maximize engagement trap users in "filter bubbles," limiting exposure to diverse viewpoints. This fragmentation undermines societal cohesion and reduces democratic deliberation.

Highly targeted advertising can be exploited in undemocratic ways to spread misinformation and manipulate public opinion, particularly during elections. Microtargeted political ads, for example, often contain falsehoods and misleading information. Because these ads are tailored to small, specific audiences based on data-driven insights, they are less visible to the general public and media. This limited visibility reduces the likelihood of public scrutiny and accountability. As well, the personalized nature of microtargeting makes it challenging for fact-checkers to monitor and address false information effectively.

A more subtle harm from constantly receiving online ads is that users become accustomed to economic disparities in voice and influence. Ad-tech structures typically amplify voices with greater financial resources, overshadowing grassroots campaigns and smaller voices in public discourse. This skews political and social debates, privileging the interests of the wealthy or powerful.

Social media postings, on the other hand, are more visible and have directly impaired voter rights. In March 2023, Douglass Mackey, a social media influencer posting under the alias Ricky Vaughn, was found guilty of conspiring with other influential Twitter users and with private online group members to deprive others of their right to vote. Mackey and others posted images on Twitter that resembled campaign ads for Hillary Clinton, falsely stating that people could vote by texting the word *Hillary* to 59925.[25] The Justice Department reported that on or around Election Day 2016, at least 4,900 unique telephone numbers texted *Hillary* or some variation to the 59925 number tweeted by Mackey and his coconspirators.[26]

What's become known as the Cambridge Analytica/Facebook scandal is a notable example of how personal data are exploited for political gain. The now-defunct data analytics firm, cofounded by Steve Bannon and Republican donor Robert Mercer, was once part of the British firm SCL Group, a private behavioral research and strategic communication company. It received $15 million from Mercer, allegedly promising Bannon, then adviser to the Trump campaign, that it would analyze American voters' personalities to influence their behavior during the 2016 presidential election. Whistleblower Christopher Wylie, who, along with subsequent investigations, exposed the use of Facebook data by Cambridge Analytica, testified before the Senate judiciary committee that he believed that voter suppression was one of Steve Bannon's goals while he was vice president of Cambridge Analytica. Wylie noted that, "One of the things that provoked me to leave was discussions about 'voter disengagement' and the idea of targeting African Americans," which he said was referenced in Cambridge Analytica documents.[27]

In total, Cambridge Analytica harvested the personal information of as many as eighty-seven million Facebook users and their friends, without their consent, through the third-party app This Is Your Digital Life.[28] Data was used to create psychological profiles for microtargeted political ads. For example, an ad appealing to "neurotic" types focused on escalating international risks and need for strong political leaders. It contrasted images of chaotic violence abroad with a young boy waving an American flag. Another ad, aimed at "agreeable" personalities, featured John Bolton, former US ambassador to the United Nations, underscoring the need for "a stronger America and a safer world for our children," given that agreeable people often value community and societal needs.[29] After whistleblowers and investigations exposed these unethical practices, Facebook admitted to the data breach in 2018.

International fallout and response to the scandal was immediate. The United States Senate Judiciary Committee called witnesses to testify about the data breach and data privacy in general. One hearing focused on Facebook's role in the breach on social media, and the other on Cambridge Analytica's role and its impact on data privacy.

In response to its compliance failures, in 2018 Facebook announced the creation of a separate private business entity, Oversight Board, to advise a narrow band of its content decisions. The Oversight Board officially began work in 2020, and according to the American Bar Association, it has indeed helped Facebook distance itself from the Cambridge Analytica affair and additional scrutiny. But the Oversight Board is narrow in scope; it doesn't answer questions about the company's back-end operations, meaning it addresses fewer than 0.01 percent of appeals to Facebook's content decisions.[30]

In 2019, the FTC found that Cambridge Analytica engaged in deceptive practices by falsely telling app users that the This Is Your Digital Life app would not collect users' names or other identifiable information. The FTC also found that Cambridge Analytica was misleading about its participation in the EU-US Privacy Shield Framework, a process that allowed companies to transfer consumer data from European Union countries to the United States in compliance with EU law (more on this in a later chapter). The FTC found that Cambridge Analytica failed to comply with the requirement to affirm to the Department of Commerce that, even after leaving the Privacy Shield program, they would continue applying its protections to the personal information they had collected. In 2019, Facebook agreed to pay a $5 billion fine to the FTC as part of a settlement over privacy violations, including those related to Cambridge Analytica. The settlement required Facebook to implement significant changes to its privacy practices and establish a privacy oversight committee.[31]

Related to the same case, in 2022, Meta Platforms, Inc., agreed to pay $725 million to settle a class-action lawsuit accusing it of granting Cambridge Analytica and other third parties access to private user data. This settlement follows a series of global penalties and actions in response to the scandal. In 2018, the UK Information Commissioner's Office fined Facebook £500,000, the maximum amount possible under the Data Protection Act of 1998, for failing to protect user data and lacking transparency regarding how user data had been harvested by third parties. In 2019, an investigation by Canada's Office of the Privacy Commissioner found that Facebook had committed serious contraventions of Canadian privacy laws in connection with the scandal.[32] Although the office did not impose financial penalties, it sought a court order to force Facebook to implement changes to its privacy practices. And in 2020, Australia's Office of the Australian Information Commissioner (OAIC) initiated proceedings against Facebook for alleged serious and repeated interferences with the privacy of Australian users. The OAIC sought civil penalties for breaches of the Privacy Act of 1988. In March 2023, proceedings were cleared to go forward after an appeal by Facebook was revoked by the High Court of Australia.

Desire Makes More $$$

There was no *ta-da!* moment when we awakened to find ourselves mid-ring in an advertising arena. We arrived here slowly, oblivious to the toxicity of slow-building threats to our autonomy.

Back in 1927, Lehman Brothers banker Paul Myer Mazur encouraged a shift from needs-based to desire-based consumer culture. President Herbert Hoover then sought the expertise of public relations and advertising professionals to instill these desires in citizens, effectively turning them into "constantly moving happiness machines" deemed vital for economic growth.

"Madison Avenue techniques" have since honed the art of tapping into human instincts to fuel purchasing desires, which now strongly drive the US economy. In 2019, US companies set a record by spending $366.4 billion on advertising, as reported by the Advertising Coalition.[33]

Our vocabulary mirrors this shift, with *consumer* now eclipsing *citizen* in usage frequency.[34] Historically, *consumer* in the early fifteenth century meant someone who was wasteful, but by the mid-1700s, it merely described someone using goods. By 1890, as *consumer goods* became commonplace in discourse, the term shed its negative undertones, aligning instead with the act of purchasing. Today, emphasizing our identity as consumers over citizens is prevalent among businesses, advertisers, politicians, and even journalists. Our lives revolve around the cycle of buying and discarding.

Meanwhile, the time and attention that people devote to shopping often sidelines their civic participation and community-oriented activities. Marketers have mastered the use of advertising to attract consumers to the superficial, sacrificing more consequential pursuits in the process. According to the International Association of Shopping Centers, in 2016, 56 percent of American adults conducted online research online before visiting a brick-and-mortar store.[35] As of 2024, shopping malls continue to attract a significant share of consumer visits, with 45 percent of shoppers primarily choosing in-store shopping.[36] The relationship between malls and online shopping has evolved into a complementary dynamic. Consumers often adopt a hybrid approach, shopping both online and in-store. This method, known as "BOPIS" (buy online, pick up in store), has gained traction, particularly for items like electronics and home furnishings. This synergy helps retailers bridge the gap between their e-commerce platforms and traditional retail, enhancing consumer convenience and maintaining engagement.

In contrast, 48 percent of Americans have engaged in a civic group or activity, according to the Pew Research Center.[37] The integration of mass media and "advertainment"—where branding blends seamlessly with entertainment content—leads us into a bleak shopping mall where communal understanding and collective problem-solving are off the market.

CHAPTER 7

Trillionaire Tech Overlords

If one considers the internet as a landscape, it's easy to imagine that we're navigating a modern-day feudal system, with tech superpowers staking claim over the territories and ruling over the users who occupy the fiefdoms. Medieval overlords controlled vast lands and wielded power over their states, providing protection in exchange for loyalty and labor. Similarly, Big Tech companies dominate digital landscapes, offering technology and connectivity in return for personal data and adherence to platform rules. Barons extracted wealth from land and labor, while Big Tech generates immense wealth through data collection, advertising, and digital services, influencing markets and global economies.

People depended on feudal overlords for security and sustenance, making escape difficult. Likewise, modern users and businesses rely heavily on Big Tech for communication, commerce, and information, which limits alternatives and fosters quasi-monopolies. Olden-day overlords operated with minimal oversight but faced resistance and power struggles. Today, influential tech companies often resist regulation, leveraging vast resources to influence legislation and shape public opinion, while facing growing demands for accountability from governments and consumers.

In both historical and modern contexts, the concentration of power and control reduces representation, accountability, and public discourse. In the digital era, the power of dominant tech players is quickly proving anathema to democracy.

Bots: Modern Yeomen

In lieu of yeomen—servants or attendants in manor households—the digital ruling elite rely on algorithms, or coded sets of rules, to mold content on social media platforms, search engines, and streaming services. Apprentice-like "bots"—software robots programmed with algorithms to automate routine tasks—carry out their masters' directives. Bots originated in the early days of computing as simple automation tools to perform repetitive tasks; as technology advanced, they began to interact more naturally with humans, process large amounts of data, and perform complex tasks autonomously. Bots work quietly in the background to control the visibility of news stories and information, determining what becomes widely known and shaping public discourse. Chatbots simulate human conversations, social bots influence discussions on social media, news bots deliver headlines, and spam bots generate fake and damaging interactions and even conduct cyberattacks, all of which pollute the web.

As bot masters, tech companies aim to maximize user engagement online. The economic impact of bots is substantial, as evidenced by the chat bot's market of $4.6 billion in 2022, projected to reach $32.4 billion by 2032, growing at a compound annual rate of 21.6 percent.[1] Research conducted by the Pew Research Center reveals that, as of 2020, approximately 66 percent of all tweeted links to popular websites originated from automated accounts, not human users.[2]

Users as Serfs

Big Tech companies have created extensive ecosystems to incentivize users to remain within their platforms by offering a suite of interconnected services. In effect, this turns users into modern-day serfs governed by tech overlords who dictate the terms of engagement within these digital realms.

Apple integrates its products, such as iPhones, MacBooks, iPads, and Apple Watches, with services like iCloud, Apple Music, and Apple Pay. Its seamless integration between hardware and software encourages users to stay within the Apple ecosystem. Users benefit from features like iMessage, AirDrop, and Continuity, which work best when all devices are Apple products.

Google's vast array of services includes Android OS, Google Search, Gmail, Google Drive, Google Photos, and YouTube, which are interconnected and made accessible through a single Google account. The convenience of having all services synced and accessible across devices, coupled with the integration of Google services in Android phones, keeps users within its ecosystem. Amazon offers a comprehensive environment with its e-commerce platform, Prime membership, Kindle devices, Alexa smart home products, and Amazon Web Services for cloud computing. Prime membership benefits like free shipping, streaming services, and discounts, along with the integration of Alexa with other Amazon services, encourage users to stay loyal to

Amazon. It's near impossible to get out from under Amazon's thumb in the digital world. Many streaming services and retail sites rely on Amazon Web Services for hosting.

Meta's digital ecosystem includes Facebook, Instagram, WhatsApp, and Oculus for VR. The network effect, where the value of the platform increases as more people use it, along with integrated services like Messenger, keeps users engaged within Meta's ecosystem. In comparison, Microsoft's ecosystem includes Windows OS, Microsoft Office, OneDrive, Xbox, and LinkedIn; the Windows OS is often preinstalled on work computers, bridging personal and professional access to one's digital footprint. Integration across these platforms, particularly for business and gaming, as well as the importance of the Windows OS in the enterprise environment, reinforces user loyalty.

These companies create walled gardens that often stifle competition and limit consumer choice. Government agencies and regulators should enforce and even update antitrust laws to accommodate the digital era, ensuring data portability, and promoting interoperability between different ecosystems. While tech companies bear primary responsibility, users also have a role in demanding more ethical practices and supporting alternatives that prioritize privacy, openness, and competition. Legislators need to craft and enforce laws that promote competition, protect user data, and prevent monopolistic behaviors. They should also focus on ensuring that users have the freedom to move their data and switch between ecosystems without undue barriers.

All-Too-Willing Subjects

With so much of our lives lived online, it benefits these trillionaire tech companies to treat American users as test subjects.

Apple's blend of stunning design and seamless functionality have captivated the masses, setting new benchmarks in the industry. It revolutionized the way people perceive and engage with computers, particularly through its pioneering work in touch-screen technology, which opened the floodgates to a constant flow of information and entertainment.

Founded by Steve Jobs and Steve Wozniak, and initially celebrated for its altruistic ethos and innovative spirit (notably introducing the first color graphics that, in tandem with the rise of Adobe, revolutionized desktop publishing), the company gradually shifted its focus toward maximizing profits over altruism.

In this pursuit, Apple's designers and engineers have honed techniques to tap into our neurochemistry, fostering addictive behaviors with our devices.

Numerous polls and statistics support the fact that we're addicted. *PC Magazine* reported in 2023 that 57 percent of Americans claim to be addicted to their phones, checking them an average of 144 times each day.[3] The intuitive design of Apple's user interface, along with its seamless app integration and the constant stream of notifications, all contribute to its addictive appeal. Notifications, though subtle, serve as captivating alerts that keep users engaged and coming back for more. A 2016 study by the platform dscout found that the average user tapped, swiped, and clicked on their phone approximately 2,617 times per day.[4] This frequent interaction with the iPhone not only sustains user engagement; it cultivates a sense of dependency.

Reliance on bots—tech overlords' silent partners—amplify addictive tendencies.

AI-powered chatbots use text or voice to simulate human conversation. The photo-messaging app Snapchat's chatbot, My AI, has sparked worries due to its addictive nature and privacy implications. With My AI, users can personalize the chatbot's name and avatar and integrate the bot into conversations with friends, making it seem more human. As young users view chatbots as companions, they may turn to them frequently for inquiries, conversations, and recommendations. Critics, including Democratic senator Michael Bennet, are apprehensive over reports suggesting that chatbots can give children suggestions about how to lie to their parents: "When [researchers] posed as a 13-year-old girl, My AI provided suggestions for how to lie to her parents about an upcoming trip with a 31-year-old man."[5]

In response to criticism for lacking age-gating features, Snapchat introduced new parental controls in 2024 that allow parents to restrict their teens from interacting with My AI. These updates give parents access to view their children's privacy settings and easier entry to Family Center, Snapchat's hub for parental controls.

Snapchatters report a high level of happiness using the platform. In an independent study conducted for Snapchat by Neuro-Insight, a neuro-analytics and neuro-marketing firm, a majority of Snapchatters said that they felt connected to friends and family while on the platform; 75 percent of those surveyed cited that as their main reason for using it.[6] Neuro-Insight used Implicit Association Testing (IAT) to measure the strength of unconscious connections between content on platforms and key emotions felt. Participants viewed several terms—such as *be me, fun, happy, true friends, judgy,* and *hurtful*—alternated with brand logos; response times were used to calculate associational strengths. Feelings of happiness while using Snapchat were 14 percent higher than on other social platforms tested, according to the IAT.[7]

Despite legitimate concerns about chatbot use, particularly regarding privacy and content moderation, studies show that educational chatbots can be beneficial for young users. One, "Role of AI Chatbots in Education," by Lasha Labadze, Maya Grigolia, and Lela Machaidze, summarizes reported benefits.[8] AI chatbots save time by managing routine tasks like scheduling, grading, and providing information, so educators can focus on teaching and student engagement. Teachers can use chatbots to enhance instruction, offer personalized tutoring, and create tailored learning materials that meet individual student needs. Chatbots help develop skills through real-time feedback on writing, problem-solving, and group discussions.

Students report that AI chatbots provide valuable assistance with homework, study guides, and exam preparation by offering feedback, clarifications, and step-by-step solutions. Their interactive nature boosts engagement and can support mental health by offering a safe space for kids to express themselves, while personalized learning adapts to each student's needs.

1984 Won't Be Like 1984.... Or Will It?

A TV ad started the shift to rule by trillionaire overlords.

Apple's iconic "1984" commercial, which aired only once, shows the power of astute corporate marketing. Referenced in introductory classes on advertising, media studies, and communications, it holds a permanent place in American advertising history. Apple, Inc.'s marketing strategy was simple: to convey "We're un-corporate."

Hollywood visionary Ridley Scott, renowned for *Blade Runner* and *Alien*, directed the groundbreaking Apple ad. Airing just two days before the Macintosh launch, it positioned Apple as the antidote to IBM's tech giant hegemony. The spot featured a runner wielding a sledgehammer, pursued by four officers, racing to smash a large projector depicting a Big Brother figure delivering a speech on unified thought. Black text and a voiceover read: "On January 24th, Apple Computer will introduce Macintosh. And you'll see why 1984 won't be like *1984*."[9] The ad portrayed Apple as synonymous with freedom and individual empowerment. Dubbed *Advertising Age*'s commercial of the decade, its single airing during Super Bowl XVIII in 1984, with its massive viewership, further elevated its status.[10]

Technological advances in the early 1980s were poised to revolutionize the global economy. Apple's Macintosh ad both capitalized on and downplayed consumers' fears around the extent and nature of corporate power. The advent of mass-market personal computers and the dismantling of the

Bell System monopoly on phone lines heralded a wave of technological innovations that would forever transform communication and reshape our perception of reality.

Innovation flourished on a grand scale, with US inventors contributing to a 19 percent increase in total telecom patents.[11] Before long, the tech industry became the darling of the stock markets, outpacing the once-dominant Big Oil energy giants and mega media companies. The Ridley Scott ad cast Apple as a beacon of user freedom, but that message is now as outdated as the Macintosh itself. Today, Apple has grown as conformist and domineering as the Orwellian world it once rebelled against, echoing the very control it condemned in IBM's dominance of the personal computer market.

From "Non-1984" to Law Enforcement's Handmaiden

Ironically, even though Apple professes freedom and personal empowerment, its business model revolves around "owning" the consumer. It boasts one of the highest customer retention rates, reaching 90 percent as of 2023.[12] Viewed positively, such high retention rates reflect the company's success; but from another perspective, the implications are somewhat sinister.

Consider the groundbreaking iPhone. Americans are tethered, many even addicted, to smartphones. This addiction is a deliberate outcome of product design. Consumer loyalty supports the notion that you don't *use* an Apple product—you *become* an Apple person.[13] That premise was personified by the 2006–2009 "Get a Mac" ads featuring comedians John Hodgman as a PC and Justin Long as a Mac. The campaign reinforced the notion that choosing Apple is not just about the product but about embracing a particular lifestyle and identity. In addition to delivering reliable and aesthetically pleasing products, Apple meticulously crafts its messaging and presentation for consistency. Other identity brands, such as Converse and IKEA, similarly broadcast mission, values, personality, position, and voice to keep customers engaged and invested in their products.

Once users enter the Apple ecosystem, they often develop strong loyalty to Apple products. As mentioned earlier, hardware and applications are tightly integrated with an operating system, facilitating seamless functionality across various Apple devices. For instance, Apple exerted control over its iPod (hardware), launched in 2003, and iTunes Music Store (content) by creating a closed ecosystem that effectively locked users into both. Music purchased from iTunes was encoded with Apple's proprietary DRM (digital rights management technology), FairPlay, which restricted playback to Apple devices like the iPod. This made it difficult for users to switch to other MP3 players without losing access to their purchased music.

Apple reinforced this control by regularly updating iTunes and iPod firmware to prevent third-party solutions, like RealNetworks' Harmony, from bypassing these restrictions. Although successful in driving iPod and iTunes adoption, this approach drew criticism for being anticompetitive. In response to growing pressure, Apple eventually removed DRM from iTunes music in 2009, affording users more flexibility to play their music on non-Apple devices.

Once hooked into its ecosystem, Apple devotees and their personal data don't receive the level of privacy protection the company claims it provides.

Despite Apple's claims of having robust privacy safeguards, in several instances the company was accused of significant privacy violations. A series of lawsuits filed against Apple highlights its alleged practice of collecting and sending analytics data from iPhone users, when they had explicitly opted out. In late 2022, Tommy Mysk and Talal Haj Bakry from the software company Mysk found that the App Store, Apple TV, Apple Music, Apple Stocks, and Apple Books were tracking users' app interactions, searches, and other activities, even when devices' analytics were disabled. Tracking extended beyond mere functional data collection and was used for analytics and marketing purposes, with the information directly related to Apple.[14]

Mysk's findings raised significant concerns about the gap between Apple's privacy promises and its actual practices. The revelation undermined Apple's credibility and highlighted the challenges users face in trusting even the most seemingly secure platforms. Digital literacy, which includes healthy skepticism, helps users understand how companies with strong reputations for privacy can engage in questionable practices. This case also illustrates the larger issue of how companies may exploit user data under the guise of improving services. People easily and willingly give up their personal data because they don't want to fight a monolith when using their devices. Locked into the Apple lifestyle means users have fewer app options that may or may not have ulterior data-gathering motives.

In response to Mysk's discovery in 2022, Elliot Libman, an iPhone 13 owner from New York, initiated a class-action lawsuit against Apple.[15] Libman argued that Apple's assurances of user control over shared information when using its default iPhone apps are "utterly false." He further alleged that Apple's practices violate the California Invasion of Privacy Act.

Apple partners with government agencies to spy on its loyal customers. This collaboration places it among, and sometimes above, its tech rivals in terms of compliance with law enforcement requests for user data. In the first half of 2020, for example, authorities requested information on more than 186,000 Apple accounts, with Apple complying 90 percent of the time.[16] While Apple markets itself as a corporate rebel, its competitors like Google and Facebook often had similar or even lower response rates.

Also troubling: not all data on Apple's iCloud server is encrypted.[17] This lack of encryption allows Apple to provide law enforcement with stored documents, photos, contacts, browsing history, messages, and iPhone operating system (iOS) backups.

And as detailed later, Apple has faced scrutiny and been issued fines for violating the General Data Protection Regulation (GDPR), notably for transparency issues and not adequately protecting user data. These fines, along with litigation, illustrate that despite its marketing rhetoric, Apple has struggled to adhere to its own privacy commitments.

Rule Without Oversight: Consolidation

The rapid consolidation of power in tech companies poses challenges to democratic processes and institutions. The so-called "Big Five"—Alphabet (parent of Google), Amazon, Apple, Meta, and Microsoft—and other trillionaire companies like Nvidia, whose chips are essential for AI applications, are reaching unprecedented sizes and controlling the digital infrastructure, reshaping national power dynamics.

Services once exclusively the domain of government—from communication to commerce to information dissemination—are now provided by tech companies who innovate and provide them more nimbly than federal agencies. American governmental entities contract and partner with tech firms for essential services such as cloud computing, data analytics, cybersecurity, and emerging technologies like artificial intelligence. The US Department of Defense's contract with Microsoft for the $10 billion JEDI (Joint Enterprise Defense Infrastructure) cloud-computing project highlights this close interaction. Such partnerships can lead to concerns that government oversight and governance structures might be compromised by decisions influenced by the business interests of these tech firms. With the JEDI contract, allegations of favoritism and conflicts of interest were raised, leading to controversy and legal challenges.[18] Amazon claimed the bidding process was biased in favor of Microsoft due to alleged political interference by the Trump administration. Lawsuits led to prolonged litigation, ultimately resulting in the Pentagon canceling the JEDI contract in 2021, opting instead for a new multi-vendor approach.

Feudal Lords: Wielding Propaganda, Not Protection

Big Tech's subtle manipulation resembles government propaganda, albeit more insidious. Historical instances of propaganda often came with identifiable sources and intention. "I Want You for U.S. Army" was an iconic 1917 recruitment poster featuring Uncle Sam, used extensively to encourage enlistment in the US Army during World War I. The image of Uncle Sam, personifying the government, pointed at the viewer with the slogan and became a well-known symbol of American patriotism and duty.

By 2003, propaganda moved online and became more sophisticated.

Decades later, tech behemoths' discourse shaping is woven discretely into the fabric of daily life through algorithms, personalized content, and targeted ads. Its pervasive nature, operating within the ostensibly neutral realms of social media platforms and search engines, makes it more challenging to detect and resist. The Cambridge Analytica scandal, discussed in chapter 6, illustrates the dangers of corporations improperly harvesting user data for political purposes.

Dissent is stifled by such subtle control. But technology has been used to more actively undermine dissent, notably among activist movements. Political opponents have used botnets, formed by grouping bots together, as weapons to launch distributed denial of service (DDoS) attacks aimed at disrupting activist websites and other communication systems. In 2016, eQualitie, an international group of activists, software developers and security specialists, documented more than four hundred DDoS attacks against social justice groups.[19]

Profit-driven priorities blur the lines between genuine information dissemination and manipulation. Given that no source will label propaganda as such, discerning it is something individuals must learn to detect on their own, especially in our age of constant information streams with little consensus. Is this ad tailored to my personal/political interests? Will I even be able to tell the difference? The influence of billionaire companies' propaganda underscores the pressing need for transparency, accountability, and critical media literacy.

Modeling Fief Mentality

From the spread of misinformation to the manipulation of public opinion through targeted ads and algorithmic amplification, tech companies have proven they are capable of wielding undue influence over political discourse and election outcomes. Knowing how these dynamics work can spur users to begin holding tech companies accountable for their actions.

So how do the major technology companies evade government oversight and regulation?

1. **They lobby.** The Big Five surpassed all other industries in spending on lobbying to influence policymakers and shape legislation in their favor. In 2023, Alphabet, Meta, and Microsoft each spent more than $10 million on lobbying, while Amazon spent $19.8 million.[20] Google consistently ranks among the top spenders on lobbying activities in the United States. By strategically deploying resources and leveraging connections, these companies sway regulatory decisions and dilute the impact of proposed regulations that might limit their control over our lives and threaten their interests.

2. **They engage in regulatory capture.** That's when regulatory agencies tasked with overseeing industries become influenced or controlled by the very entities they are supposed to regulate. Tech behemoths often employ former government officials or industry insiders, blurring the lines between the regulators and the regulated. A lenient regulatory environment allows large companies to operate with minimal interference. In the revolving door between Silicon Valley and federal agencies, individuals move seamlessly between tech-industry roles and regulatory positions.

3. **They employ complex transnational corporate structures.** Complex corporate structures and international tax arrangements minimize Big Tech's tax liabilities, regulatory burdens, and tethering to the nation-state. Companies like Apple have shifted profits to subsidiaries in low-tax jurisdictions abroad, like Ireland and the Netherlands, to avoid higher tax rates and generate substantial revenue. Intricate arrangements like this make it difficult for regulators to enforce tax laws and other regulatory measures.

4. **They engage in legal maneuvering.** Under increased scrutiny from antitrust regulators around the world, tech giants employ vast teams of attorneys to engage in protracted legal battles, challenging antitrust allegations and delaying regulatory interventions. A prime example is Google's legal dispute with the European Union, which began with a record 2.42 billion euro ($2.6 billion) fine imposed by the EU on Google in 2017 for abusing its dominance as a search engine by

favoring its own comparison-shopping service over competitors.[21] Google appealed the decision, challenging the EU's interpretation of antitrust laws and seeking to overturn or reduce the fine. But in September 2024, Google lost its battle when the EU Court of Justice upheld the fine imposed by the EU antitrust regulators.[22] This legal maneuvering has prolonged the case, with Google employing numerous legal strategies to delay or mitigate the impact of the ruling.[23]

When game developer Epic Games filed a lawsuit against Apple in 2020, discussed later in this chapter, accusing the company of anti-competitive behavior by monopolizing app distribution and in-app payments on its iOS platform, Apple's legal maneuvering was extensive. Apple filed counterclaims against Epic, arguing that the game developer had breached its contract by introducing an alternative payment system within *Fortnite*. The case has involved multiple legal arguments and appeals, with both companies using legal tactics to influence the outcome and delay any final resolution.

5. They launch international jurisdictional challenges. Operating on a global scale, often spanning multiple jurisdictions with different regulatory frameworks, tech goliaths exploit regulatory arbitrage, capitalizing on regulatory disparities between countries to minimize compliance costs and legal liabilities. Companies like Facebook have faced challenges in complying with the European Union's General Data Protection Regulation (GDPR), while also navigating less stringent privacy laws in other regions.

Digital Literacy as Fiefdom Liberator

There are several ways that Americans can begin to reclaim their autonomy from tech titans in the digital age. The first is understanding how they collect, store, and use—and often misuse—personal data. Consider, if you will, the cookie. Instead of quickly accepting "all cookies" on banners to reach their desired destination online, it is well worth taking the extra thirty seconds to read the choices and eliminate "marketing cookies," or nonessential trackers.

Digital literacy involves recognizing the algorithms that shape our online experiences and understanding how they too often perpetuate biases and manipulate content. It involves knowing how algorithms on social media platforms create filter bubbles, reinforce users' existing attitudes, and limit exposure to diverse views. Once aware of this, users can seek out alternative viewpoints to expand their bubbles and take in other perspectives of current events.

Awareness of monopoly power and market dominance changes how we view large tech companies. By learning about antitrust laws and the concept of monopolies, users can advocate for regulatory measures that promote competition. As Americans realize how anticompetitive practices that stifle innovation limit their choices as consumers, it becomes clear that their lives can be enriched by not having tech giants dictate their default settings.

The Anti-Competitors

In recent years, both the United States and the European Union have pursued antitrust actions against the Big Five. In the US, a series of high-profile cases indicate a concerted effort to rein in their dominance. These include the attempt to block Microsoft's acquisition of the video game publisher Activision; a lawsuit against Google over ad tech; the FTC's scrutiny of Meta's virtual reality startup acquisition; and ongoing state-level cases against Google and Amazon. Similarly, the EU has levied hefty fines against Google and Apple for anticompetitive behavior and is investigating Amazon and Meta for potential violations. While these legal battles signal concern about tech monopolies, their impact on diminishing the overlords' dominance remains to be seen, as their market power and influence continue to shape the digital landscape.

In addition to antitrust lawsuits, regulatory reforms are another means by which to rein in the power of mega tech firms. Reforms include implementing stricter regulations on data privacy and protection, ensuring fair competition in digital markets, and enhancing transparency in algorithms and content-moderation processes. Fostering innovation through policies that promote interoperability and data portability could encourage a more diverse and competitive tech landscape. Data portability enables users to transfer their personal data between different services or platforms, promoting user autonomy, encouraging competition, and safeguarding privacy. Collaborative efforts between government, tech companies, and other stakeholders to establish industry standards and codes of conduct could play a key role in lessening tech dominance while fostering a healthier digital ecosystem.

One court victory has highlighted the aggressive tactics—indeed, the brute force—used by a tech giant to prevent smaller entities from thriving. It underscores the importance of promoting fair competition, innovation, and consumer choice in digital ecosystems.

An Epic Ruling

In the realm of mobile apps, Apple's App Store and Google's Play Store reign supreme as the default distribution channels for mobile applications, reaching billions of users worldwide. This control over app availability significantly influences users' choices and ultimately molds their digital behavior. While these platforms offer unparalleled access to potential customers, they come at a cost to smaller app developers.

Epic Games, the developer of the widely popular *Fortnite* game, learned this firsthand in 2020 when it introduced a direct payment system within *Fortnite*. This system allowed players to purchase in-game currency (V-Bucks) directly from Epic at a discounted price, bypassing Apple's and Google's in-app payment systems, which charge developers a 30 percent commission fee for transactions. As a result, both Apple and Google removed *Fortnite* from their app stores, sparking a legal battle over app store policies. Epic filed two separate lawsuits in August 2020—one against Apple and another against Google. Though both suits involved similar allegations about monopolistic practices and anti-competitive behavior, the lawsuit against Apple focused on iOS-specific issues, while the one against Google addressed the Android platform. Both cases criticized the companies' control over their app distribution channels, mandatory in-app payment systems, and anti-steering provisions.

Epic accused Google of using the Games Velocity Program (GVP) to "bribe or block" developers from distributing their games through alternative channels or app stores under an initiative known internally as "Project Hug." Through GVP, Google offered lucrative deals to developers, including a $360 million agreement with Activision Blizzard, the developer of *Call of Duty* and *World of Warcraft*, and a $90 million offer to Riot Games, the developer of *League of Legends* and *Valorant*. These agreements were reportedly aimed at deterring developers from seeking alternative platforms and mitigating the impact of the 30 percent revenue cut imposed by Google.[24]

Additional evidence supported Project Hug's strategy of enticing around twenty developers with favorable agreements to discourage them from exploring other options.[25] Internal communications and documents revealed that this was indeed the objective. Purnima Kochikar, director of Google Play, Apps, and Games, wrote in an email about their efforts to sway one smaller company: "We pulled all stops (promised them $10M marketing before they signed GVP for example) to get Riot to stop their inhouse 'app store' efforts and bring their billion-dollar League of Legends franchise and other mobile games to Play."[26]

As for its case against Apple, Epic claimed that Apple's policies created a "walled garden" that barred developers from using alternative app stores or payment options on iOS. Specifically, Apple required developers to use its in-app payment system, taking up to a 30 percent commission, and prohibited developers from directing users to alternative payment methods. These restrictions, according to Epic, paralleled Google's efforts to lock in developers and reinforce its app distribution monopoly, ultimately limiting user choice and developer freedom on both platforms.

On December 11, 2022, in a landmark victory, the jury ruled in favor of Epic Games. Following the verdict, the game developer celebrated on its website, stating, "Thank you to the Court for hearing this important case and for the next steps determining the remedies that will right Google's decades of anticompetitive conduct. And thank you to the jury for their historic decision. The one million game developers who couldn't be here thank you!"[27]

There was a partial victory for Epic Games in its case against Apple. In September 2021, a US federal judge ruled that Apple could no longer prohibit developers from directing users to external payment options outside the App Store. This decision allowed developers to inform users about alternative, often cheaper, ways to make purchases, bypassing Apple's 30 percent commission. However, the court did not require Apple to allow third-party app stores on iOS, and it upheld Apple's right to charge a commission on in-app purchases.

While the court ruled in favor or Epic regarding Apple's "anti-steering" practices, Apple retained its overall control over the iOS app ecosystem, and Epic did not succeed in forcing Apple to make broader changes to its App Store policies. Both sides appealed aspects of the decision, but in 2024 the US Supreme Court declined to hear the appeals, leaving the lower court's ruling in place.[28] As a result, while the specific legal dispute concluded, discussions about App Store policies and antitrust concerns continue in the broader tech industry.

Old Tricks, New Illusions

Apple's tactics for stifling competition are as old as the robber barons: acquire competitors, leverage their money and influence to crowd out alternatives, and undercut prices to force rivals out of business.

By 2023, Apple had absorbed more than one hundred companies through its acquisition spree. Apple CEO Tim Cook told CNBC in 2019 that Apple acquires on average one company every two to three weeks.[29] As a result, Apple has been hauled into court in numerous antitrust claims, unfair trade practice lawsuits, privacy class actions, price-switching class actions, corporate espionage accusations, and more.

As for the "1984" Apple ad, at least one commentator highlighted its hypocrisy three decades after its airing. In 2014, writer Rebecca Solnit described in *Harper's Magazine* how Apple helped usher in a new era of oppression:

> I want to yell at that liberatory young woman with her sledge-hammer: 'Don't do it!' Apple is not different. That industry is going to give rise to innumerable forms of triviality and misogyny, to the concentration of wealth and the dispersal of mental concentration.... If you think a crowd of people staring at one screen is bad, wait until you have created a world in which billions of people stare at their own screens even while walking, driving, eating in the company of friends—all *of them eternally elsewhere.*[30]

The fantasies depicted in Apple's "1984" spot—that Apple broke the mold of corporate domination—fed hopeful, if irrational, assumptions that users would be valued as humans rather than mere consumers. Remarkably successful in selling a product, the ad effectively hooked loyal consumers into the Apple ecosystem.

Google: Partners and Rivals

When you open your iPhone's browser, what search engine pops up? Do you even have to think about it anymore?

In 2021, Google paid Apple a staggering $18 billion to ensure its search engine remained Safari, the default option on iPhones.[31] During the government's 2023 antitrust investigation, its lawyers alleged that Google's agreements with Apple, as well as with Samsung and Mozilla, funneled traffic to Google's search engine.[32]

Google's dominance over users' online activities poses a threat to the open internet, which is vital to democratic discourse. Through sheer financial prowess, the company secures its position as the default search engine on a wide range of devices and platforms. This "pay-to-play" practice, also referred to as "search engine bundling," limits user choice and reinforces Google's stranglehold on the search engine industry.

Users who don't actively modify their default search engine settings unwittingly end up using Google by default, allowing it to accumulate vast amounts of user data, further entrenching the company's dominant position in the online-search landscape. Users may not be aware of alternative search engines or may find it inconvenient to switch from the default option, even if they prefer another search engine's privacy features or search results.

Another strategy Google uses is ad-revenue sharing. In certain cases, Google shares a portion of the advertising revenue generated through searches conducted on its search engine with companies or platforms that promote it as the default choice. This financial incentive encourages partners to continue favoring Google's search engine over alternatives.

Autonomy for Users

Apple, Google, and other tech giants have engineered a vice grip on consumers. They wield their influence through a combination of hardware, software, and ecosystem lock-ins. These tactics curtail user choice and foster a reliance on their products and services. For these reasons, more people are calling on these tech overlords to embrace a moral responsibility—a duty of care to their customers—to address the harm caused by their products.

The court victory of Epic Games against Apple serves as a significant milestone in conveying that feudal-like practices have no place in a democracy.

Design ethicist Tristan Harris's Time Well Spent movement advocates for an alternative to Big Tech's relentless pursuit of "time spent" advertising. Harris, founder of the Center for Humane Technology and a former Google project manager, proposes a paradigm shift wherein companies like Apple and Google design smart phones to safeguard rather than manipulate users' minds. Instead of fostering addiction to tech and social media, individuals would be empowered to make autonomous choices. This vision includes the establishment of a digital bill of rights outlining less intrusive design standards for apps and websites. These platforms would offer direct pathways to users' desired content, prioritizing their preferences over algorithm-driven distractions.

Based on the digital bill of rights' vision, companies would take the lead to mitigate "slot machine effects"—design strategies that exploit and maintain our attention—by implementing more ethical design practices. Rather than being tethered to social media platforms out of fear of missing out, individuals would reclaim control over relationships with friends and businesses, defining them on their own terms.

To safeguard the public's welfare, an independent organization akin to the Federal Drug Administration for the tech industry would be established.[33]

This consortium, consisting of diverse experts, would define and enforce standards, intervening when technology companies abuse them. Among the consortium's experts would be technology and software engineers, economists, data-privacy and data-security professionals, consumer-rights advocates, ethics experts, legal and regulatory specialists, artificial- and machine-learning specialists, and communications and media experts.

For those nostalgic for the days of the underdog startups and longing for a return to the early promises of the World Wide Web, Harris's manifesto offers hope:

> The ultimate freedom is a free mind, and we need technology that's on our team to help us live, feel, think and act freely. We need our smartphones to be exoskeletons for our minds and interpersonal relationships that put our values, not our impulses, first. Let's protect our minds with the same rigor as privacy and other digital rights.[34]

CHAPTER 8

Surveillance

The New Critical Infrastructure

A small action will not be noticed when it is done while making a
broader gesture for which there is an obvious reason.
—John Mulholland, magician (1898–1970) [1]

During the Cold War, the CIA paid magician John Mulholland $3,000 to
share his tips on the art of misdirection and deception.[2] Magic tricks, the
agency knew, were invaluable to their covert operations. That was during the
industrial age.

In the information age, federal agencies and multinational tech companies employ similar sleights of hand to conceal what Mulholland termed
their "obvious reason": implementing mass surveillance—and control—of
the populace. As civil liberties attorney Frank Donner wrote in his 1980 classic *The Age of Surveillance*, "Intelligence as a means of containing movements
for change, as a system of control, is simply too powerful a weapon in a highly
conservative economic and social order lightly to be abandoned."[3] Social control and containment proved too tempting for the US government to ignore
after the 9/11 attacks.

Cultural Reinforcement: A Monument to Fears

The 9/11 Memorial & Museum, along with its associated programs, com-
memorates the attacks of September 11, 2001, and reinforces national narratives about the War on Terror. These messages often perpetuate Islamophobia, normalize the acceptance of a national surveillance apparatus, and justify
US impunity for mass deaths resulting from the invasions of Iraq and Afghanistan. The museum's awesome size is designed to evoke strong emotions.
Visitors must pass through a full-body scan, reinforcing a sense of potential

danger and the perceived necessity of constant surveillance. The physical descent via ramp to bedrock below the fallen towers symbolizes the recovery efforts at the site of devastation. It culminates at the remains of the Vesey Staircase, which many occupants used to escape.

Museum exhibits—including one called "Revealed: The Hunt for Bin Laden"—further serve to evoke emotional reactions from visitors and to convey the idea that the United States remains vulnerable to distant threats.

A twenty-foot cross of steel beams found in the rubble of 6 World Trade Center was installed in the museum before any other exhibits, which some believe conveys the notion that the United States is a Christian nation. Some former staff members and critics have questioned whether the 9/11 commemoration crosses the line into perpetuating a culture of fear and surveillance.

"I can't tell you how many times I said the words 'honor and remember' in the 9/11 Memorial & Museum," recalled a former museum staff member, who asked to remain anonymous, in a 2023 email correspondence. "I would think about how much more there was to do in terms of contextualizing the attacks, and how to package programming that went against the party line and remain factually accurate."[4]

They weren't the only museum employee to consider the implications of presenting the 2001 attacks as fear-inciting government propaganda. Speaking of their colleagues, they note that "a few of us educators did what we could to do more than just weaponize the memory." But, they assert, the 9/11 Memorial & Museum has moved beyond implying that mass surveillance can improve our safety. Now, they note, "it *outright advocates* for surveillance packaged as security." Since 2019, the museum has even hosted an annual "Summit on Security" for security and cybersecurity professionals.

Absent from the museum's exhibits is an explanation of how our mass-surveillance apparatus came into existence. Such an explanation is increasingly necessary given that the media became more nationalistic, security focused, and uncritical of government actions in the immediate aftermath of the attacks. But that would run counter to the museum's raison d'être.

Critics have pointed out that the museum's narrative is more about airing resentment than education. "Overwhelmingly, the message of the museum wasn't educational as much as it was about grievance....There's been little discussion of how 9/11 actually changed America, how we're all under surveillance. Our phones tapped, our emails collected."[5] That's according to Philip Kennicott, the chief art and architecture critic for the *Washington Post*, in *The Outsider*, a documentary about the museum.[6] The 9/11 museum has faced criticism for failing to distinguish between one violent faction of Islam and the majority of Muslims who reject that ideology. Some family members of victims have voiced displeasure with the gift shop and the commercialization of their loved ones, deeming it insensitive.[7] A ceramic cheese platter in the shape of the United States, with three small red hearts marking the areas where the 9/11 attacks occurred, was removed in 2014 after receiving public backlash.[8]

As advancements in digital technologies coincided with the deadliest attacks on American soil, the government seized the opportunity to use the powerful weapon of digital surveillance to spy on its citizens. By exploiting fears of another terrorist attack, they lured us into consenting to mass monitoring of our daily lives and most intimate activities. In return, they influence our thinking and profit handsomely from marketing troves of personal data.

While the government had some preexisting plans and infrastructure for surveillance, the attacks provided the impetus for vast expansion. The passage of the USA PATRIOT Act in October 2001 lowered the legal barriers for government surveillance, enabling broader monitoring of communications, financial transactions, and other personal data.

Tech companies, meanwhile, became increasingly involved in surveillance over time. Initially, many tech companies were either compelled by government requests or cooperated under the belief that they were aiding in the fight against terrorism. As technology evolved, companies like Google, Facebook, and telecommunications firms found themselves holding vast amounts of personal data, which became valuable to government surveillance programs. And that data became highly lucrative to the industry. The revelations by whistleblowers like Edward Snowden in 2013 highlighted the extent of collaboration between tech companies and government agencies, showing that this relationship had evolved for decades.

If fighting terrorism was the government's true aim, they could have continued to use an existing NSA counterterrorism program called Thin Thread—it was excellent at detecting potential terrorist activity while also protecting citizens' data. Instead, the NSA created a "wasteful failure" program called Trailblazer that linked with NSA's warrantless surveillance of Americans.[9]

Now, decades later, surveillance has become normalized through the electronic home-security industry, educational systems reliant on education tech, and multiple types of entertainment showcasing high-tech surveillance tactics.

With citizens' mass desensitization to its risks, surveillance has become a significant part of America's cyber infrastructure—the essential systems, assets, and networks integral to a nation's security, economy, and safety. Of the sixteen sectors identified by the Department of Homeland Security—including chemical, energy, and financial services—information technology (cyber) is arguably the most important; all sectors depend on it to function. And like other infrastructures, cyber and surveillance can be harmful if mismanaged, poorly maintained, or intentionally targeted.

Surveillance has indeed been mismanaged, poorly maintained, and often intentionally targeted. It erodes constitutional protections, such as the Fourth Amendment, which guards against unreasonable searches and seizures. The awareness of being monitored has stifled activism, journalism, and other forms of individual autonomy and civic engagement. As a result, digital literacy must include recognizing biases and omissions in the portrayal of historical events to understand how narratives are shaped to exclude uncomfortable truths, and how, as the following examples show, surveillance has become normalized.

Normalized Surveillance: Neighborhood Watch

Seventy-three-year-old Gino Colonacosta and his fifteen-year-old son received an alert from their Amazon Ring doorbell, indicating motion at their front door in Winter Haven, Florida. Father and son grabbed .45 caliber firearms and rushed outside. They saw a woman sitting in her car, using her cell phone. They pointed their weapons at her and ordered her to exit the vehicle. Frightened, she put the car in reverse, crashing into the parked vehicle behind her. The Colonacostas proceeded to open fire, a total of seven shots at her car. The victim sped away unharmed but terrified.[10] This incident from late 2022 illustrates how heightened fears can displace common sense.

Instilling a constant fear of criminal activities, whether acts of terrorism or everyday street crime, normalizes constant surveillance in Americans' backyards, turning people into self-appointed neighborhood informants, or worse, vigilantes. Hyperbolic industry messaging about theft or violent crime fosters an exaggerated preoccupation with safeguarding property interests. Residents may view routine actions, like walking past a house or ringing the doorbell, through a fear-driven lens. Innocent bystanders, particularly from communities of color, can be wrongly accused of crimes or become victims of violence at the hands of vigilantes or the police.

Devices such as Ring along with its Neighbors App, boasting more than ten million users in 2024, keep many users in a perpetual state of vigilance.

Continuous streams of alerts and endless scrolls on social media tether many homeowners to applications from companies like Amazon (Ring), Google (Nest), and Wyze Labs. Tens of millions share videos and images captured by these cameras to neighborhood watch platforms like Citizen App—previously known as Vigilante before a prudent rebranding—and NextDoor. This fosters a normalization of surveillance where individuals may monitor neighbors as if they were citizen deputy police officers.

It was perhaps inevitable that citizen-collected data would be shared with law enforcement. Amazon's free Ring Neighbors app is marketed as helping communities stay informed about safety and crime in their area with real-time updates. Law enforcement agencies can join as well. In 2022, the New York Police Department—the largest in the nation—announced it would join Ring Neighbors. With the app, Ring owners can post camera videos for the public to watch. Amazon established partnerships providing Ring video footage to approximately two thousand cooperating police and fire departments, all without search warrants. Neighbors often share tips regarding "suspicious people." A 2019 analysis by Motherboard (reporters for which formed 404 Media in 2023 after Vice Media's Motherboard filed for bankruptcy) revealed that a majority of reports concerning "suspicious people" on Ring's platform involved people of color.[11] In 2024, Amazon announced it would no longer comply with warrantless requests from law enforcement for footage from Ring users.

The TV show *Ring Nation* also desensitizes viewers to surveillance. It premiered in August 2022 on Amazon-owned MGM. Widely criticized by tech media and US senator Ed Markey (D-MA), it features viral video captured by smartphones, Ring cameras, and other surveillance devices. Turning monitoring snippets into entertainment, *Ring Nation* diminishes their privacy-invading nature. Capitalizing on humorous interactions desensitizes others to hateful rhetoric and actions, not unlike the way white supremacists use memes and humor.

Many groups, including Media Justice and Fight for the Future, have called on MGM to cancel *Ring Nation*. In a letter to MGM studios, they wrote: "It's irresponsible for MGM to promote dangerous surveillance devices, like Ring, as family-friendly. Ring is not safe for families or anyone else."[12] Ring opponents include Alternate ROOTS; Athena; Center for Race and Digital Justice; For Us, Not Amazon; WITNESS; and the Surveillance, Tech, and Immigration Policing Project, a program of the Immigrant Defense Project.

But Amazon's branding of surveillance is strategic and lucrative. The company owns the show's producer, Big Fish Entertainment, as well as the distributor, MGM. From a branding point of view, Ring Nation is a perfect vehicle for electronic surveillance propaganda.

Normalized Surveillance in Entertainment

In the 1998 Hollywood thriller *Enemy of the State*, a retired NSA official played by Gene Hackman tells Will Smith, who plays a lawyer the rogue agency is trying to kill: "The government's been in bed with the entire telecommunications business since the '40s. They have infected everything. They can get into your bank statements, computer files, email, listen to your phone calls."[13] The film caused such a stir within the National Security Agency (NSA) that its new director at the time, Michael Hayden (whose directorship began in March 1999), invited CNN to produce a profile to help counter the film's negative portrayal of the agency.

While films like *Enemy of the State* may embellish some of the capabilities of surveillance agencies, they usually contain truths that resonate with real-world concerns. Government and corporate infiltration into telecommunications have been well established for decades, portrayed in films from 1967's *The President's Analyst*, about the intrusion of a telecommunications alliance and a microelectronic implant device, to Francis Ford Coppola's 1974 film *The Conversation*, about the moral implications of surveillance.

The entertainment industry, through the portrayal of advanced surveillance technologies in movies, TV shows, and video games, plays a key role in normalizing mass monitoring. That's because repeated exposure to media content can distort viewers' understanding of real-life consequences and expectations. The immersive nature can blur the line between fiction and reality.

Popular espionage, police procedurals, and crime dramas often depict sophisticated monitoring tools used by law enforcement and intelligence agencies to catch criminals or prevent terrorist attacks. Shows like *Mr. Robot*, *Westworld*, *24*, *Black Mirror*, and *Person of Interest* routinely use high-tech gadgets and omnipresent surveillance systems to solve problems and save lives (or, in the case of *Black Mirror*, satirize our growing hyper-dependence on mediated reality). This constant exposure to surveillance as a heroic and necessary tool for maintaining security and justice can desensitize audiences to the intrusive nature of these technologies, making the idea of being constantly monitored seem acceptable or even desirable for safety.

Then there are online video games. For example, *Grand Theft Auto V* features various missions where players must evade or utilize surveillance systems, reflecting the pervasive nature of surveillance in both criminal and police activities. In *Watch Dogs*, each player assumes control of a hacker pro-tagonist who uses surveillance technology to manipulate the city's infrastruc-ture and gather information on targets, highlighting the omnipresence of sur-veillance in urban environments. Just like smart devices used in Americans' homes, in the game, a fictional computing network links all electronic devices in a city to form one system that stores the personal data of its citizens.

Because entertainment media depict surveillance as a normative aspect of society, viewers are more accepting of intrusive technologies and the govern-ment deployment of them.

Normalized Surveillance in Classrooms

Technology companies have discovered a lucrative market in students. Google introduced its Chromebook in 2011, followed by the launch of its Classroom app in 2014. Both have become integral components in education. By 2017, more than half of the nation's primary and secondary-school pupils regularly used Google apps such as Classroom, Workspace for Education, Gmail, and Docs.[14] Google provides Chromebooks at a low enough cost that schools can give them to all students. It even offers Classroom for free to educational institutions. Many teachers rely on Google Classroom to create assignment templates, streamline submissions with Google Docs and Forms integration for easy grading, and use tools like standardized rubrics and com-menting features to provide direct feedback. The platform allows for efficient grade management and exporting, though some teachers prefer traditional methods depending on their comfort with technology.

Through strategic partnerships with cash-strapped school systems, tech providers instill loyalty among students, ensuring they become lifelong con-sumers of their industry products. A 2019 report by the Tech Transparency Project, *Capturing the Classroom,* highlights Google's strategic approach to dominating classrooms in the US and globally. First, Google targeted teach-ers directly, offering lucrative consulting contracts and turning them into advocates for its products among their peers. Second, the company shifted the cost of teacher training onto school boards by leveraging schools' "pro-fessional development" budgets, fueling a gold rush for EdTech companies that now train teachers on tools from Google, Apple, Microsoft, and others. Finally, Google utilized its relationships with influential education officials to lobby for its products, partnering with EdTech allies to shape national educa-tion policy through key working groups.[15]

Michael Vakian, a 2025 graduate of the University of Southern California, notes, "My school required us to set up Google Classroom accounts in 6th grade and through senior year. Since then, I have never considered anything but the Google ecosystem. Other platforms, such as Microsoft Office, feel foreign to me."[16]

During the pandemic, schools distributed laptops and tablets to millions of students who lacked access to them, according to the Center for Democracy and Technology.[17] More than 80 percent of surveyed teachers reported that their schools used surveillance software on the devices they provided. In fact, there was a 500 percent increase in use of proctoring tools, according to the Electronic Frontier Foundation.[18] In 2020, more than half of higher-education institutions used "remote proctoring" services such as ProctorU, ExamSoft, Respondus Monitor, Honorlock, Examity and Proctorio, with another 23 percent considering doing the same.[19]

In addition to remote proctoring, many schools use anti-plagiarism software. TurnItIn, a widely used tool, aims to help educators identify unoriginal content and promote original writing. "My school used TurnItIn.com, a plagiarism checker designed to generate 'similarity scores' to ensure that students' papers were not plagiarized," continues Vakian. "The inaccuracy of this platform was a constant source of frustration for me and my classmates. Our teacher set a strict similarity percentage limit, warning that any student exceeding this limit would receive a failing grade. Students frequently received unusually high similarity percentages even when they had not plagiarized at all. This often led to uncomfortable follow-up discussions to explain to teachers that the similarity percentage was inaccurate."[20]

In 2024, TurnItIn announced it was making changes to reduce the number of inaccurate similarity scores. But what is equally concerning is the issue of user privacy and intellectual property. Its database includes student submissions, which can be used to train its algorithms to compare against future submissions.[21] This raises ethical questions about the use of students' submissions beyond their original educational context, as students' intellectual property is used in ways they might not fully understand or consent to.[22]

Another insidious and inescapable element of continuous monitoring is discrimination. Biases in software have resulted in disabled students being wrongly flagged for cheating more frequently. Surveillance software frequently fails to properly recognize Black and brown faces. There are serious consequences of these errors: a high "suspicion score" on a student's record can trigger investigations into academic misconduct. When students challenge these claims, they are confronted with labyrinthine school bureaucracies, with a resolution potentially taking months.

In October 2021, US senators Elizabeth Warren (D-MA) and Markey (D-MA) investigated monitoring software companies including Gaggle, Bark Technologies, GoGuardian, and Securly. They found that 43 percent of teachers used monitoring software to identify violations of disciplinary policies, that companies were *not* evaluating their products for potential discriminatory biases, that schools and parents were *not* being notified about potential misuse of students' data, and that regulatory and legal gaps heightened the risks posed by student-activity-monitoring software.[23]

As students graduate, familiarity with Google facilitates the seamless transfer of their extensive collection of school-related Gmail, Docs, and other files to regular Google consumer accounts. Because schools encourage this practice, they foster new generations' lifelong reliance on the company's ecosystem. Michael Vakian recalls that "Google Classroom was non-negotiable at my school; there were no analog alternatives. We took quizzes, wrote essays, and did in-class assignments all online. I hate taking quizzes online; I find it easier to focus when there is a paper and pencil in front of me. As someone who occasionally struggles to finish exams on time, I feel more pressure typing my answers into a computer. For multiple-choice exams, I felt much less comfortable reading the questions on a laptop as opposed to on paper."

Vakian also commented on the overall effect of e-learning software.

"I believe using Google classroom from 6th to 12th grade impaired my organization and time management skills. Google Classroom handled the scheduling of due dates and exam dates for me. However, when making the transition to college, I had a steep learning curve in how to manage a hectic college schedule."[24]

Normalized Surveillance: Selling Security

The surge in school shootings and heightened public anxieties about student safety served as a catalyst for security companies to promote their electronic monitoring programs to schools nationwide. Overwhelmed school districts eagerly adopted new security measures, especially those that appeared grounded in science or technology. Prominent players in the field alongside Gaggle include Bark, Lightspeed, Securly, and Gnosis IQ.

Joining Google in the classrooms is Gaggle, a Dallas-based student digital safety company founded in 2019. That year, it announced its partnership with schools and districts using Google Workspace or Education to monitor Google accounts for red flags indicating students in crisis.

Gaggle is another aggressive marketer that claims to enhance student safety. It integrates with Google's G Suite and Microsoft 365, and monitors notifications from X, Facebook, and Instagram accounts linked to school email addresses. Using artificial intelligence, Gaggle autonomously analyzes students' communications against a list of keywords associated with suicide, self-harm, harm to others, signs of depression, and bullying. This list includes profanities and words and phrases such as *drunk, end my life, hate myself,* and *hit me.* Gaggle's AI extends to handling images through its "Anti-Pornography Scanner."

The effectiveness of such programs is limited. While models can identify keywords associated with self-harm, interpreting context is a subjective task. A student might use a keyword in a nonthreatening or metaphorical way, which the AI might misinterpret as a risk. AI can generate false positives (flagging harmless content as risky) and false negatives (failing to detect genuine risk), depending on the sophistication of the model and the data it was trained on. AI models might not fully account for cultural nuances or individual differences in how students express themselves, leading to potential misinterpretations. And the use of AI in this context raises questions about student privacy and the ethics of monitoring personal communications.

It's difficult to find an independent evaluation that has assessed whether these measures reduce harassment, violence, or self-harm. Despite the lack of evidence about the effectiveness of school-monitoring technologies, tech companies market them with bold claims of hundreds of lives saved, particularly in the context of preventing youth-suicide attempts. Gaggle, for instance, asserts that its products monitor 4.5 million students across 1,400 school districts, and that during the 2018 to 2019 academic year its technology "helped districts save the lives of more than 700 students who were planning or actually attempting suicide."[25] Another company, Securly, reports that its products safeguard 10 million students across 10,000 individual schools. In 2019, Securly claimed that it assisted school officials in intervening in 400 situations that presented "imminent threats."[26]

Positioning their technology as highly advanced and reliable can give businesses a competitive edge in a crowded market, attracting more customers and justifying higher prices. Not surprisingly, the way these companies interpret and report data can be selective, emphasizing success stories while downplaying false positives, false negatives, or contextual errors. This can create a misleading perception of AI's true effectiveness.

In response to the 2018 Parkland High School shootings in Miami, Florida, Bark offered schools free trials of its automated, twenty-four-hour-a-day surveillance system. Without Bark, parents relied on their child's friends to report concerning issues to an adult, which could make the friend feel guilty for disclosing information. The software monitors content in students' school emails, shared documents, and chat messages. When key phrases are detected, it alerts school administrators. For instance, if Bark flags a student discussing self-harm, the principal will contact the student's guardian or parent to inquire about their child's safety. In situations such as domestic abuse, however, notifying the guardian may not be the best first step.

Bark's feature has already come under fire for flagging abortions, gender-affirming care, and outing students about their gender identity and sexual preferences.[27]

Targets du Jour

Mass surveillance lengthens the arm of the privacy police. Subjects of surveillance by law enforcement vary over the decades, often determined by current events, political rhetoric, or moral panic.

Today, with the passage of antiabortion legislation in conservative state legislatures across the country, women are increasingly vulnerable to targeted surveillance.

Before the landmark case *Roe v. Wade* was decided in 1973, law enforcement lacked the technology and surveillance capabilities to enforce abortion laws. But half a century later, with the overturning of *Roe* and with limitations and bans on abortion that vary by state, police possess the tools necessary to track down people seeking to exercise control over their own bodies.

Digital data being tracked may include location data to show if someone has visited an abortion clinic, or data from online-search histories for medication abortion, clinic locations, and abortion information in general. Other potential surveillance methods include tracking data from menstrual cycle tracking applications, and monitoring communications data regarding pregnancy and abortion, such as text messages to friends and loved ones.[28]

Authorities can often access much of this information without a warrant. Traditional restrictions on police searches may not uniformly apply to every instance of law enforcement seeking access to personal data.[29] Legal requirements for obtaining digital evidence, such as location data, can vary: there are limitations on compelling information from suspects or third parties like Google, but a substantial amount of data can be acquired without a warrant simply by purchasing it from data brokers.

Several senators have urged Apple and Google to implement more robust regulations on data privacy to protect abortion seekers. In a letter to Google

CEO, Sunder Pichai, US senator Ron Wyden (D-OR) and forty-one other Democratic lawmakers wrote: "We are concerned that…Google's current practice of collecting and retaining extensive records of cell phone location data will allow it to become a tool for far-right extremists looking to crack down on people seeking reproductive health care."[30]

This is not a trivial concern: Google receives tens of thousands of court orders, search warrants, and subpoenas for user data from law enforcement agencies each year. In approximately 80 percent of these cases, Google discloses some information. One out of every four court orders it receives pertains to "geofence" data, which provides information about a person's location at a specific time. Geofences are virtual boundaries that rely on GPS, Wi-Fi, or Radio Frequency ID technology to monitor when mobile devices enter or exit a designated area. GPS signals from tracking devices pinpoint their location and define the boundaries of a specific area. Such data could potentially be used to track women visiting reproductive health clinics or abortion providers.[31]

Even before the reversal of *Roe*, police departments have investigated online activities of pregnant women and presented digital evidence in court. Take the case of Purvi Patel, a resident of Granger, Indiana, who in 2015 was found guilty of feticide and neglect of a dependent after taking abortion drugs. In the prosecutor's case, data retrieved from Patel's cell phone and iPad played a central role in her conviction. Text messages to a friend about her pregnancy and the purchase of pills were introduced as evidence. Patel was initially sentenced to twenty years in prison, but her conviction was eventually overturned on appeal following public outcry and a protracted legal battle.[32]

Latice Fisher, who is Black, faced accusations of second-degree murder in Mississippi following the home birth of a stillborn baby in 2018. Police conducted a search of Fisher's phone and presented her internet searches for abortion pills as evidence in her trial. As in Patel's case, prosecutors eventually yielded to public pressure and dismissed the charges against her.[33]

Tracking pregnant women once seemed dystopian. That it now feels less so may be linked to how we have taught new generations to embrace surveillance in their lives.

Digital Illiteracy and Surveillance

A proliferation of mobile apps collect and share users' location data without their full comprehension—a consequence of digital illiteracy. A 2019

Washington Post report revealed that numerous popular mobile apps, including weather and shopping apps, transmit precise user location data to third-party trackers, usually without users' awareness or explicit consent.[34] With apps expanding into niche services from telecommunications to finance management, to airlines, to healthcare, users' lack of practicing digital literacy and data hygiene can lead to sharing sensitive information that, if security is compromised, can be pilfered by unscrupulous actors.[35]

For example, researchers Narseo Vallina-Rodriguez and Srikanth Sundaresan from the Madrid Institute for Advanced Studies built Lumen, an app to monitor communications between smartphone apps and third-party trackers. They found that more than 70 percent of smartphone apps share personal information with third-party tracking companies; 15 percent of apps were connecting to five or more trackers.[36] These apps also send sensitive information to third-party software "libraries" that pass the gathered info to their online servers or to other companies. If apps with different data share the same library, the library's developer can combine them to form a more complete user profile.

Equally concerning is the potential misuse of personal information by law enforcement and government agencies when accessed through data brokers. Agencies can construct comprehensive profiles using this information, enabling surveillance or investigations, even in cases where no wrongdoing has occurred. A 2023 study by the Consumer Financial Protection Bureau (CFPB) on the data-broker industry found widespread concerns about how consumer data is collected, used, and shared.[37] Researchers received numerous submissions from the public warning about the disproportionate risks that unregulated data sharing can have on minorities, seniors, immigrants, and victims of domestic violence.

"Reports about monetization of sensitive information—everything from the financial details of members of the military to lists of specific people experiencing dementia—are particularly worrisome when data is powering 'artificial intelligence' and other automated decision-making about our lives," CFPB director Rohit Chopra said in a statement.[38] Chopra emphasized the CFPB's commitment to taking measures to ensure that data brokers understand that unlawful data collection and sharing will not be tolerated.

Widespread lack of understanding about online surveillance means we're ill-equipped to avoid or mitigate its damage, continually contributing to a reservoir of data that fuels targeted advertising, profiling, and invasive monitoring. These practices pose worrisome threats to personal privacy and data security. Assisted by advanced technologies like artificial-intelligence software, the industry's rapid growth makes it more challenging to evade its invasive reach—but not impossible.

Rolling back mass surveillance involves legal reforms, stronger judicial oversight, and increased transparency and accountability of tech companies. Promoting safeguards like encryption and anonymization of data, raising public awareness, protecting tech whistleblowers, and fostering international cooperation are necessary to maintain citizen autonomy.

Digital literacy can help protect privacy and civil liberties. Literate citizens can advocate for stronger legal protections, enhance public awareness, and support technological safeguards. Together, they can strive to reclaim privacy and ensure a free and open society.

PRACTICES FOR THE PEOPLE

The web is at a tipping point. How we respond to this crisis will determine whether the web serves humanity well for decades to come or whether it's subverted to serve a narrow agenda.

—Sir Tim Berners-Lee, inventor of the World Wide Web[1]

CHAPTER 9

Disrupters for Democracy
Open Source, Blockchain, and More

Historic battles for market dominance shaped the industrial age, and now they are shaping the cyber age. Major companies in both industrial and digital epochs have vied to control emerging technologies and markets. Fortunately, several disruptive forces play a key role in preserving democracy, offering alternatives to anticompetitive practices led by billionaire tech titans.

As power becomes concentrated in the hands of a few behemoth technology companies, initiatives like the World Wide Web Consortium (W3C) have played a crucial role in establishing open standards for the web, promoting interoperability, and preventing monopolistic control. Decentralized platforms, such as those based on blockchain technologies, provide alternatives to the centralized systems of internet giants, giving users more control over their data and transactions. Open-source projects, like the Linux operating system and the Apache web server, enable developers worldwide to contribute to and improve technologies, reducing reliance on any single company and fostering both innovation and efficiency. Additionally, international legislators have enacted sweeping privacy-preserving regulations, encouraging America to follow suit.

These innovators seek to democratize technology and offer consumers more choices, challenging the dominance of a few major market players. As a result, resisting the tech industry's negative effects on democracy is becoming a more achievable goal.

An early battle known as the "browser wars" catalyzed the rise of open-source software and a movement against corporate dominance in the tech space. During this battle it became clear to many that corporate control over key internet technologies could stifle innovation and limit user choice.

Cannon Fire Between Netscape and Microsoft

The first "browser war," from 1994 to 2001, pitted Netscape Communications Corporation, founded in 1994 by Marc Andreessen and Jim Clark, against Microsoft in a struggle between profit and accessibility, mirroring older historic rivalries. The conflict led to the development of key web technologies such as JavaScript, CSS, and HTML. But the tactics were as ruthless as those of earlier corporate rivalries, foreshadowing massive tech companies' domination over American culture, politics, economy, and personal autonomy.

A year before the war began, Mosaic, one of the first widely used web browsers, was released in 1993 by the National Center for Supercomputing Applications (NCSA) at the University of Illinois. Mosaic is often credited with popularizing the World Wide Web due to its graphical interface, which allowed users to view images alongside text on web pages, making the internet more accessible and visually appealing. Netscape Navigator, developed by Netscape Communications Corporation and released in 1994, was created by a team that included several developers from the Mosaic project, such as coauthor Andreessen.

Netscape Navigator was faster, more feature rich, and more robust than Mosaic, introducing innovations like the ability to display pages incrementally as they loaded. This improved user experience and helped Navigator quickly became the most popular web browser in the mid-1990s, capturing 90 percent of the market share.[1] Unlike earlier browsers, which were dull and uninspiring, Navigator was visually exciting and user-friendly. It transformed the web by introducing vibrant photos, video clips, sound snippets, and clickable hyperlinks; a first user's experience was akin to Dorothy stepping from a black-and-white landscape of Kansas into the colorful land of Oz.

Marc Andreessen recalls the seminal moment of Netscape's release. "The night of the first release we set up a computer in one of the conference rooms to watch the downloads and we had a sound effect where there'd be a cannon shot. Every time someone downloaded it there'd be a shot and after a while it sounded like a war 'cause it was just continuous cannon shots."[2]

Microsoft, led by Bill Gates, was caught off guard by Navigator's rapid success. Former Microsoft program manager Thomas Reardon remembers, "We'd never seen anything like this in the history of software. In thirty days, 90 percent of the people who were on the web switched from Mosaic [Netscape's predecessor, released on January 23, 1993] to Netscape."[3]

On May 26, 1995, Gates sent an all-staff memo titled "The Coming Tidal Wave," in which he declared, "A new competitor 'born' on the Internet is

Netscape. Their browser is dominant, with 70% usage share.... We have to match and beat their offerings including working with MCI [telecommunications company providing long-distance calling], newspapers, and others who are considering their products."[4] A few months later, on December 7, 1995, the fifty-third anniversary of the bombing of Pearl Harbor, Gates held a press conference effectively declaring war on Netscape. Microsoft's response, Internet Explorer (IE), would be bundled with its Windows 95 operating system, leveraging its monopoly to gain a competitive edge.

The browser wars intensified as both companies released frequent updates and enhancements. In 1997, Microsoft released Internet Explorer 4.0, pressuring vendors to preinstall its browser on all their personal computers, which ultimately crushed Netscape to win the early browser battle.[5] By 2001, Internet Explorer had cornered approximately 96 percent of the web-browser usage share. That same year, the Justice Department filed an antitrust lawsuit against Microsoft, eventually leading to a settlement that required Internet Explorer to be separated from the Windows operating system.[6]

Microsoft soon faced challenges during the second browser war sparked by the release of Mozilla Firefox in 2004 and Google Chrome in 2008. This period saw competition among browsers like Internet Explorer, Apple's Safari, and Opera, leading to rapid advancements in speed, security, and standards compliance.

As Netscape began losing its dominant market position the company decided to release the source code of its browser code, launching the Mozilla project. This initiative aimed to foster innovation through community involvement and was named Mozilla—short for "Mosaic Killer"—reflecting its goal to surpass Mosaic's success. The name also inspired the creation of Mozilla's mascot, a playful fusion of Mosaic and Godzilla, the iconic sea monster from the 1954 Japanese film directed by Ishirō Honda.[7] Over time, Mozilla created new browsers like Firefox that carried forward Netscape's original mission.

Following the Cambridge Analytica data scandal, Mozilla demonstrated its commitment to privacy and democracy online. It protested Facebook's practices by pulling its ads from the platform and launched a petition urging Facebook to change its app permissions to protect users' privacy by default.[8] Mozilla also developed the Facebook Container, a Firefox add-on that limits Facebook's ability to track user data by isolating Facebook activity in a separate "container," or fenced-off area, within the browser. This containment strategy prevents Facebook from tracking user movements across other websites.

Mozilla also developed other privacy-centric tools and technologies that shield individuals from online tracking and data surveillance. Firefox, its flagship browser, is designed with user privacy as a top priority. Enhanced Tracking Protection was initially introduced as an optional feature in pre-release versions of the Firefox browser in 2018. By September 2019, it had transitioned to being automatically enabled by default under the "Standard" setting in the Firefox browser. This feature effectively blocks known third-party tracking cookies, bolstering users' privacy.

Mozilla's ongoing commitments to privacy and democracy extend beyond its products and services. The organization actively advocates for policies like net neutrality, which ensures that internet service providers treat all data impartially without unfair prioritization or throttling of specific content. Mozilla organizes the Mozilla Festival, also known as MozFest. Launched in 2010, MozFest is a dynamic digital maker festival and educational summit that brings together developers, designers, activists, and creatives from around the world. It provides a collaborative space to explore and build a healthier internet, focusing on privacy, digital inclusion, and open-source innovation through interactive sessions, workshops, and other critical topics.

From Silicon Valley's browser wars and subsequent competitions, many innovative counterforces have emerged, dedicated to preserving online transparency and equity.

Disruptive Challenger: Hello, Open Source!

Open-source software is software whose source code is made available to the public, allowing anyone to view, modify, and distribute it. This collaborative approach fosters community-driven development and transparency, often resulting in more robust and secure software solutions.

Netscape's decision to open-source its browser significantly bolstered the open-source movement, advancing user choice, online freedom, and transparency. Inspired by this move, Bruce Perens and Eric S. Raymond co-founded the Open Source Initiative (OSI), a nonprofit that educates about, and advocates for, the benefits of open source. The OSI also maintains the Open Source Definition, which outlines the criteria for open-source software and was adopted in late February 1998. Mozilla continued to innovate in the open-source realm, with releases like the email client Thunderbird. In 2003, Mozilla established the Mozilla Foundation to manage its operations, promote an open internet, and support web-accessibility improvements.

Companion efforts in the open-source movement include the Linux operating system, which has significantly contributed to the principles of democracy and technological innovation. Linus Torvalds, a Finnish computer science student, created the Linux kernel—the core program that manages a computer's operating system—and released it as a free and open-source project on August 25, 1991. Linux quickly gained popularity and attracted a community of developers and enthusiasts who helped develop it into a robust and versatile operating system.

Linux is more than just the kernel. It also includes a wide range of software and components from the broader open-source community. The combination of the Linux kernel with various software applications, utilities, and libraries forms a complete operating system, commonly referred to as a "Linux distribution." Popular Linux distributions such as Ubuntu, Debian, Fedora, and CentOS build upon the Linux kernel to provide comprehensive and user-friendly computing environments.

Linux is favored for its security, flexibility, and cost-effectiveness, and is widely used by government agencies and departments. For example, the Department of Defense and various other government websites rely on Linux for diverse applications, including servers and embedded systems. Open-source software is also considered a vital component of the US Cyber Defense Agency's efforts to mitigate cyber threats to federal agencies and infrastructure. Linux is ubiquitous in embedded systems found in automobiles, smart devices, and appliances.

Corporations use Linux extensively in their data centers, where it allows them to customize and adapt the operating system to their specific needs. Linux is often chosen for server deployment due to its scalability and reliability, powering a significant portion of the internet's back-end systems. Tech titans like Google, Facebook, Amazon, and X use Linux-based servers to run their services. Additionally, Linux powers 85 percent of all smartphones, and is the third most popular desktop operating system.[9] Its use reduces software licensing costs and provides greater control over computing environments.

Mike Little and Matt Mullenweg are the architects of a transformative open-source project designed for people who want to create their own website or blog but lack coding experience. In the early 2000s, Little, a resident of Stockport, England, reached out to fellow blogger and University of Houston freshman Mullenweg. Both were users of the open source b2/cafelog platform. When the creator of b2/cafelog, Michel Valdrighi, stopped releasing updates, Mullenweg and Little decided to "fork" the software—modifying and updating it to suit their needs—so they could continue blogging.[10]

Building on the same source code of b2/cafelog, Little and Mullenweg developed a new open-source platform that was user-friendly, free, accessible, community-driven, with no licensing fees or vendor lock-ins. In 2003, they launched WordPress, empowering more people to have a voice online regardless of their technical skills. Its ease of use attracted a growing number of users, and the platform's features and capabilities continued to expand. As of 2024, WordPress—whose motto is "Code is Poetry"—continues to release regular updates, staying true to its roots as a free and open-source platform.

This democratization of web publishing through WordPress aligns with the early promise of the internet to allow everyone to share information and express themselves online. As of 2024, WordPress powers more than 43 percent of all websites worldwide, making it the most-used content management system (CMS) on the internet, with a 63 percent market share.[11] WordPress has transformed the digital publishing landscape and demonstrated the strength of open-source development. Unlike proprietary content management systems like Wix, Weebly, and Squarespace—which offer more limited customization options—WordPress invites users who want more advanced customizations to learn how to code, further enhancing its flexibility and appeal.

Disruptive Standard Setters: W3C

The World Wide Web Consortium (W3C) is an international community that develops open standards to ensure the long-term growth of the web. Founded in 1994 by web inventor Tim Berners-Lee, the W3C brings together member organizations and the public to develop web standards. These principles define the fundamental technologies upon which the web is built, ensuring that it remains an open and accessible platform for all users, from designers to innovating organizations of all sizes.

W3C has developed several well-known protocols and standards that form the backbone of the modern web. They include HTML (hypertext markup language), the standard markup language for creating web pages and web applications, one of the fundamental technologies of the web, along with CSS and JavaScript. HTML provides the structure of web pages, allowing users to embed text, images, links, and other media. Other developments are ARIA (accessible rich internet applications) and WCAG (web content accessibility guidelines), guidelines and principles to make web content more accessible to people with disabilities. These guidelines form the basis for many accessibility laws and policies worldwide.

HTTP is the foundation of data communication on the web, enabling the transfer of information between web servers and clients. You'll recognize it at the beginning of most URLs: http://. Although HTTP (hypertext transfer protocol) was developed before the W3C's establishment, the W3C has played a significant role in advancing and maintaining it.

Many major tech companies actively align with and contribute to W3C protocols. As would be expected, Mozilla's strong commitment to web standards and open web principles make it a key player in W3C initiatives and working groups.

Other companies take part in W3C working groups, including IBM, Samsung, Adobe, Intel, and Amazon. Google, for example, is a significant contributor to web standards and an active participant in W3C working groups. Its Chrome browser is known for its strong adherence to web standards. Apple supports W3C standards through its Safari browser and actively contributes to the web ecosystem by supporting projects like WebKit, an open-source browser engine that powers Safari and ensures robust web compliance, and Swift, an intuitive programming language designed to build high-performance apps across Apple platforms. Apple participates in various W3C working groups related to web performance and security. Meta contributes to web standards development, particularly related to social media and web performance, and is involved in W3C working groups. After initial reluctance, Microsoft now supports W3C standards too.

Despite these companies' histories of violating US antitrust laws and the GDPR, it is not surprising that they are part of the W3C and its working groups. Participation offers both strategic and practical benefits. By contributing to the development of web standards, these tech giants can ensure these standards align with their technological frameworks and market strategies, maintaining influence over the digital ecosystem. Participation also allows them to address and shape policies on emerging technologies that will affect their products and services, sometimes preemptively addressing regulatory scrutiny. In the process, they can build a public image of commitment to open standards and collaborative development, potentially offsetting criticisms of privacy violations and GDPR issues, as these initiatives can give the appearance of transparency and alignment with broader web security and performance goals.

The vast resources that industry representatives dedicate to participating in the W3C raise concerns that their undue influence might overshadow and marginalize the needs and voices of smaller stakeholders, nonprofits, and individual developers, leading to standards that don't fully meet the needs of a diverse web community. Dominance of corporate influence could favor business models and proprietary technologies that benefit large corporations over those that benefit smaller entities, stifling innovation and competition.

The W3C has mechanisms in place to mitigate these risks and ensure a balanced and inclusive approach to developing web standards. Its consensus-based model means that decisions are made through discussions and agreement among a wide range of stakeholders, not just the most powerful ones. They include academia, nonprofits, individual developers, and smaller companies, to ensure a diversity of perspectives. The W3C also has advisory committees and councils that include representatives from various sectors, helping to balance corporate influence. Transparency in processes, with public documentation of discussions, decisions, and standards, allows for scrutiny and input from the broader community. Draft standards are often published for public review and feedback, allowing anyone to contribute their insights and concerns before finalization.

While the involvement of Big Tech companies in the W3C brings valuable expertise and resources to the table, the consortium remains vigilant about fostering an inclusive and balanced approach to ensure that web standards serve the interests of the entire web community.

Market Challenger: Blockchain

Blockchain is a ledger-type electronic system of recording transactions that cannot be altered, thus enhancing its trustworthiness. As a decentralized method of storing information, all users, rather than one person or group, retain control. Multiple copies of information are saved in blocks—like spreadsheets cells—and then encrypted. A series of blocks are then chained together.

Blockchain, as we know it today, was conceptualized in 2008 by an anonymous person or group of people using the pseudonym Satoshi Nakamoto, who described it in the whitepaper "Bitcoin: A Peer-to-Peer Electronic Cash System."[12] The first blockchain was implemented as a core component of the cryptocurrency Bitcoin, released in 2009. Earlier research had been influential in developing concepts for blockchain technology, particularly in cryptographic security and decentralized trust, where trust—emphasizing user privacy and security—is distributed across a network rather than centralized. In his 1982 dissertation, David Chaum described cryptographic protocols that laid the groundwork for secure, decentralized systems.[13] In 1989, he founded DigiCash, a company specializing in electronic money. Between 1989 and 1994, DigiCash developed and tested its groundbreaking eCash system, which used Chaum's "blind signatures" to enable secure, anonymous digital payments. The company also collaborated with banks and promoted its vision of privacy-preserving digital payments, leading to the 1995 launch of products like cyberbucks and eCash. Although DigiCash was not decentralized like Bitcoin, it pioneered digital money outside traditional banking systems, advancing privacy in digital payments through innovative cryptographic techniques.

Blockchain technology offers a compelling alternative to Big Tech by decentralizing control and empowering users with greater autonomy. Unlike traditional centralized systems, blockchain's distributed ledger allows transactions to be verified by a network of nodes, ensuring transparency and security without a central authority. This reduces the risk of data breaches and censorship, as no single entity controls the entire network.

The voting platform Voatz demonstrates the transformative potential of blockchain technology. Traditional voting methods, whether paper based or electronic, face challenges ranging from fraud and lack of transparency to inefficiencies. The state of West Virginia piloted the Voatz app during the 2018 midterm elections to allow military personnel stationed overseas to vote using their smartphones. Cryptographic technology ensured that each vote was securely recorded and could not be altered once submitted, theoretically enhancing both security and transparency. In practice, however, Voatz has faced criticism for failing in both areas, prompting efforts to improve its security protocols and increase independent audits.

Blockchain's potential for transparency enables it to be used to address issues such as financial inequality, corruption, and data security, with great potential to create a more equitable and secure digital future. But in one area, blockchain falls short: it can't store large amounts of data "on chain." Merely storing a video could run in the millions of dollars. But, as we'll soon learn, one young inventor has devised a way to store extensive amounts of data cost-effectively and with data integrity.

Interplanetary Files

In May 2014, Stanford University graduate Juan Benet invented the InterPlanetary File System (IPFS), a protocol designed to enhance the speed, security, and openness of the web while making content accessible to everyone, regardless of location or background.

Here's how IPFS works: Instead of relying on centralized servers, IPFS distributes web content across a peer-to-peer network. When users upload a file, it's broken into smaller, uniquely identifiable chunks, encrypted, and distributed across the network. When someone requests a file, their computer retrieves the chunks from the nearest or most available nodes, reducing latency and improving download speeds. Any computer can join the network by downloading IPFS software. That ensures that content remains accessible even if the original server goes down.

The mission of PFS aligns with the original vision of Web 1.0, that of a borderless and resilient network. It addresses key challenges of the traditional internet, such as overreliance on central servers and vulnerability to censorship.

Researchers and scientists can use IPFS to distribute and share large datasets and scholarly content, ensuring long-term accessibility even if their servers go offline or their institutions undergo changes. Libraries and archivists can use IPFS to preserve cultural heritage and historical records for future generations. Internet of Things (IoT) devices can leverage IPFS to securely share data with centralized or decentralized applications; for example, environmental sensors in a smart city could publish their data to IPFS for secure and efficient access.

Traditional cloud storage providers may incorporate IPFS into their services, giving users greater control over their data. In regions with limited internet infrastructure, IPFS can be used to create local networks to share content, reducing dependence on distant servers.

Critics point out several drawbacks of IPFS, including issues with reliability, difficulty in verifying data integrity, and a lack of economic incentives. Since there is no profit motive, peers are less likely to store large volumes of data for free over the long term, making IPFS less reliable for private data storage. Storing encrypted data on a peer-to-peer network like IPFS may also complicate duplication or caching. Additionally, verifying the integrity of the data stored on IPFS is challenging because peers are not required to submit proofs of storage or uptime.

From "The World Wide Wait" to Edge Computing

In the late 1990s, Tim Berners-Lee issued a challenge to solve the issue of the "World Wide Wait," a term used to describe the slow speed of the early internet due to analog modems.[14]

In response, Akamai Technologies, a Cambridge, Massachusetts–based company founded in 1998, laid the groundwork for reducing latency and improving content delivery by developing CDN (content delivery networks) services. CDNs use distributed servers to deliver digital content more efficiently by bringing it geographically closer to users. When a user requests content from a website, the CDN redirects the request to the nearest server in its network, which then delivers the content. This not only speeds up load times but also helps manage high traffic volumes and protects against certain types of cyberattacks, like distributed denial of service (DDoS) attacks. CDNs are commonly used by businesses and websites to enhance user experience and ensure quick and reliable access to digital content globally.

The concept of edge computing began to emerge in the late 1990s and early 2000s, gaining more formally recognition in the early 2010s. The term *edge computing* gained traction around 2014, driven by the rapid growth of internet-connected devices (the Internet of Things), which required processing data closer to where the data is generated, rather than relying solely on centralized cloud data centers. Edge computing represents a shift from traditional cloud-based computing to a decentralized network where data processing occurs closer to the data source, or "edge" of the network. This approach allows local devices and systems to operate independently of centralized infrastructure, providing faster, more secure, and more efficient data handling. Edge computing can drive innovation across multiple sectors by creating smarter, safer, and more responsive environments.

Tech leaders like Mozilla support the development and implementation of edge computing because it enhances data privacy, reduces latency, and can lead to more efficient use of bandwidth compared to centralized cloud servers typically run by Big Tech companies. By moving computation and data storage to local devices, edge computing can help alleviate bottlenecks and vulnerabilities of centralized systems.

Edge computing enables real-time data processing by bringing computation and data storage closer to the devices where it is needed. In smart cities, for example, edge computing is used in traffic management systems where cameras and sensors analyze traffic flow and adjust signals instantly to reduce congestion. Smart street lighting employs edge devices to detect pedestrian and vehicular movement and adjust lighting in real time for energy efficiency and safety. In applications such as autonomous vehicles and industrial automation, even milliseconds can make the difference between success and failure. With edge computing, data generated by sensors and cameras in these environments can be processed locally, ensuring faster response times.

Netflix uses edge computing by deploying content delivery networks closer to users, which reduces buffering times and improves streaming quality.

Local nodes can cache popular content, allowing users to access shows and movies with minimal delay.

Edge computing also holds promise for healthcare applications. Medical devices and sensors can process data locally to monitor vital signs and detect anomalies in real time, providing immediate feedback and alerts to healthcare providers. This capability can improve patient outcomes, especially in critical and time-sensitive situations. By processing and storing sensitive medical data locally rather than in a central cloud, patient privacy is better protected.

Urban environments can also benefit from edge computing. Smart grids can more effectively balance energy loads by integrating renewable energy sources and ensuring a stable power supply. During natural disasters, if central networks fail, edge devices can provide critical information to first responders. In remote areas, environmental monitoring systems can use edge computing to analyze data, detect changes in air quality, water levels, or wildlife patterns, and send alerts when anomalies are detected, aiding environmental preservation and prompt responses to ecological threats.

While edge computing can be expensive in the short-term, many large tech companies have already adopted it. Smaller tech companies can implement it through hybrid models that combine edge computing for real-time processing with cloud computing for less critical tasks. This approach allows them to leverage existing resources, start with pilot projects to assess feasibility, or use flexible service models like subscription-based services (such as Amazon Web Services, IoT Greengrass, Microsoft Azure IoT Edge, and Google Cloud Anthos) instead of investing in entirely new equipment. Additionally, open-source edge computing platforms, such as Open Horizon and EdgeX Foundation, can help minimize software licensing costs.

Coexisting

Guarding against potential dominance of any single model, regardless of its intentions, is crucial for maintaining online equity. Visionary author and National Humanitarian Medalist Walter Isaacson emphasized the importance of coexistence among different software development models, including open and closed, proprietary and free, and bundled and unbundled. He noted, "Windows and Mac, UNIX and Linux, iOS and Android: a variety of approaches competed over the decades, spurring each other on—and providing a check against any one model becoming so dominant that it stifled innovation."[15]

Maintaining online democracy requires similar checks against dominance, not just from software developers, but from all stakeholders. It involves learning to use our digital tools effectively in this space. For those who value diverse ways of navigating the information world, this is a collective responsibility. This duty falls on users, advocacy groups, lawmakers, and technology companies to understand how technology works. The strategies needed to counter potential abuses of power aren't insurmountable: they begin with basic digital literacy, whether self-taught or through formal education. Once one is familiar with the digital terrain, it becomes not only possible but essential to advocate for principles that prioritize user rights, competition, and innovation.

While the browser wars are a thing of the past, a new challenge has emerged: the urgent task of navigating the digital world with vigilance against those seeking to monopolize control. With newfound skills and community engagement, cyber citizens have a fighting chance to reclaim and maintain our democratic rights online.

CHAPTER 10

Bending to the GDPR

Technology leaders have each made public pronouncements about the importance of privacy and its preservation. Apple's CEO Tim Cook has called privacy a fundamental human right. Sundar Pichai, CEO of Google, wrote in a *New York Times* op-ed that "privacy is at the heart of everything we do." Posting on Facebook, Meta CEO Mark Zuckerberg acknowledged the company's past missteps and stressed the importance of giving users more control over their data. Satya Nadella, Microsoft's CEO, at the company's 2019 annual Build conference, aimed at developers and software engineers, affirmed that privacy is a human right and that users will only trust technology if it's secure and protects privacy. Jeff Bezos of Amazon echoed the claim that privacy is essential in earning users' trust.[1]

From a business perspective, savvy technology leaders understand that showcasing a commitment to privacy is vital for building and sustaining public confidence, as well as retaining market share. It also helps these companies navigate regulatory environments and avoid scrutiny from authorities, showcasing their dedication to legal obligations. In an increasingly privacy-conscious market, promoting privacy serves as a competitive advantage: A pro-privacy stance enhances a company's reputation, aligning its brand image with broader societal values and expectations. Such a stance positions tech companies as responsible and ethical, which helps mitigate the risk of backlash from data breaches or misuse, aiding in damage control and maintaining a positive public image.

These neatly packaged statements from Big Tech CEOs were made in 2018 and in 2019, coinciding with the rollout of the European Union's comprehensive privacy law, the General Data Protection Regulation (GDPR), which imposes strict rules on data handling and requires transparency from organizations.

What Is the GDPR?

Initially proposed by the European Commission in late 2012, after extensive negotiations and revisions involving the European Parliament, the Council of the European Union, and various stakeholders, the GDPR was formally adopted by the European Parliament on April 14, 2016. It entered into force on May 25, 2016, and gave organizations a two-year transition period to comply with the new rules.

The GDPR came about as a response to growing concerns over privacy, data security, and the protection of personal data in the EU. The drive for GDPR was a mix of governmental and consumer and grassroots concern and advocacy, with strong leadership from both EU policymakers and a growing public demand providing the social impetus and legitimacy for strong data-privacy protections.

The GDPR replaced the EU's 1994 Data Protection Directive, which had been adopted when the internet was in its infancy and was the first major attempt to regulate data privacy across member states. The directive lacked specific regulations on data-processing practices that became common in the digital age. For example, it was ill-equipped to address new technologies such as social media platforms, cloud computing, and mobile apps that make it easier for businesses to gather and analyze vast amounts of personal information.

The directive also allowed for significant flexibility in how EU member states implemented its principles, leading to a fragmented regulatory landscape. Each country had its own data-protection laws and enforcement mechanisms, which created inconsistencies and legal uncertainties for businesses operating across borders. The need for a more uniform, updated framework that could better address the realities of the digital era became increasingly clear.

Unlike the 1994 directive, the GDPR applies directly to all EU member states without the need for additional national legislation. That ensures a more consistent application of data-protection rules. It also introduced several new principles and requirements, such as the right to be forgotten, data portability, stricter consent requirements, and mandatory data-breach notifications, to better protect individuals' privacy and empower them with greater control over their personal data.

For their violations of the GDPR, large technology companies have faced, and will continue to face, investigations and significant fines. Early penalties included Amazon's $887 million fine in 2021 by the Luxembourg National Commission for Data Protection for improper processing of personal data.[2] The Irish Data Protection Commission fined Meta $1.3 billion in 2023 for breaching data-privacy rules.[3] Google has been fined several times, including a $166 million penalty in 2021 by France's Commission Nationale de l'Informatique et des Libertés for the operating rules of its ad platform, Google Ads. The commission described them as "opaque and difficult to understand," also noting that it applied them in "an unfair and random manner."[4] Apple and Microsoft also remain under scrutiny for GDPR compliance.

A Different Commitment to Privacy

In contrast, the United States lacks federal privacy legislation, preferring a state-by-state and sector-specific approach that varies significantly in terms of scope, protections, and enforcement. For example, the 1996 Health Insurance Portability and Accountability Act (HIPAA) protects sensitive patient healthcare data, while the Gramm-Leach-Bliley Act, passed in 1999, outlines responsibilities and standards of financial institutions to protect the confidentiality and security of consumers' private data. And the Federal Information Security Management Act, passed as part of the E-Government Act of 2002, requires federal agencies to create, document, and implement agency programs to provide data security.

There is confusion about what data can be lawfully collected and what cannot. This fragmented approach has left current privacy laws in the US inadequate for the digital world. They lack consistency, with different requirements leading to inconsistent protections and obligations. They have gaps in coverage as some laws apply only to specific sectors or types of data, leaving other areas under-regulated. Many contain outdated provisions; legislation predating the internet cannot account for modern data collection, processing, and sharing practices. Like the EU's early privacy laws, many US laws, such as the Privacy Act of 1974 (governing how federal agencies handle personal data), were enacted before the internet era, rendering them increasingly obsolete.

While some legislators have shown interest in enacting a comprehensive federal data-protection package like the GDPR, it has yet to happen. Instead, it's been up to the states to pass privacy protections. As of 2024, nineteen states have passed comprehensive data-privacy laws: California, Colorado, Connecticut, Delaware, Florida, Indiana, Iowa, Kentucky, Maryland, Minnesota,

Montana, Nebraska, New Hampshire, New Jersey, Oregon, Tennessee, Texas, Utah, and Virginia.[5]

The California Consumer Privacy Act (CCPA), enacted in 2018, exemplifies how states are stepping up to address the lack of federal privacy protections. The CCPA provides Californians with rights like those granted by the GDPR, such as the right to know what personal data is being collected, the right to request deletion of their data, and the right to opt out of the sale of personal information. By adopting these GDPR-like provisions, California has set a precedent for other states and potential federal regulations.

A growing patchwork of corporate self-regulation efforts suggest a concerted movement toward enhancing data-privacy protections in line with global best practices. Various American companies have proactively adopted GDPR principles in their data-handling practices to ensure compliance, especially if they operate internationally or handle data of EU citizens. That includes implementing more transparent data policies and strengthening user-consent mechanisms. Initiatives like the Global Privacy Control, allowing users to universally opt out of data sharing across websites, exemplify this.

Global Privacy Control

With a simple click of their browsers, people can now exercise their right to opt out of data sharing and selling and communicate that preference to websites across the internet. The premise owes credit to a creative professor and his eager students.

On October 7, 2020, Sebastian Zimmeck, assistant professor of computer science at Wesleyan University, and his collaborator, Ashkan Soltani of Georgetown Law, announced the beta launch of the Global Privacy Control (GPC). Its universal switch permits users to make one decision across all websites, or to pick just some. The initiative was backed by several partner organizations, including Mozilla, the *New York Times*, and other weighty players in the tech and media worlds. GPC's wide acceptance has been due to a combination of regulatory support, industry collaboration, consumer demand for privacy tools, and the ease with which it could be implemented across various platforms. Its growing recognition as a standard that aligns with legal requirements and consumer expectations has driven adoption across various sectors.

Zimmeck notes that the success of privacy regulations, such as California's Consumer Privacy Act, and the GDPR, "doesn't amount to much if it is hard for people to take advantage of their new rights."[6] After he had the idea for a new global opt-out, he began, with his students, building an extension for the Chrome web browser called OptMeowt.

At the time, Zimmeck said, "My students are doing an excellent job. I am mostly taking on the role as an engineering manager and the students are really the ones implementing the various technologies." He added that a perk of the project was helping students to acquire real-world software engineering skills.[7]

Of the GDPR's central data-privacy law, Zimmeck notes, "I think we should take a lesson from what was learned in the European Union." Prior to the GDPR, when privacy online was addressed at the national level, the patchwork of laws across the European continent made it difficult for consumers to know exactly what protections they had, especially if they traveled across the EU's visa-free zone, with openings for profit exploited by businesses.

As Americans increasingly gained the right to opt out of the selling or sharing of their personal data by website operators, operators in turn must give users ways to object, and must honor user requests in a timely manner. The typical user experience involves accepting or rejecting advertising cookies, filling out forms, or making selections in a provided preference center, among other interactions.

Global Privacy Control (GPC) streamlines this process. It was designed to be a simple signal that users could enable in their browsers or through extensions to automatically communicate a user's preferences to opt out of data tracking and sales to websites. As awareness grew, some browsers, such as Mozilla Firefox and DuckDuckGo, integrated GPC support, allowing users to easily enable the signal. Additionally, some websites and organizations recognized the GPC signal as a valid method for users to opt out of data sales, contributing to its widespread adoption.

The GPC signal gained traction when the California Attorney General clarified that businesses subject to the CCPA must honor GPC as a valid consumer request to opt out of the sale of personal information. This endorsement by a regulatory body elevated GPC's importance and increased its adoption by companies seeking to comply with privacy laws. As GPC continued to be recognized by more privacy regulations and adopted by more browsers and privacy tools, it has become a de facto global standard for expressing user privacy preferences.

As of 2024, companies are required to recognize GPC signals if they are doing business with residents of California, Colorado, Connecticut, Montana, and Texas. Since California is often the standard for other states' (and eventually federal) laws, businesses should anticipate global privacy signal recognition becoming a de facto national requirement.

The GDPR's Effectiveness in Europe

In the European Union, the GDPR has had a profound impact in several ways. It promotes the concept of "privacy by design and by default," encouraging organizations to consider data protection from the beginning of product and service development. It has led to the integration of privacy features in technology and business processes.

The law has granted individuals greater control over their personal data, control that many people likely didn't realize they had lost. As a result, public awareness about data privacy among individuals and businesses has risen. Europeans are now better informed about their data rights, and organizations are more conscientious about their responsibilities concerning data protection.

The GDPR has also resulted in more user-friendly—and thus more effective—consent mechanisms. Websites and apps now frequently provide clear options for users to opt in or out of data processing, making it easier for individuals to make informed choices about their data.

The GDPR principle of data minimization encourages organizations to collect only the data necessary for their purposes. This ensures that individuals have more control over their data and can access it, correct inaccuracies, or request its deletion. Overall, the regulations have empowered European consumers to exercise their data rights and have motivated businesses to conduct data-protection impact assessments to identify and mitigate privacy risks.

In an important advance in public transparency and corporate accountability, the GDPR also introduced mandatory data-breach reporting requirements, compelling companies to report data breaches to supervisory authorities and affected individuals within seventy-two hours. This has led to quicker response times and improved transparency when addressing data breaches.

While the GDPR has been effective in enhancing data protection and privacy in Europe, it is not without challenges. Continuous monitoring of data-breach trends and adaptation is essential to effectively address emerging data-privacy issues. Enforcement can vary among member states, and organizations must continuously adapt to evolving privacy expectations. Some critics argue that the GDPR's strict requirements may impose a heavy burden on small businesses. Research by Dean Li at MIT, Diego J. Jiménez

Hernández at the Chicago Fed, and Sida Peng at Microsoft found that GDPR compliance increased data storage costs by 20 percent, disproportionately burdening smaller firms, akin to a 25 percent tax. Compliance costs range from $1.7 to $70 million, with $5 billion in fines issued. If the GDPR focused on regulating the most sensitive data, it could better balance privacy protection with economic impact.[8]

The Information Technology and Innovation Foundation (ITIF), a think tank focused on public policy, also criticized the GDPR for imposing what it sees as onerous obligations on small and medium-sized enterprises. The ITIF argues that the GDPR's data-protection officer requirement, data-breach notification rules, and consent regulations are particularly challenging for smaller companies with limited legal and administrative resources.[9]

Despite its criticisms, the GDPR has had a positive impact on raising the bar for data protection and shaping global discussions about privacy regulation.

The GDPR's Influence on the United States

The European Union's commitment to data protection drives ongoing innovations and legal requirements in digital privacy. The GDPR significantly influenced data mining and surveillance practices of US companies, emphasizing informed and explicit consent for collecting and processing personal data. This has prompted American businesses to improve user-consent mechanisms and privacy policies, helping users understand data usage.

In 2023, the EU-US Data Privacy Framework was adopted to govern the protection of personal data transferred between the European Union and the United States. This framework replaces the invalidated EU-US Privacy Shield, addressing concerns from the European Court of Justice about US surveillance. Under the new agreement, personal data can flow freely from the EU to participating companies, so long as these companies comply with privacy obligations, such as deleting personal data when it is no longer needed. US-based companies now focus more on data minimization, collecting only necessary data for intended purposes.

The GDPR's stringent data-security requirements and the obligation to report data breaches within seventy-two hours have led US companies to enhance their data-security measures and response protocols. This has improved data-protection practices and raised public awareness about data privacy and accountability in the American business landscape.

Data-Protection Impact Assessments

In contexts where data processing might significantly affect individuals' rights and freedoms, such as in education, healthcare, finance, and other sectors handling sensitive personal data, data-protection impact assessments (DPIAs) have become a crucial standard practice for organizations to assess, evaluate, and mitigate potential risks associated with data-processing activities. A DPIA is a structured process that helps organizations systematically analyze how their data-processing practices could impact the privacy of individuals and what steps they can take to minimize those risks.

In many cases, especially when dealing with complex or high-risk data-processing activities, organizations may choose to involve third parties in conducting DPIAs. Engaging external consultants or auditors can provide an objective, unbiased assessment of the data-processing activities and associated risks. This external perspective is especially valuable when the organization lacks the necessary expertise in-house, or when a neutral evaluation is required to ensure compliance. Third parties often have specialized knowledge and experience in conducting DPIAs and can help organizations navigate the complexities of data-protection laws and regulations, identify less obvious risks, and recommend appropriate mitigation strategies. Using a third party to conduct or review a DPIA can enhance the credibility of the assessment, particularly in highly regulated sectors or where there is a high potential for public scrutiny, such as in education, healthcare, or finance.

Put in Practice: DPIAs in a Public School Setting

Consider a public school that is deciding whether to use biometric data, such as fingerprints or facial recognition, to track student attendance and for security purposes. To inform its decisions, the school conducts a DPIA to assess potential privacy risks and ensure that the processing of biometric data complies with data-protection laws and standards.

The DPIA would analyze the sensitivity of biometric data and the risks associated with its collection, storage, and use. The DPIA would evaluate the school's data-security measures, such as encryption and access controls, to ensure that biometric data is protected against unauthorized access, data breaches, or misuse. It would also consider the risks of potential data misuse, such as unauthorized surveillance or profiling of students, and assess if the proposed use of biometrics is proportionate to the need for enhanced security or efficiency in attendance tracking. The risk assessment might find that biometric data is highly sensitive because it's unique to each individual. If compromised, identity theft or other security issues could follow.

The assessment might advise the school to implement mitigation measures, collecting only the biometric data necessary for the specific purpose of attendance tracking and deleting it once it is no longer needed. Consent and transparency might require ensuring that students and their parents or guardians are fully informed about the use of biometric data, the reasons for its collection, and the measures in place to protect it. The school might also seek explicit consent from parents or guardians before collecting biometric data from students. Implementing strict access controls can also limit who can access the data and for what purposes. This could include role-based access, logging access attempts, and regular audits to detect any unauthorized access or misuse.

Alternatively, privacy-enhancing technologies (PETs) are tools that help protect people's privacy while still allowing data to be used for analysis. Think of a PET like a lockbox that keeps your data safe but still lets researchers look inside without opening the box. Two examples of PETs are homomorphic encryption, which lets computers perform calculations on encrypted data without ever needing to see the actual data; and secure multiparty computation, which allows different parties to jointly compute a result without revealing their own private information.

These technologies have introduced new possibilities for responsible data handling. For instance, the Boston Women's Workforce Council used PETs in reports on gender pay gaps, in partnership with Boston University's Hariri Institute for Computing, to ensure confidentiality and security.[10]

As awareness of the GDPR grows among consumers, privacy-conscious choices are becoming normalized in daily life.

Cookies Reform

Cookies reform is another key component of the GDPR. It significantly impacts how organizations use and handle cookies—you know, those pesky data trackers that appalled Jay Schwedelson back in the day (see chapter 6). The GDPR's provisions on cookies are further complemented by the ePrivacy Directive (known as the "Cookie Law"). Passed on July 12, 2002, the directive is a set of rules that protect privacy and data in the EU's electronic communications sector. It covers topics like cookie usage, email marketing, and data minimization, and aims to protect online privacy while browsing the internet using mobile phones and other internet-connected devices.

According to the GDPR, organizations must now obtain explicit consent from users before placing nonessential cookies on their devices, meaning that users must actively opt in to accept cookies.

Pre-ticked boxes or implied consent are *not* sufficient. This passive-consent approach does not require users to actively choose whether they agree to the use of cookies, or even understand what they're agreeing to. Often, there is no clear information about what types of cookies will be used (i.e., essential cookies versus marketing cookies), what data will be collected, or with whom it will be shared. As a result, many users may not notice these boxes or may not realize they have to *untick* them to withhold their consent. Many users may feel that the quickest way to proceed or access the content they want is to simply accept the default settings, which are often designed to favor data collection. This process does not reflect an informed or deliberate choice, which undermines the concept of genuine consent.

As per the GDPR, users have the right to withdraw their consent at any time, and organizations *must* make this process easy. To do this, companies should implement strategies that involve simplifying the cookie-consent interface with a user-friendly design. Rather than overwhelming users with lengthy text or too many options, companies should provide clear and prominent options like "Manage Cookies" or "Withdraw Consent" next to the consent button. The buttons for withdrawing consent should be just as visible and easy to access as the button for accepting cookies. Using contrasting colors and straightforward labels like "Reject All" or "Manage Preferences" can make these options more noticeable.

Additionally, clear and plain language should be used to explain what cookies are, how they function, and the implications of consenting to them. Instead of generic statements like "We use cookies to enhance your browsing experience," companies should specify the types of data being collected and the purposes for which it is used. It is important to clearly communicate users' right to withdraw consent at any time, through unobtrusive banners or prompts that do not disrupt the user experience. Phrases like "You can change your cookie preferences at any time" or "Click here to withdraw consent" should be prominently displayed.

The process to withdraw consent should require as few steps as possible to emphasize user accessibility. Companies should include a dedicated section on their website or app for managing cookies, which should be easy to find and accessible from every page, often in the footer or through a settings menu. If the website's cookie policy changes, users should be notified and asked to review the updated policy, and given a straightforward way to adjust their consent preferences.

Finally, companies must adhere to legal standards and best practices for consent management, such as those outlined by the GDPR and the California Consumer Privacy Act (CCPA). By combining intuitive UX/UI design with clear, plain language and easy access to consent settings, companies can significantly enhance the user experience around cookie management and ensure compliance with legal and ethical standards.

Cookies Reform vs. Ad Tech

In 2024, the ad-tech industry underwent a radical change when Google discontinued support for third-party cookies in its Chrome browser. This change was driven by evolving privacy regulations, including the GDPR, the EU Cookie Direction, the California Privacy Rights Act, and the Children's Online Privacy Protection Act.

Google's plan includes creating a Privacy Sandbox, designed to protect user privacy through anonymization methods while still allowing advertisers to measure ad performance and attribute ads to specific actions, such as page views and purchases. It reduces the amount of data shared across different websites and does not reveal individual user identities.

Sandbox potentially reshapes the competitive landscape in digital advertising, as it influences not only how ads are delivered and measured, but how different companies can compete in the advertising space. With Google controlling the development and implementation of these new technologies, there are concerns that it could further entrench its position in the advertising ecosystem, giving it a competitive advantage over other companies that rely on third-party cookies for targeted advertising.

Third-party cookies are generated when a user visits a website containing elements from other sites, like ads or third-party images. For instance, if someone plays a YouTube video embedded on a site, the YouTube server sets cookies on their device. These cookies then track user preferences and suggest related videos when they visit YouTube, leading to ads following users around the internet. The data used to create user profiles can be exploited for personal-data theft or malware delivery.

While Mozilla Firefox and Apple's Safari have already introduced features to prevent cross-site tracking, some methods for tracking users go beyond traditional third-party cookies. These methods include browser fingerprinting and using first-party cookies in a way that mimics third-party cookies. Deceptive practices, also known as "dark patterns," are user-interface designs or user experience strategies that intentionally manipulate or trick users into taking actions that may not be in their best interest, in order to benefit the company that designed the interface. Deceptive techniques exploit psychological biases and user behavior to steer people to specific decisions, such as signing up for a subscription, sharing more personal information, making unintended purchases, or not canceling a service because the process for canceling is too difficult. Dark patterns are often subtle but can significantly impact user autonomy and privacy. Examples include confusing language on consent forms, hidden fees, and default settings that favor data collection.

Some websites use assumed-consent approaches: a consent management platform displays a default option like "OK" to encourage users to give consent in a single step. Additionally, some websites justify the use of third-party cookies by claiming that advertising is a "legitimate interest" of the site.[9] As for so-called trust tokens, or private state tokens, which convey a user's authenticity across different contexts, they won't enhance privacy unless Chrome and other browsers eliminate all other forms of tracking. In aiming for a simple user experience around consent, companies may be taking shortcuts or deliberately misleading users with their own policies.

Cyber citizens should advocate for alternatives to trust tokens that prioritize transparency, consent, and user control. We should push for consent-based data collection and the use of first-party data to minimize tracking risks. We should also support the development and adoption of privacy-enhancing technologies like differential privacy and decentralized identifiers, which protect personal information without compromising functionality.

GDPR and Beyond

The shift from "open data networks" to a "closed data network model" has been accelerated by GDPR enforcement since 2018, prompting US executives to pay more attention to privacy concerns. In open data networks, data is freely accessible, reusable, and shared among various users and organizations, promoting transparency, collaboration, and innovation. A closed data network restricts access to its data, allowing only specific individuals or organizations, often through proprietary systems or exclusive agreements. Closed networks may prioritize privacy and security, but they can also inhibit collaboration and innovation by keeping valuable data siloed and inaccessible to the broader community.

The ad-tech industry is undergoing a transformative period as privacy regulations reshape the landscape, with Google and Apple playing prominent roles as global regulators. Compliance with new regulations and meeting consumer expectations will remain critical challenges in this evolving ecosystem.

Let's Talk Privately: Signal and Mastodon

While the GDPR has set a global standard for data protection, some organizations in the United States are taking significant steps to protect their users' data. For example, the Signal Foundation is dedicated to safeguarding privacy through its commitment to developing open-source, encrypted communication tools. The Signal messaging app, founded in 2012, is owned and operated by the Signal Foundation. Because Signal's code is open source, its encryption protocols and overall security can be reviewed and verified by independent security experts, ensuring that vulnerabilities can be identified and patched quickly. The app's focus on privacy has earned it endorsements from prominent figures such as Edward Snowden and entrepreneur Jack Dorsey, cofounder and former CEO of Twitter, further boosting its credibility and user base. As a nonprofit organization, Signal is funded by donations, so it doesn't rely on ads, tracking, or selling user data for revenue. Signal is available on both Android and iOS, and it offers a desktop app so users can maintain secure communication across different devices.

Unlike many mainstream messaging apps, Signal uses end-to-end encryption (E2EE) for all communications, which means that messages, calls, photos, videos, and files are encrypted on the sender's device and only decrypted on the recipient's device. This ensures that no one, including Signal, can read the messages or access the content of your communications while they are in transit. Once messages are delivered, Signal does not keep metadata or store messages on its servers; even if someone were to gain access to Signal's servers, they wouldn't find any message histories there. Messages on Signal are designed to be untraceable and unrecoverable by anyone who doesn't have access to the devices involved in the conversation.

In January 2021, Signal experienced a surge in downloads, reaching over fifty million installs on the Google Play Store alone.[11] This spike was partly driven by heightened privacy concerns following changes to WhatsApp's privacy policy, in which it clarified that it could share data such as user phone numbers, transaction data, service-related information, and IP addresses with Facebook and its other subsidiaries to improve ad targeting and overall user experience on Facebook platforms. Many users feared it signaled a broader data-sharing agreement between WhatsApp and Facebook, potentially compromising the privacy and security of their communications. Confusion and concern over the policy change led many to seek out messaging apps perceived to be more secure and private, like Signal and Telegram.

On the downside, unlike some other messaging apps, Signal does not integrate easily with other apps and services. While Signal offers robust security features, it lacks some of the more advanced functionalities available in other messaging apps, such as extensive media-editing tools or integration with third-party services like payment apps. Signal requires users to register with a phone number, which can be a privacy concern for those who wish to remain completely anonymous. And the disappearing-messages feature is a double-edged sword; while it enhances privacy, it also means that important messages or information are lost if not saved before they disappear.

Mastodon, a decentralized social media platform, offers a compelling alternative to traditional social networks like X, Instagram, Threads, and Facebook (the latter three all owned by Meta). German software developer Eugen Rochko launched Mastodon in 2016 as an alternative to mainstream social networks, aiming to provide users with greater control over their data and the communities they participate in. Rochko has been a vocal advocate for decentralized web technologies and privacy, focusing on building a platform that avoids the pitfalls of centralized social media, such as data exploitation and corporate control.

Mastodon operates on a federated model. Unlike traditional social media platforms which are centralized—owned, controlled, and operated by a single company—Mastodon is made up of a network of independent servers, known as "instances," that operate independently and that can interact with each other. Administrators and community members set their own rules and guidelines. This decentralized structure allows users to choose instances that align with their privacy preferences and values, ensures that no single entity controls the entire network, and fosters a more user-centric and privacy-respecting environment. In contrast, Meta controls all data, user accounts, content, and interactions that are managed and stored on their servers. Decisions about moderation, privacy, and platform policies are made centrally by Meta.

As of October 2024, Mastodon had grown to nearly nine million monthly users.[12] The success of platforms like Mastodon and Signal demonstrates a shifting paradigm in the tech industry, in which privacy-centric alternatives are gaining traction and challenging the dominance (and financial model) of traditional tech giants.

Coming Around to Privacy

Recent studies indicate that a significant portion of Americans are adopting tools and strategies to enhance online privacy. Password-manager use has risen notably, with about 32 percent of Americans using them compared to 20 percent in 2019. Younger adults, particularly aged eighteen to twenty-nine, are more likely to use these tools, revealing improved personal-data management among younger demographics.[13]

A study by the International Association of Privacy Professionals found that 93 percent of Americans would switch to companies that prioritize data privacy.[14] This trend suggests that consumers are not only aware of privacy issues but are also willing to take their business elsewhere to ensure their data is protected.

Many citizens are concerned about specific privacy risks, such as the sharing of location data and the use of personal information for targeted advertising. The Pew Research Center found that 72 percent of Americans believe there should be more regulation of what companies can do with their personal data.[15] Even more, 78 percent, trust themselves to make sound decisions about managing their personal information. This widespread concern underscores the importance of both individual actions and regulatory measures to safeguard privacy in the digital age.

End users can contribute to cookies reform by advocating for Comprehensive Privacy Laws, similar to the GDPR and the California Consumer Privacy Act, which give users greater control over their data by requiring clear consent mechanisms, the right to access and delete data, and strict penalties for noncompliance. End users can also advocate for regulations that prohibit "dark patterns"—deceptive design practices that trick users into making choices they might not otherwise make, such as agreeing to extensive data collection.

CHAPTER 11

Becoming Digitally Literate Citizens

Knowledge of our system of governance and our rights and responsibilities as citizens is not passed along through the gene pool.
—Justice Sandra Day O'Connor[1]

There are several common misconceptions about what civics classes teach. These myths may stem from outdated views of the curriculum, haziness about the goals of civics education, or a lack of exposure to modern approaches. One mistaken belief is that civics classes only teach the structure of government and how a bill becomes law. Although those topics are important, modern civics often includes broader topics like civic engagement, community involvement, digital literacy, and critical thinking about political processes. Studies have shown that effective civics education also emphasizes the importance of civic duties, such as voting, volunteering, and staying informed about current events.[2]

Another misconception is that civics is boring and irrelevant and focuses on rote memorization of historical facts and dates. In fact, much of contemporary civics education aims to be interactive and relevant, engaging students in discussions about current events, ethical dilemmas, and their individual roles in society. This helps students understand the practical implications of civics in their daily lives and encourages active participation in democracy.

Many believe that civics promotes political neutrality and avoids discussions about controversial or political issues. In truth, effective civics instruction often involves exploring contentious topics to help students develop critical-thinking skills and understand different perspectives. This approach prepares students to navigate complex political landscapes and become informed, engaged citizens.

There is also a misconception that civics doesn't teach digital literacy. But modern civics courses increasingly incorporate topics like the critical evaluation of online sources and the impact of social media on public opinion and democracy.

Estonia's Example

One nation's commitment to digital literacy and the integration of technology into society is a model for others. Estonia, with a population the size of San Diego, California—1.3 million—is arguably the most digitally enabled in the world. Nearly all Estonians, in both urban and rural areas, have access to high-speed internet. Digital services are a fundamental part of their daily routines. From e-governance and e-residency to online voting and digital healthcare, Estonian technology serves citizens efficiently and securely.

Estonia's "Tiger Leap" program, or Tiigrihüpe, was pivotal in fostering digital literacy among citizens and transforming Estonia into an egalitarian e-society. Launched in 1996 by the Estonian Ministry of Education and Research, Tiigrihüpe introduced information and communication technology into schools and ensured that students and teachers had access to computers and digital resources.

Students are proficient in using digital tools, learning coding and other essential skills from a young age. Early and consistent exposure ensures that students are well-prepared for the demands of the transnational workforce. Although Tiger Leap ended in the early 2000s, its legacy continues to shape Estonia's approach to digital education and literacy. A popular public-private program, ProgeTiger, launched a nationwide campaign to teach school children ages seven to nineteen to write code.

Estonia's e-residency program exemplifies its forward-thinking approach. It allows non-Estonians to access the country's digital infrastructure, enabling them to start and manage businesses online from anywhere in the world. Encouraging open competition among digital services providers reduces reliance on tech giants and monopolies.

Take the case of three young entrepreneurs.

Merve Cankız Çoruh, Samet Ozkale, and Gabriel Betancourt shared a common dream of starting their own tech-related companies. Çoruh and Ozkale created Roadmape, an AI-powered project-road-mapping software that helps companies refine and structure their ideas.[3] Betancourt's venture, Petme, is a social media platform that simplifies how pet owners create and manage profiles.

All three entrepreneurs became Estonian e-residents. In 2023, Betancourt applied for and collected his e-residency kit at the Estonian embassy in

Buchares. Çoruh and Ozkale followed suit, incorporating their company in Estonia after picking up e-residency kits at the Estonian embassy in Ankara, Turkey.

"Everything related to startups and running a business in Estonia is easy, everything is digitized," explains Çoruh. E-Residency provided easier access to the European market, allowing Roadmape to work with services like Stripe, the online payment system which is not available everywhere.

In early 2024, Betancourt made his first visit to Estonia to meet with investors. Before visiting his e-citizenship country, he said, "Of course, I want to go there. This is the country that made my dream come true."[4]

Estonia excels in many areas essential to a democracy: it has among the highest levels of economic freedom, internet freedom, and press freedom worldwide. Estonia's innovation as a member of the cyber society has made this possible.

Granted, replication of such services in some countries is not as easy to implement. The US, for example, lacks Estonia's small population and a strong, consistent government vision for digital transformation, both of which allow for quicker and more uniform implementation of e-initiatives. Extensive legacy computer systems and a complex regulatory environment in America also present challenges, as does the fact that many users are awestruck by influential tech titans' addictive devices and tactics.

Democracy's Ally: Digital Media Literacy in the United States

If more internet users develop a healthy skepticism, check multiple sources, evaluate platforms' credibility, and identify bias, they may mitigate unnecessary political divisions and civic complacency. *The key lesson for the literate cyber citizen is always: consider the source.*

Fortunately, many organizations and individuals encourage us to be more discerning. Dr. Andy Lee Roth is one. A sociologist, he has been associate director of Project Censored, a nonprofit media watchdog, since 2005. In 2022, the project copublished *The Media and Me*, a primer dedicated to fostering critical media literacy in young people.[5]

"The critical dimension of critical media literacy is thinking about power, about the distribution of power and life chances. Not all media literacy programs do that," says Roth. *The Media and Me* provides user strategies for remaining aware of biases and potential manipulation in information, such as navigating media fallacies, deciphering advertising language, and examining power structures. Understanding power structures empowers users to advocate for their rights, demand transparency, and push for changes that ensure technology serves the public good. Understanding who controls the narratives and what mechanisms are at play can help citizens participate more effectively in democratic processes and hold powerful entities accountable.

Roth uses a favorite metaphor. "Imagine an old-fashioned wristwatch or clock with the big hand pointing to the minutes and the small hands pointing to the hours. You can read time by knowing the relationship between those hands and the numbers on those clocks." Media use, he suggests, is as essential as being able to tell time. "What critical media literacy does is say, 'Let's go beneath the surface.' What's underneath the face of the clock, what are the gears and the wheels and the springs that drive the hands of the clock? If you understand what is going on beneath the surface, the structures, the framing, you can look at media with a different set of eyes." The different set of eyes in this case is more discerning, and ultimately more empowering.

Roth notes that, "Right now, strong corporate-based movements are promoting media literacy, but not of the sort that my coauthors and I are thrilled about." As efforts to promote media literacy are underway across the nation, Roth cautions that there's a battle over whose version will prevail. Several courses are funded by corporations, including the online-learning company Coursera's *Making Sense of the News* and the News Literacy Project's *Checkology*, according to Fairness and Accuracy in Reporting, another media watchdog. Such programs often promote status quo standards of "objectivity," but don't address ways to analyze power dynamics, profit incentives, or bias in the reporting and selection of sources.

He continues, "A media literacy that says we should trust members of the Department of Defense to tell us who's producing reliable news stories is not the sort of critical media literacy I'd hope for in our future."[6]

Momentum for media literacy in public education is building. State legislators, educators, and a host of nonprofit organizations and individuals understand the necessity of teaching digital literacy and citizenship at the K–12 level.

Media Literacy Now, founded in 2013, reports that legislatures in more than half the states are holding hearings or voting on media literacy education, with eighteen governors enacting laws related to K–12 media literacy or digital citizenship education, as of 2024.[7] As discussed earlier, in 2013 New Jersey became the first state to mandate K–12 information literacy instruction, defining information literacy as "a set of skills that enables an individual to recognize when information is needed and to locate, evaluate and use effectively the needed information. Information literacy includes, but is not limited to, digital, visual, media, textual, *and technological literacy*" (emphasis mine).[8]

As of 2024, nineteen states in the US have implemented some form of media literacy action, through legislation mandates or instructional resources.[9] The nation's largest K–12 school population, California, passed a comprehensive media literacy law in 2023, directing resources to media literacy curriculum and professional development. The law mandates media literacy curriculum development to help students critically evaluate media content, understand the impact of media on public opinion and behavior, recognize the influence of digital and social media on society, and discern credible sources of information from misinformation and disinformation.

California's privacy legislation allocates funding and resources for professional development programs to train teachers in media literacy education. Trainings include workshops, seminars, and online courses focusing on the principles of media literacy, the ethical implications of media, and how to address controversial or sensitive topics in the classroom.

The law also encourages giving students real-world insights into how media shapes public discourse through partnerships with media professionals, technology experts, and academic researchers.

Evaluation and assessment tools are included in the legislation so that data collected can inform future curriculum adjustments and identify areas where additional support or resources are needed. The law encourages initiatives to raise awareness about media literacy among parents, community members, and policymakers as a critical life skill, with emphasis on community involvement supporting media literacy education in schools.

The mere existence of laws requiring media literacy action doesn't necessarily mean that actual programs have been enacted. A 2024 survey by the National Association of Media Literacy Educators revealed a disconnect in several states with existing media literacy legislation. Some respondents from these states reported being unaware of the legislation or mandates. Overall, responses indicated confusion about the specific state requirements, how these policies or mandates will be implemented, and how teachers will be trained or should adjust their standards and curriculum. This disconnect may be partly due to a lack of consensus on what constitutes media literacy.[10]

Educating Students and Teachers

As noted earlier, in 2023, the Surgeon General; the National Academies of Sciences, Engineering, and Medicine; and the American Psychological Association urged K–12 media literacy education to address the growing problem of student health and wellness related to internet and social media use. The Media Education Lab, Media Literacy Now, the National Association for Media Literacy Education, the Center for News Literacy, and the Critical Media Project are among many organizations that, as of 2024, are developing curricula and solutions to emerging online challenges. Common Sense Media's digital literacy curriculum is used in over ninety thousand schools, reaching millions of students on topics of online privacy, responsible social media use, critical thinking about online information, and cyber security.[11]

Typically, at the elementary level, students are introduced to the basics of digital literacy through interactive lessons on how to use search engines, assess the credibility of online sources, and practice responsible online behavior. In many classrooms, students are tasked with researching a topic online and presenting their findings, emphasizing the need for critical thinking and source evaluation.

In middle and high schools, digital literacy education becomes more advanced. Students learn the ABCs of digital citizenship, online privacy, and ethical behavior in digital spaces. They discuss the consequences of cyberbullying, the importance of respecting intellectual property rights, and the power of social media for advocacy and positive change. Real-life case studies are often incorporated into the curriculum to illustrate the impact of digital choices.

In the wider digital literacy landscape, emphasis is growing on teaching practical digital skills relevant to future careers, such as coding and programming, digital storytelling, data analysis, and multimedia production. Students may use coding platforms to create their own websites or apps, analyze real-world datasets to draw meaningful conclusions, or produce multimedia projects that convey complex ideas effectively.

In a 2023 Pew Research Center digital knowledge survey, respondents ranging in age and educational background correctly answered a median of five out of nine questions on topics related to cybersecurity practices, facts about major tech firms, and federal laws pertaining to artificial intelligence and online privacy. About a quarter were able to answer at least seven of the nine queries, with age and educational levels influencing results. Younger adults, ages eighteen to twenty-nine, had a higher rate of correct answers, a median of six. That number dropped to five respondents in the thirty to forty-nine-year-old age group, and to four among those aged fifty and older.[12]

The younger adults were the first in the e-generation, growing up in a technology-driven environment at school and at home. Those whose formative years were in the analog era understandably face a steeper learning curve, reflecting the rapid evolution of digital landscapes and the need for ongoing literacy education to keep up with changes.

Action Civics

Peyton Amaral is a fast-talking eighth grader from Morton, Rhode Island. In April 2021, Amaral addressed the Fall River City Council to urge a citywide ban on single-use plastic bags.

"Pollution is making our community dirty and unlivable. We, the youth of Fall River, want to stay here, but we can't bear to stay in a city that is dirty."[13]

Welcome to action civics.

The term was coined in 2007 by the Mikva Challenge, a group founded in 1998 by former White House counsel Abner Mikva, his wife, and a few friends. The all-volunteer pilot education program began in four Chicago schools to inspire city youth to partake in electoral experiences. The Mikva Challenge contends that its model of raising the voices of youth leaders in civic endeavors strengthens schools, thereby enriching and strengthening communities.[14]

In 2022, Massachusetts enacted the nation's first law requiring students to take part in at least two student-led, nonpartisan civics projects.[15] They do so in eighth grade, then in high school. Advocates say that it's a tool to engage, and thus prepare, students to be active citizens.

The nonprofit Generation Citizen also uses action civics to teach young people to be active and engaged citizens. It began in 2008 as a student project at Brown University; eight students sought to address a perceived weakening of democratic spirit among young people. Generation Citizen collaborated with local classrooms in Providence, Rhode Island, to teach action civics to inspire civic participation in real-life contexts. It has become a formidable force helping students around the nation actively engage in civics in real-life situations.

Arielle Jennings, executive director of Generation Citizen's New England chapter, says, "Students need to interact with the issues to understand the complexity of them, and the complexity of Generation Citizen has action-focused civic hubs in California, Massachusetts, New York, Oklahoma,

Rhode Island, and Texas."[16] Amaral found the experience of testifying in Rhode Island "nerve-wracking" but "rewarding." "I learned that if you present the facts, and show genuine concern, people will take you seriously, even if you're young," she said.

Savannah Slayton is a Generation Citizen alumna from Oklahoma who was involved in action civics in 2020 at Northwest Classen High School. Later, at the University of Oklahoma (OU), she pursued a degree in political science and constitutional studies, while remaining civically engaged on campus. She was a policy and advocacy fellow at Let's Fix This, a student advisory board Indigenous chair for Campus Vote Project, a programming chair for Oklahoma Votes at OU, and an activist with Rock the Native Vote OKC. Slayton says she plans to continue to advocate for Native rights and empower young people through civics education. She cites her experience with Generation Citizen as a key influence that taught her to recognize the strength of her voice and guided her to advocate for education policy, especially in Indian education in Oklahoma and elsewhere in the United States. Slayton notes the importance of project-based civics education for transforming students' passion and creative ideas into tangible projects.[17]

This project-based focus is what defines action civics, and what many advocates cite as its strength. However, action civics also has its critics.

Many assert that low scores on national civics and history tests suggest that schools should devote more in-class time to teaching the US system of government, versus encouraging students to tackle hands-on community action projects. Research fellow David Davenport at the conservative Hoover Institution says, "In science, you don't run around doing a bunch of experiments—you start with knowledge and develop a hypothesis first."[18]

The similarly conservative National Association of Scholars formed a coalition dedicated to protecting traditional civics education from "sustained assault by radical activists."[19] The Texas Public Policy Foundation, with the website banner "Freedom, Prosperity, and Opportunity," writes that action civics "tends to politicize civics, spurning more apolitical activities like volunteering at a soup kitchen." They criticize the practice as focusing only on actions that challenge power dynamics, namely government entities.[20]

Action civics leaders emphasize that their approach engages students in real-world democratic practices, empowering them to participate actively in their communities. They argue that this hands-on learning fosters a deeper understanding of democratic processes and encourages lifelong civic engagement. Rather than promoting any specific political agenda, action civics educates students on how to critically analyze issues, deliberate, and take informed action.

Democracy Games: A Companion to Civics Education

During her career, former Supreme Court Justice Sandra Day O'Connor was increasingly troubled by the mass misunderstanding of our system of government. Americans were disengaged from civic life. When she retired in 2018, O'Connor wrote a public letter announcing that she would dedicate her remaining years to advancing civics education and engagement:

> I've seen firsthand how vital it is for all citizens to understand our Constitution and unique system of government, and participate actively in their communities. It is through this shared understanding of who we are that we can follow the approaches that have served us best over time—working collaboratively together in communities and in government to solve problems, putting country and the common good above party and self-interest, and holding our key governmental institutions accountable.[21]

She explained how eight years earlier, in 2009, at age eighty-two, she founded the Boston-based nonprofit organization iCivics. In her 2018 letter, she announced that more than half of US social studies teachers use iCivics in the classroom.

Louise Dubé, iCivics's executive director, responded to the nation's 2023 report card on the day the National Association of Educational Procurement (NAEP) released it. "Today's results are indeed a report card for our nation, reflecting a failure to prioritize and invest in civics education—the knowledge and skills fundamental to the responsibilities of citizenship in our self-governing society."[22]

Dubé urged policymakers at the federal, state, and local levels to pass legislation that ensures schools are supported to provide high-quality civics education for all students. iCivics noted that a poll of more than three thousand voters conducted just before the 2022 midterm elections, by the political and public affairs consulting firm Cygnal, revealed that nearly 80 percent—from both sides of the political aisle—believe that civics education is more important now than it was just five years ago, with 65 percent saying they would support more funding of civics.[23]

iCivics offers creative role-playing games and other resources for educators to use in animating civics education. In *Court Quest*, players get behind the wheel of the Justice Express bus and must decide which courthouse to drop off all passengers based on the nature of their cases. For example, a woman whose boss is engaging in gender discrimination against her goes to a federal circuit court, while a misdemeanor complainant hops off at county court. This and other games cover topics such as voting, the branches of government, activism, immigration, and more.

One of iCivics' advocacy initiatives focused on passage of the Civics Secures Democracy Act in 2023. The bipartisan spending bill (which was reintroduced in 2024) allocates resources to expand educational programs on the state level for US history and civics. iCivics urged the private sector to add the act to the list of priority legislation supported by the governmental affairs teams in several companies, while also adding corporate bylines to op-eds that support the act.

Beyond Curricula

Combating Deepfakes

The most common method of preventing deepfakes relies on training a "good" machine-learning model to identify or disrupt the manipulation. Because the process is time- and resource-intensive and unique to an organization's network, many researchers are seeking more systematic and reliable methods of identification.

Some researchers have developed methods to produce images and videos that can't be easily modified, basically hardening the target against tampering. This would be particularly useful for artists and creators with respect to protecting their intellectual property. But while promising for newly produced media, this approach doesn't protect the vast amounts of unfiltered media already published on the internet.

Undergrads at the University of Virginia School of Engineering created a way to detect and prevent deepfake images, videos, and other online manipulations.

Ahmed Hafeez Hussain, a computer engineering and physics major, and Zachary Yahn, a computer engineering and computer science major, developed an end-to-end method for the automatic detection and integrity of digital media. Their method leverages blockchain technology to prevent tampering and uses cryptographic hashes for rapid verification of whether internet media has been altered or deepfaked.[24] Hussain and Yahn's solution enhances current verification methods by generating unique signatures for videos at the time of upload, which allows straightforward content integrity checks across various platforms. This approach protects newly created media and quickly authenticates existing internet content. Unlike other solutions that only work well with media that is difficult to modify, their web-based framework benefits all media consumers and uses machine learning only when necessary.

Hussain and Yahn's method would be useful for X, Facebook, Instagram, and YouTube security departments.

Yahn explains that "whenever a publisher uploads a video to a platform's website or channel, a video hashing algorithm produces a unique signature for the video; the signature can later be used to determine whether two videos are the same. When the image is released, its hash is saved in the publisher's blockchain, like a virtual ledger, with all previous video hashes. Once something is added to the ledger, it is immutable and publicly available."[25]

Potential privacy downsides might arise from storing video hashes on a public blockchain which makes these hashes publicly available, if the videos contain sensitive or private information. And as more videos are uploaded and hashed, the blockchain's size could grow significantly, leading to scalability and storage issues that might make the system less efficient over time. Maintaining a blockchain requires significant computational resources, which could be a barrier for widespread adoption, especially among smaller publishers or platforms with limited technical infrastructure.

"Pants on Fire"

Fact-checking organizations play a key role in identifying and debunking misinformation. For years, professional fact-checkers manually reviewed and analyzed assertions by culling a range of resources to assess accuracy. It's painstaking work.

In the information age, the process has largely become automated as algorithms employ natural language processing, machine learning, and deep learning to comb through datasets looking for patterns and correlations. Automation has its own problems; huge troves of data and emerging forms of disinformation often can't keep pace with rapidly spreading information. And some developments, such as deepfakes, require human intervention.

Snopes is the oldest online fact-checking site, founded in 1994 by Barbara and David Mikkelson. As of 2022, it was averaging about 6.4 million page views per month.[26] Snopes became a major player in debunking disinformation after the 9/11 attacks, dispelling false claims such as one that CNN had faked footage of Palestinians celebrating in the streets after the Twin Tower attacks. Over the years, the site underwent management and financial problems until 2022, when it was purchased by tech entrepreneurs Chris Richmond and Drew Schoentrup.

As recently as 2024, Snopes was deemed compliant with the International Fact-Checking Network principles, after being vetted and evaluated by external assessors. To be deemed compliant, organizations must demonstrate a commitment to nonpartisanship and fairness; transparency of sources, funding, organization, and methodology; and a commitment to open and honest corrections.

The International Fact-Checking Network is a project of the Poynter Institute for Media Studies. "Through teaching, publishing, convening, fact-checking and media literacy, Poynter creates a crossroads where communities come together to use journalism to confront society's complex problems," Poynter says regarding its mission.

The institute operates PolitiFact.com, which began in 2007 as a project of the *Tampa Bay Times*. The site's Truth-O-Meter ratings have six levels: true, mostly true, half true, mostly false, false, and Pants on Fire. To slow the spread of online disinformation, Meta and TikTok retain PolitiFact to flag posts they think may be inaccurate or misleading. These platforms also share potential misinformation to fact-checkers using signals, such as community feedback or similarity detection algorithms.

One study by researchers at Harvard University found that Snopes and PolitiFact have both developed "consistent and reliable fact-checking practices."[27] As online platforms increasingly turn to fact-checking as a way to reduce disinformation, such consistency is integral to countering falsities and establishing credibility among the public.

As early as 2020, platforms like X began lowering their standards for combating false claims, setting the stage for the proliferation of blatant misinformation. By 2024, when PolitiFact examined election-related misinformation policies at YouTube, X, TikTok, and Meta, it found inconsistent enforcement, with X and Meta also reducing their content-moderation staff. In September 2023, X eliminated the feature allowing users to report misleading information, relying instead on its Community Notes program. Personnel cuts, and a 2024 policy change at YouTube to no longer remove videos containing false information about the 2020 presidential election, signal a broader shift away from regulating misinformation.[28] Elon Musk's own posts on X have further fueled that shift. Between September 30 and October 14, 2024, PolitiFact identified over 450 of his posts—including reposts and replies—that contained misleading or false claims about voting. These included mischaracterizations of a new California voter-ID law.[29]

By verifying the information they encounter online, individuals can better protect themselves from misinformation and contribute to the integrity of democratic institutions. Other sites, such as FactCheck.org, BBC Reality Check, and Reuters Fact Check, are accessible go-to platforms for people who rely on online sources for their news. Encouraging users to make fact-checking a regular part of their information consumption is crucial for a healthy democracy, as many media platforms, especially social media, do not verify content before it reaches the public.

An Eye on Algorithms

Efforts to counteract the harmful effects of algorithms have been largely driven by watchdog organizations and educational institutions.

The Ada Lovelace Institute in London was launched in early 2018 by the Nuffield Foundation with a mandate to ensure data and artificial intelligence work for people and society. It's a collaborative effort, with partners like the Alan Turing Institute, the Royal Society, the British Academy, the Royal Statistical Society, techUK, and the Nuffield Council on Bioethics. Together, they're tackling some of the thorniest issues surrounding data and AI, like human rights, equity, and the democratic principles at stake as technology advances.

The institute's 2021 report, *Exploring Legal Mechanisms for Data Stewardship*, analyzed innovative ways to manage data through models like data trusts, providing guidance on how these structures can be leveraged to safeguard individual and community data rights.[30] It's had a significant impact, shaping policy discussions around data-sharing practices that actually prioritize public benefit and ethical considerations, and is a valuable reference for organizations advocating for responsible data governance.

The Algorithmic Justice League (AJL), founded by Joy Buolamwini in 2016, has played a crucial role in exposing and addressing biases in artificial intelligence systems. Through projects like "Gender Shades," which revealed significant racial and gender biases in commercial facial recognition technologies, AJL brought global attention to the discriminatory impacts of these AI tools. Their work has pressured major tech companies to reassess and improve their algorithms, leading to industry-wide changes in how AI systems are evaluated and deployed. Additionally, AJL's advocacy and research have influenced policy discussions, emphasizing the need for accountability, transparency, and fairness in AI development to protect marginalized communities.

AJL research highlights how bias is built into commercial algorithms that disproportionately misidentify women and people of color, leading to advocacy for more stringent regulatory measures and the ethical development of AI.[31]

The AI Now Institute studies the social implications of artificial intelligence. Founded in 2017 by Kate Crawford and Meredith Whittaker, faculty members at New York University's Tandon's Department of Technology, Culture and Society, in 2022 it became an independent policy research organization. Its mission is to study the increasing application of AI technologies and machine-learning systems in industries such as healthcare and law and to understand its technological impact on people and their civil rights, safety and infrastructure, and labor and automation, as well as the implications of biased data.

The institute's 2023 report, *Confronting Tech Power*, provides a road map for regulators to rein in the unchecked development of AI technologies.[32] The report's core recommendation is to make tech companies responsible for proving that their AI systems won't harm society before they're deployed—akin to FDA regulations for new drugs. Instead of relying on after-the-fact audits, which often fail to address systemic issues like racial bias, AI Now argues that the threshold question should be whether certain AI tools should even exist. For example, the authors urge bans on pseudoscientific AI applications such as emotion recognition, which they note are inherently prone to misuse and discrimination, rather than superficial attempts to make them "less biased."

Also suggested are cross-policy strategies, combining data privacy laws with antitrust regulations to curb data collection and dismantle tech monopolies. Recognizing "AI policy" as deeply interconnected with privacy and competition laws can strengthen regulators' control over AI's trajectory. Importantly, the AI Now report dispels the myth that AI development is inevitable, urging policymakers and the public to assert popular control over which technologies we allow, reminding us that societal values—not corporate interests—should dictate the future of AI.

Holding Platforms and Others Accountable

Another ongoing challenge to digital users is curbing online intimidation and threats, especially when linked to real-life violence. Dominant tech players often use heavy-handed tactics to avoid being accountable for the threats posted or publicized using their platforms. Despite that, some tenacious victims have had victories.

In 2013, New York attorney Carrie Goldberg fell into a whirlwind romance that quickly turned into a nightmare. Her jealous ex threatened to send intimate photos of her to her colleagues and boss—the practice known as revenge porn. He *did* reach out to more than a dozen of her friends and family members with lies that she had STDs, was pregnant, and was a drug addict. He filed false police reports, forcing her to move. When police and courts failed to help, Goldberg opened her law firm in January 2014.[33]

"My whole purpose was to become the lawyer I needed," says Goldberg, author of *Nobody's Victim: Fighting Psychos, Stalkers, Pervs, and Trolls*.[34] Goldberg notes that an estimated ten million Americans have been victims of revenge porn.

After years of advocacy, New York State joined forty-one others in outlawing revenge porn. The Unlawful Dissemination or Publication of an Intimate Image law, which Goldberg helped draft, allows victims to sue the person who shared the explicit content without consent and request that web hosts remove offending images.[35] Initially introduced in 2013, the law gained momentum after a 2017 *New York Post* exposé on the Panama-based porn site Anonymous Image Board (Anon IB).[36] Despite Google's last-minute campaign to kill the bill in 2018, it passed.

Google now bans revenge porn and allows victims to request the removal of links to such content from search results. However, removing the content from the source website requires victims to contact the site directly. Goldberg notes the difficulty of this process, emphasizing that the content can reappear elsewhere even after being taken down.

Victims can claim ownership of images to request their removal from sites like Pornhub, but the process is lengthy, and images can quickly go viral. "Even if we got it taken down from one place, it can then pop up somewhere else," Goldberg says. She encourages clients to become warriors, transforming their victimhood into empowerment through the fight to remove improperly shared photos.

Always Consider the Source

Digital literacy and civics education in the information age have become as fundamentally important as learning the alphabet. Without such competence, each day we hand over the reins controlling our data privacy to tech companies, allowing purveyors of disinformation to dominate our online content. Furthermore, we forfeit civic agency by not understanding citizen rights and responsibilities in the face of technology companies wielding power over our everyday decisions and activities.

As an industry of online literacy education arises, it's inevitable that some businesses will prioritize profit ahead of societal well-being, and that certain ideologies may creep into the mix. The 2023 lawsuit by *Consortium News* (*CN*) alleged that the digital news rating agency NewsGuard acted as a proxy for military interests and engaged in censorship. NewsGuard labeled some *CN* reporting as unreliable, thus limiting their visibility and advertising revenue. According to *CN*, these actions aligned with military or governmental objectives by suppressing dissenting perspectives that challenge mainstream narratives, particularly on issues related to foreign policy and national security. Even conservative websites like *The Federalist* and the Daily Wire accused the government of financing firms like NewsGuard or attempting to compile a list of websites critical of government positions, all while directing readers to news sites with more favorable views.[37]

Project Censored's Andy Lee Roth's insights into critical media literacy underscore the importance of scrutinizing power distribution when it comes to where we source our information—a consideration not always integrated into literacy programs. The same applies to the myriad apps and features developed by companies like Apple, Google, and others to make users feel they're exercising self-control over their screen time. Apple's Screen Time and Digital Wellbeing and apps like Forest, Freedom, and RescueTime *appear* to empower users by letting them block distracting websites and apps or tracking their productivity. Although these tools seem designed to provide a sense of control, tech companies have done little to address fundamental addictive properties build into the devices themselves. Still, tech monopolies frequently make public proclamations of helping users decipher fake news or reduce reliance on their devices. Google's Digital Wellbeing site, for instance, invites users to reflect on their relationship with technology and offers tips to achieve personal digital well-being.

For readers committed to becoming responsible digital citizens, it's crucial to exercise discernment and prudence when considering advice on digital well-being from companies like Google. This demonstrates mastery of the first and most fundamental lesson of critical digital literacy: *always consider the source.* Relying on others to do this work for us is not an option; we must get into the habit navigating the complexities of the digital world ourselves.

CHAPTER 12

A Safer Digital World: Cyber Hygienists

We spent several chapters learning about the many loopholes that unsavory actors in society are exploiting in our digital world. Now it's time to learn about the mass of citizens fighting back.

Much like the Rebel Alliance in *Star Wars*, a critical mass of citizens is committed to safeguarding our digital infrastructure. While *cyber hygiene* doesn't sound grandiose or heroic, the cyber hygienists described in this chapter defy stronger forces in small yet impactful ways, making all systems more resilient. They include educators, nonprofit organizations, cybersecurity clinics in higher education, whistleblowers, litigators, regulatory agencies, and ethical hackers who quietly find and report software vulnerabilities. From librarians, cryptography researchers, and developers creating encryption tools to the Mozilla Foundation advocating for an open and accessible internet, the heroes of cyber hygiene are legion.

Organizations like the Electronic Frontier Foundation (EFF) have been pivotal in raising awareness and advocating for stronger digital rights alongside groups like the Center for Democracy and Technology (CDT) and Access Now, which promote internet freedom and protect user privacy globally. Academic institutions increasingly offer digital literacy programs, such as the University of Washington's Information School, which integrates cybersecurity and privacy education into its curriculum to equip the next generation with the tools to navigate and secure the digital world. Grassroots initiatives like Tactical Tech's Data Detox Kit empower individuals to take control of their digital footprints. The collective efforts from these diverse fronts, including advocacy, education, and practical resources, show that progress in digital hygiene is not just aspirational—it's actively happening.

E-Rates for Cyber Hygiene

The federal E-Rate program, officially known as the Schools and Libraries Program of the Universal Service Fund, was created in 1996 by the Federal Communications Commission under the Telecommunications Act of 1996. It is a critical initiative aimed at providing affordable internet access and tele-communications services to schools and libraries across the United States. Administered by the Universal Service Administrative Company under the oversight of the FCC, the E-Rate program helps ensure that all students and library patrons have access to the educational and informational resources available online, regardless of their location or economic status. It provides financial support to schools and libraries to help them obtain affordable broadband internet and telecommunications services. This includes discounts on services such as high-speed internet access, Wi-Fi networks, data transmission, and voice services. The level of discount varies from 20 percent to 90 percent, depending on the economic needs of the student population and the location of the school or library, with higher discounts given to institutions serving low-income communities and rural areas.

With E-Rate funding, schools can implement technology-driven teaching methods, such as blended learning, digital textbooks, online assessments, and interactive classroom tools, which are essential for preparing students for a technology-centric future. Libraries benefiting from the E-Rate program provide critical access points to the internet for members of the community who lack reliable internet access at home. This support fosters lifelong learning opportunities, allowing patrons to engage in online education, access digital resources, participate in job-training programs, and connect with essential services.

Librarians as Digital Dentists

Libraries advocate for cyber hygiene by participating in coalitions that influence national cybersecurity policies, as evidenced by a collaboration of leading education and library nonprofits responding in 2024 to the FCC's Notice of Proposed Rulemaking on a $200 million Cybersecurity Pilot Program.[1] This coalition, which includes the American Library Association and other key educational organizations, emphasizes the need for modernized firewall definitions (the criteria or rules used by firewall systems to control the flow of network traffic, deciding what is allowed or blocked) and immediate cyber-security enhancements for E-Rate-funded networks in schools and libraries.

The Library Freedom Project (LFP) knows that libraries and librarians are fundamental to democracy. It was founded in 2013 by librarian and social justice activist Alison Macrina, who was inspired in part by library-activists who had earlier opposed the USA PATRIOT Act in the 2000s, at a time when public dissent was frowned on. LFP raises awareness and provides extensive privacy training to librarians, including about how to respond to law enforcement requests for information on patrons' checkout history. LFP trains library staff on privacy rights and relevant laws, ensuring they understand their legal obligations and patrons' rights. It advises minimizing data collection to limit information available to law enforcement and suggests appointing a trained privacy officer to handle requests. When a request is overly broad or lacks proper authority, LFP recommends challenging it in court to protect patron privacy; it also advocates for transparency by encouraging libraries to report law enforcement requests publicly, raising awareness about privacy issues.

LFP trains librarians to teach their patrons how to use the Tor browser to enhance online privacy and security. In Lebanon, New Hampshire, librarian Chuck McAndrew took a bold and successful stand in defense of the library's use of Tor after the Department of Homeland Security (DHS) visited the library, expressing concern that the library's efforts to maintain privacy might protect terrorists. McAndrew refused to remove Tor from the library's computers despite the DHS's implicit pressure. He argued that providing access to the Tor browser was crucial for protecting user privacy and supporting open access to information without surveillance or censorship. McAndrew's actions underscored his commitment to intellectual freedom and digital privacy, demonstrating a staunch resistance against government overreach into public library operations and patron privacy.

Education for a Secure Wired World

Several nonprofit organizations teach young persons about digital hygiene and cybersecurity, both in schools and in community programs. As mentioned earlier, Common Sense, founded in 2003, offers independent age-based ratings and reviews of media and provides extensive resources to teachers and schools to foster digital citizenship among students. Their award-winning Digital Citizenship Curriculum prepares young people with the skills needed to safely navigate the digital terrain. It also trains teachers and involves families and communities, offering practical advice and tools.

Reminiscent of the early hacker movement that emphasized openness, sharing, creativity, and the belief in the positive potential of technology, organizations like Code.org and Girls Who Code strive to create a more equitable and knowledgeable digital society. These groups teach young people how to code and share a commitment to break down barriers, foster innovation, and promote a free and secure internet for all. Both nonprofits are focused on expanding access to computer science education and emphasize the importance of personal cybersecurity.

Some federal efforts are under way to protect schools' data. In 2022, President Joe Biden signed into law the State and Local Cybersecurity Improvement Act, authorizing $1 billion in grants to state, local, and tribal governmental entities, including school districts, to address cybersecurity threats and risks to their IT systems.[2]

On a smaller scale, but equally important, are initiatives open to the community. For twenty-five dollars, the University of South Florida's continuing education program offers a five-hour cybersecurity course for seventh- to twelfth-grade students and their parents. This affordable course should be emulated nationwide, as schools may fall short in teaching cyber hygiene alongside digital media literacy. The course description acknowledges how new technologies have changed adolescence, from schoolwork to gaming to social interactions. The course covers essential cybersecurity concepts in an accessible format featuring interactive content, videos, and quizzes across five modules. Topics include online safety for families, creating strong passwords, identifying social-engineering tactics, recognizing and avoiding malware, and implementing best cyber-hygiene practices in your home immediately.[3] Participants have thirty days to complete the coursework at their own pace and receive a digital badge upon completion.

The University of South Florida has several degree programs in the field and has been designated a National Center of Academic Excellence in Information Assurance/Cybersecurity, an academic recognition program cosponsored by the NSA and Department of Homeland Security. CAE designations confirm that USF's programs have passed rigorous curriculum and program requirements. Initiatives like this are a cost-effective way to significantly improve digital hygiene education in schools nationwide.

Cybersecurity Clinics to the Rescue

University cybersecurity clinics and nonprofit educational programs—well positioned because they're trusted in their respective communities—are shoring up local cyber capacity.

Stillman University, MIT, the University of Texas at Austin, the University of Georgia, and University of California, Berkeley, are among many institutions with clinics helping to protect local organizations from cyberattacks. Students provide free cyber-risk assessments, offer recommendations, or even design and implement custom solutions to supplement and shape future incident response.[4]

In May 2021, the Consortium of Cybersecurity Clinics was founded with financial support from Newmark Philanthropies, the Public Interest Technology University Network, and others. The Consortium works with university-based clinics nationwide.

In 2022, Congressman Mark Veasey (D-TX), introduced the Cybersecurity Clinics Grant Program Act, to create a Department of Homeland Security (DHS) grant program to fund higher education–based cybersecurity clinics at community colleges and minority-serving institutions.[5] The legislation would require DHS to create an experiential cybersecurity curriculum for grant recipients. Veasey stressed that the clinics are interactive and personalized, educating about the importance of safeguarding devices, data, and identity from both physical and digital compromise. "It's my belief that this model can really empower students and we can start working with people while they're young—before they start their businesses and have to worry about their own households being compromised—on how they can protect themselves."[6]

In an era of extensive electronic storage and transmission, and without a federal privacy law, it's imperative for all computer users to acquire defensive online skills. That includes administrators and others responsible for protecting vast amounts of confidential data.

UNICEF, the United Nations agency charged with providing humanitarian and developmental aid to children, took a stand on digital literacy in its report, *The State of the World's Children 2017: Children in a Digital World*, which emphasized the urgent need to protect young users from digital dangers. It assigns significant responsibility to the private sector, including technology and telecommunication industries, to establish ethical standards on data and privacy. UNICEF calls for teaching digital literacy to guide and support young users to be informed, engaged, and safe online.[7]

Absent a federal initiative, the task of educating young internet users about online safety is left to projects like the higher-education cybersecurity clinics funded by the NSA and Google, along with Google's Be Internet Awesome initiative. Be Internet Awesome promotes digital safety and citizenship among students, teachers, and parents, teaching people how to protect personal information, recognize scams, and understand the consequences of online behavior. It also educates students on how to safeguard their online accounts and personal data, by creating strong passwords and using two-factor authentication and secure websites. Be Internet Awesome encourages responsible online behavior, emphasizing the importance of being respectful and kind to others online, and understanding the implications of our actions in the digital world. It provides guidance on recognizing and addressing online harassment and cyberbullying and encouraging empathy and respectful communication.

Features include an online adventure game called *Interland*, which engages students in scenarios related to online safety and digital citizenship, reinforcing the concepts in a fun and interactive way. Educators can access free lesson plans and classroom activities that align with Be Internet Awesome principles, making it easier to incorporate digital safety and citizenship into their curriculum. Resources, tips, and conversation starters help parents guide their children in developing safe and responsible online habits.

Despite these efforts, entrusting computer hygiene education to companies like Google, which has contributed to digital threats through its market dominance and data practices, highlights an irony. Resources are skewed toward addressing the consequences of poor hygiene practices rather than prioritizing prevention.

A top priority of parents, educators, philanthropists, and both the public and private sectors should be to foster a culture of digital responsibility from an early age.

Whistleblowers Expose Hygiene Lapses

Whistleblowers play a crucial role in exposing inadequate security practices in the technology industry, especially when such lapses compromise the overall security of the ecosystem. Historically, whistleblowers have been instrumental in uncovering safety hazards, corporate misconduct, and government abuses, leading to increased awareness, regulatory changes, and improved safeguards for the public.

In July 2022, Peiter "Mudge" Zatko, Twitter's former head of security and a well-known cybersecurity expert and government advisor, filed a complaint against Twitter with the Securities and Exchange Commission, the Department of Justice, and the Federal Trade Commission.[8] He alleged widespread malfeasance and fraud and testified before Congress and federal agencies that the company's security practices posed grave threats to national security. This wasn't his first time testifying; in 1998, and again in 2008, Zatko and other members of the Boston-based hacker collective L0pht (pronounced "loft") warned Congress about internet-related national-security threats.[9]

They warned that the internet was inherently insecure, with major weaknesses in its core protocols and software that could be exploited for large-scale attacks. Notably, they claimed they could shut down the entire internet in thirty minutes by exploiting flaws in the Border Gateway Protocol, demonstrating the fragility of internet systems. They also pointed out the lack of incentives for software companies to prioritize security, leading to widespread vulnerabilities that put users at risk.

L0pht emphasized the need for better collaboration between the government and private sector to address these cybersecurity threats and called for greater accountability from software developers. Its members also stressed the importance of being proactive about emerging threats, warning that as the internet expanded and technology advanced, the potential for more sophisticated cyberattacks would grow.

At his 2022 appearance, Zatko claimed that Twitter had given access to critical controls to about half of its staff—numbering in the thousands—and suggested that one or more of them could be working for a foreign intelligence agency. He alleged that the company did not adequately protect the security of user data, using servers with outdated software that lacked essential security features like encryption and granting too much access to employees. Because Twitter wasn't properly tracking data access, it couldn't address threats to national security, including potential foreign agents working within the company. The former hacker posited that because the platform lacked sufficient security measures, "it's not far-fetched to say an employee inside the company could take over the accounts of all the senators in this room."[10] Zatko also said he was discouraged from sharing the full extent of the company's security problems with its board.[11] Twitter fired Zatko in January 2022, citing poor performance and subpar leadership. He received a $7.75 million severance check as part of his exit agreement.[12]

Zatko's allegations drew significant public attention and even influenced Elon Musk's legal strategy when he tried to back out of his agreement to purchase Twitter, arguing that the company was not transparent about its security practices and citing the prevalence of fake accounts on its platform.

Zatko's whistleblower report highlights how social media platforms pose privacy risks to users and national security. Despite warnings from as far back as 1998 about the internet's vulnerabilities, it has taken time for lawmakers to acknowledge the severity of the issue. Now, some congressional leaders are finally recognizing that social media companies, data aggregators, and similar entities cannot be trusted to maintain their own data collection, sharing, and security standards.

Another whistleblower case involves the Penn State Applied Research Lab. Matthew Decker, the former chief information officer at the lab, claims that Penn State University falsified compliance reports related to cybersecurity standards required by federal government contracts. The complaint, filed in 2022 and unsealed in 2023, asserts that Penn State failed to properly secure controlled unclassified information, which includes sensitive but not classified data that requires strict handling to prevent security breaches.[13]

Decker's accusations include that Penn State intentionally used unsecure cloud services and provided false attestations of compliance with federal cybersecurity standards. He noted that the university moved a version of its cloud services to a non-FedRAMP-certified version of Microsoft 365 OneDrive, which may not meet the stringent security standards required for handling sensitive or regulated data, potentially compromising data security. The lawsuit also highlights that Penn State used template documents to address missing compliance records instead of conducting proper assessments.

In 2022, the Department of Justice took up the case as part of its Civil Cyber-Fraud Initiative, aimed at enforcing cybersecurity compliance among federal contractors. In this case, federal cybersecurity standards require Penn State to self-assess more than one hundred required cybersecurity standards outlined in the National Institute of Standards and Technology (NIST) *Special Publication 800–171*.[14] These standards are mandated for federal contractors handling controlled unclassified information.

In late 2024, Penn State agreed to pay $1,250,000 to settle the case, resolving allegations that, between 2018 and 2023, it failed to implement cybersecurity controls that were contractually required. US Attorney Jacqueline Romero said, "Federal contractors who store or access covered defense information must take required steps to protect that sensitive information from bad actors. When they fail to meet their cybersecurity obligations, we and our law enforcement partners will use every available tool to remedy the situation."[15]

Three other cases related to the Civil Cyber-Fraud Initiative have become public. While the cybersecurity requirements in each were less complex than those in the Penn State case, they still required prolonged investigations before reaching settlements. It took more than four years for the Justice Department to settle a lawsuit in 2022 against the contractor Comprehensive

Health Services for $930,000 for allegedly failing to securely store the health records of State Department and Air Force personnel.[16] In March 2023, three years after a hacking incident, the Justice Department settled a case that the Florida Healthy Kids Corporation brought against Jelly Bean Communications Design. The lawsuit alleged that Jelly Bean, despite claiming to have designed and hosted a HIPAA-complaint website, failed to properly secure sensitive patient data on the Florida Healthy Kids website, leading to potential breaches of protect health information.[17]

Litigating Our Way to Hygiene

In addition to whistleblowers, elected officials and citizens take legal actions to hold technology companies accountable for privacy infractions. In 2023, a bipartisan group of forty-two state attorneys general launched a lawsuit against Meta, alleging that Facebook and Instagram's features are intentionally addictive and target children and teens. Thirty-three state attorneys general filed a federal suit in the Northern District of California, while nine others filed separate suits in their respective states.[18] The attorneys general accuse Meta of designing Facebook and Instagram to prolong user engagement and encourage frequent return visits. They assert that Meta was aware of the adverse effects its design had on young users, citing the design of algorithms, excessive alerts, notifications, and infinite scroll features. They claim that Meta violated the Children's Online Privacy Protection Act by collecting personal data from users under thirteen without parental consent. The states are seeking an end to these alleged harmful practices, along with penalties and restitution.

In 2023, the software company Blackbaud settled claims relating to a 2020 ransomware incident that affected more than thirteen thousand customers, with attorneys general from forty-nine states and the District of Columbia. Before the $49.5 million settlement, Blackbaud was fined $3 million earlier in the year by the Securities and Exchange Commission (SEC) for making misleading disclosures about the 2020 attack.[19] Both Blackbaud payouts show the companion powers of litigation and regulatory enforcement.

Such litigation has the potential to drive industry-wide settlement discussions or encourage individual litigation against other companies. It also serves an important public educational function by bringing the malfeasance of tech giants to the public fore.

As online monitoring of students grows, and cyberattacks escalate in school systems, more students are heading to court to challenge privacy invasions. In

2023, an Ohio court held it unconstitutional to scan students' homes during remote testing, a practice enacted during the pandemic to prevent cheating.

Two hours before a remote exam was administered by Cleveland State University, Cleveland State Testing Services emailed chemistry student Aaron Ogletree that the exam proctor would be checking his ID, exam materials, and surroundings.[20] Ogletree initially objected, claiming he had confidential materials in his bedroom and didn't have time to move them for the room scan recording that would be shared with other students.

Judge J. Philip Calabrese held that this kind of scanning could create a slippery slope to more unlawful searches. He agreed with Ogletree that the room scans violated his Fourth Amendment right to be free from unreasonable searches, finding that in part, "room scans go where people otherwise would not, at least not without a warrant or an invitation" and that the home has long been deemed a basic protected space with the assumption of privacy.[21]

Illinois was the first state to enact a biometrics data-privacy law. Enacted in 2008, the Biometric Information Privacy Act (BIPA) requires entities using and storing biometrics—fingerprints, iris scans, hand- and face-geometry scans, and voiceprints—to comply with certain mandates. It affords a way for aggrieved users to sue when companies collecting and storing biometrics fail to do so. The law states, in part, that Social Security numbers, "when compromised, can be changed. Biometrics, however, are biologically unique to the individual; therefore, once compromised, the individual has no recourse, is at heightened risk for identity theft, and is likely to withdraw from biometric-facilitated transactions."[22]

In 2021, students Rutvik Thakkar, William Gonigam, and Andrea Kohlenberg, at the University of Illinois at Urbana-Champaign, sued ProctorU for alleged biometric violations.[23] The students were taking online exams, such as a test of English as a foreign language, a Graduate Record Examination, and a law school admission test, and claimed that ProctorU engaged in illegal actions by "collecting, storing and using" their biometric data, including their eye movements, facial expressions, and keystroke biometrics. They asserted that the company failed to protect their data in violation of BIPA and thus that it was vulnerable to a breach.

Thakkar, Gonigam, and Kohlenberg's lawsuit alleged that from at least June 2019 onward, ProctorU didn't protect biometrics in its possession, resulting in a data breach. ProctorU doesn't specify a time limit for how long it retains biometrics, nor does it provide information on its biometrics-destruction policies, as required by BIPA.

Instead, ProctorU's Privacy Policy states that it retains information for as long as it needs to perform any contract with the user or institution, or as long as needed to comply with legal obligations.[24] It also lacks a section regarding the deletion of biometrics. The three students suing ProctorU said that the data breach involved records dating back to 2012 to support their argument that ProctorU held onto records well beyond the timeframe for the initial purpose of collecting such data.[25]

In 2022, the ProctorU case was dismissed, after a contract clause required it to be moved to Alabama.

Another case had a different outcome. In 2023, the testing company Respondus agreed to a $6.25 million settlement to resolve a class action lawsuit. The plaintiffs alleged that Respondus had violated BIPA by collecting biometric identifiers from students who took an exam using Respondus Monitor while in Illinois between November 11, 2015, and June 2, 2023.[26]

The surge in biometric privacy class action lawsuits and arbitration, coupled with a rise in proposed legislation and broad criticism of facial and voice recognition technologies, signals that biometrics will continue to be a focal point for legal professionals, policymakers, technology developers, privacy advocates, and the general public.

Federal Agencies Catch Up

Regulatory agencies such as the Cybersecurity and Infrastructure Security Agency (CISA) and the Department of Defense play a crucial role by implementing and enforcing policies that enhance cybersecurity and data protection across various sectors

In 2023, CISA launched the Secure Our World program, emphasizing fundamental cyber hygiene in public service announcements and through various media channels to educate the public on these practices.[27] In a sixty-second PSA, Kevin gives his son, Max, a phone and says, "Happy Birthday, Max." The phone, with a face, starts talking: "I'm Joan the Phone, here to show you four easy ways to stay safe online." They swirl into an animated world. "Strong Passwords" pops up, and Joan sings about using strong passwords, a manager, and multi-factor authentication with icons of a phone, a text box, and a fingerprint on screen. "Update!" flashes as Joan sings, "Update apps ASAP." "Phishing" appears with a money hook, and Joan warns, "Beware offers too good to be true—they might be scams!" Kevin yells, "That's phishing!" Joan says, "Report it." The group sings, "Install updates, make better passwords, think before you click, use multiple factors. That's how we secure our world!"[28]

CISA's Secure by Design initiative, launched in 2023, urges software manufacturers to incorporate security into the design and development process from the outset. This aims to ensure that products are inherently secure, reducing the need for constant patches and updates.

The Department of Defense has also worked to enhance its cybersecurity posture by implementing basic cyber-hygiene practices. According to a report from the Government Accountability Office (GAO), cybersecurity experts estimate that up to 90 percent of cyberattacks could be prevented through proper cyber hygiene. The DOD has focused on training and awareness, emphasizing the need for regular updates and adherence to cybersecurity protocols across all its departments.[29]

In the corporate sector, AI technologies are being used to analyze vast amounts of data, detect anomalies, and predict potential threats before they manifest. This proactive approach transforms cybersecurity from a reactive stance to a more preventive one. AI's capability to automate repetitive security tasks and provide predictive insights helps organizations stay ahead of emerging threats. Regular updates and adherence to secure-development principles are crucial for maintaining robust cybersecurity defenses.

In recent years, the Federal Trade Commission (FTC) has intensified efforts to protect the public from increasing losses due to fraud by promoting cyber hygiene and enhancing cybersecurity measures. In October 2023, the FTC updated its Safeguards Rule, requiring financial institutions to implement comprehensive security systems to protect customer information, including specific criteria for limiting access to consumer data and using encryption to secure data. A 2023 amendment requires non-banking financial institutions to report breaches.

In 2023, the FTC released a Privacy and Data Security Update, detailing its actions to protect consumer privacy and secure data.[30] This included enforcement actions against companies mishandling consumer data and the development of policies to prevent misuse of personal information. The FTC also focused on issues related to artificial intelligence, health privacy, and children's online privacy. In the same year, the commission reported that consumers lost over $10 billion to fraud, with investment scams leading the reported losses. The FTC continues to work on preventing these scams and educating consumers on self-protection.

The agency has also been proactive in public outreach through various campaigns aimed at educating consumers about cyber hygiene. This includes providing advice on how to avoid scams, protect personal information, and understand the risks associated with digital transactions. Together, these efforts enhance cybersecurity and promote better cyber-hygiene practices across different sectors.

Every Person's Role—Basics First

There are several reasons why people are slow to take responsibility for digital hygiene.

One reason is that citizens do not understand the significant relationship between their cybersecurity practices and democracy—plain and simple. Because we don't know, we don't feel the need to care so much. We bat away cookie-consent forms like gnats.

Another is a lack of comprehensive digital education. Unlike the citizens of Estonia, for example, many Americans haven't received proper training and education on topics such as online privacy, cybersecurity, and the importance of strong passwords. Few fully understand the risks and consequences associated with poor digital hygiene practices such as falling victim to cyberattacks, identity theft, or data breaches.

Complacency and convenience are other reasons. Human nature steers us to frequently opt for the easiest and quickest ways to access and use digital services, even if it means sacrificing security.

And while it's changing, for many years there has been a widespread and blind trust in technology and the companies providing digital services. That began to change in 2013, with former NSA contractor Edward Snowden's revelation of mass and warrantless NSA surveillance of Americans. Too many people, however, still put faith in tech companies to protect their data and ensure their security.

Missing is a nationwide initiative to educate children about basic digital hygiene from the moment they create their first passwords. It's incumbent on educators and parents to teach them early on to protect themselves and the computer systems they interact with, yet this is still not happening, with the exception of scattered efforts discussed earlier. As UNICEF noted in its report about children using the internet, each day a staggering 175,000 children join the online world for the first time.[31] With numbers like this, educating young people about navigating the virtual realm is as necessary as teaching traditional literacy and numeracy skills.

Equally important is fostering an appreciation for online privacy and the importance of protecting personal information. Teaching children about privacy settings, secure passwords, and the implications of oversharing online helps safeguard their personal information from potential misuse, especially in educational environments where students' personally identifying information is gathered, stored, and shared with third-party vendors.

Digital safety education goes hand in hand with teaching critical thinking and responsible digital citizenship. Students learn to question the information they encounter online, assess the credibility of sources, and engage in respectful and ethical online behavior. Such skills are increasingly important for academic and professional success. By introducing digital safety concepts early, schools prepare students for future educational and career opportunities for which digital competence is prerequisite, especially in the global job market.

Teaching digital safety in schools must extend to parents as well. When children learn about digital safety in school, they're more likely to discuss these topics at home, leading to a collaborative effort between parents and educators to create a safer online environment.

It Starts with You: Some Basic Digital Hygiene Practices

The complexity of the digital ecosystem—with its numerous devices, platforms, and apps interconnected in our daily lives—makes managing hygiene across this vast ecosystem seem overwhelming, causing some to feel powerless or uncertain about where to start. Some tech users might avoid taking responsibility because they view security measures like complex password management, two-factor authentication, and regular software updates as too much of a hassle.

When incorporating new digital hygiene practices, it is crucial to start slowly and gradually, at levels that are manageable and not overly challenging, ensuring that they can be consistently maintained over time.

Device Protection

1. Safeguard all your devices used to access sensitive information by running security software on each one. Routinely check for software updates or set up automatic updates for security software.

2. Set up auto-lock and require a strong password to unlock your devices.

3. Avoid leaving your devices in insecure locations such as public tables, airport waiting areas, or hotel lobbies, where they can be easily accessed, stolen, or tampered with. Always keep your devices close to

you or secured in a locked bag or compartment, especially in crowded or high-traffic areas.

4. Only install software from trusted sources, such as official app stores and verified vendor and reseller websites.

Other essential practices of good cyber hygiene require a little more self-awareness when navigating cyberspace.

Data Protection

Encrypt all sensitive data and make regular backups.

- When in doubt, err on the side of encrypting information.
- Regularly back up your data to another secure personal device to avoid potential loss.

Secure Connections

Avoid accessing sensitive information over free public Wi-Fi networks.

- Minimize use of public Wi-Fi for sensitive activities.
- Favor the more secure cellular service connection, which can often be shared among multiple devices through your phone's "mobile hotspot" feature.

Proper Authentication and Passwords

Ensure that every individual accessing essential systems has their own distinct profile and login credentials. Additionally, provide a separate login for shared family accounts when needed.

- Avoid sharing passwords for online banking, email, social media, etc., with family members or significant others.
- Use strong and distinct passwords for your most sensitive accounts.
- Don't take Facebook or Instagram quizzes or questionnaires. They are an excellent way for hackers to find password-potential data.

Sharing Information

Be cautious about oversharing personal information on social media and other platforms.

- Understand that cyber criminals may use shared data to manipulate or deceive individuals by crafting personalized phishing scams or fraudulent messages that appear legitimate, increasing the likelihood of gaining access to sensitive information.

- Limit the amount of personal information you disclose to reduce the risk of scams or identity theft affecting you and your loved ones. Personal information is any data that can be used to identify you as an individual, such as your name, address, phone number, or email, as well as more sensitive details like Social Security numbers, medical records, or financial information. There is a layer of personal information that is too private to be shared publicly, including intimate details about one's health, mental well-being, or financial status, which are distinct from the basic information typically included in a profile bio and should be safeguarded to protect one's privacy and security.

CHAPTER 13

Correcting the Tilt

Some Americans are already full-fledged cyber citizens. Pitched political rhetoric and information overload has *not* dulled their truth- and justice-seeking antennae. Their innovative tactics are gaining traction, drawing more people into the fold of online social justice activism. Singly or in combination with others, their strategies may help freedom and equality fighters tilt the balance back in favor of democracy.

Let's explore some of these tactics.

Pop Culture to the Rescue: Fandoms

Sarah Mortenson was completing her undergraduate degree and figuring out what she wanted to do with her life. She likes to say she was radicalized spending time on Tumblr, the microblogging and social networking platform. There, she was exposed to concepts like feminism, racial justice, and the importance of accessibility. This exposure broadened her perspective, helping her understand how systemic social inequalities caused widespread suffering.

Mortenson is also an expert on fandoms—communities of enthusiasts who share passion, empathy, and camaraderie for a particular interest or entity. These communities can revolve around films, TV shows, celebrities, hobbies, sports, and many other subjects. Popular fanbases include Trekkies, Potterheads, Whovians, and Thronies. Annual conventions dedicated to celebrating some fandoms, such as Gamescom, Comic-Con International, and Dragon Con, attract substantial followings of people seeking community to nurture an otherwise isolating or lonely appreciation for their respective niches.

Some fandoms are channeling their energy to support social justice activism. One international nonprofit, Fandom Forward, in its own words, "turns fans into heroes."

Mortenson recalls her introduction to the organization. "When I went to a Harry Potter convention in 2014 (called LeakyCon) and came across the booth for Fandom Forward (then called the Harry Potter Alliance) and realized that there was an organization combining my love for stories with my desire to get involved in social justice, I was sold."[1] She began volunteering with Fandom Forward in 2015 and joined the senior staff as campaigns director in 2022.

Founded in 2005 by Australian comedian Andrew Slack and the wizard rock band Harry and the Potters, Fandom Forward started by collecting contributions for Amnesty International during rock shows. The organization operates on the principle that fans can apply their passions to activism to improve the world. Fan activism, in their view, is an accessible entry point into the broader social justice movement.

"Fans join our community because our actions are a fun thing that their fandom friends are doing or a good place to meet new friends with similar interests," says Mortenson. "But in joining they learn to become leaders and organizers of anti-racist campaigns and actions. Similarly, when someone is a hardcore fan of a piece of media it is because, at least in some part, their personal values are being reflected in that piece of media."

As organizers within the fan community, Fandom Forward recognizes the importance of understanding the values of a particular fandom before launching a campaign connected to it.

"For example, our 2010 to 2014 campaign to compel Warner Brothers to make all Harry Potter–branded chocolate fair trade or Utz certified worked well for Harry Potter because there was a narrative connection with the chocolate frogs as well as storylines to do with forced labor," says Mortensen. However, she points out that a campaign centered on chocolate might not resonate as effectively with the Game of Thrones fandom because the narrative and values connections are different.

"Fans are consuming their media critically, meaning that they love the story but they are also naturally analyzing the similarities with the real world. Our role is to take fans one step further and help them learn the skills they need to realize a better world."

The issues they focus on include LGBTQ+ equality, gender equity, youth advocacy, racial justice, education and libraries, media reform, and climate change. In 2022, Fandom Forward launched the Book Defenders initiative to combat book bans and advocate for universal access to books. It trained five hundred activists through free online workshops to fight book bans in their communities and offered a free writing workshop series that trained three hundred writers to keep sharing their stories about book censorship.

Fan activists donated twelve hundred books in three countries; each donated book and action taken counted as points toward their "house cup," which was themed after favorite book genres.

Fandom Forward hosts live events aimed at addressing the pressing issue of book bans and ways to get involved in keeping challenged books on library shelves. In 2022, participating groups included Black Nerds Create, We Need Diverse Books, the National Coalition Against Censorship, and PEN America, along with "some rockstar trans and nonbinary authors, student activists from across the country, and more."[2] Fandom Forward's book club also read three banned books: *All Boys Aren't Blue* by George M. Johnson, *Here and Queer* by Rowan Ellis, and *Persepolis* by Marjane Satrapi. Workshops focused on crafting uncolonized narratives, the importance of writing stories that might face challenges, and exploring how cultural expectations inform storytelling.

Edha Gupta is a nineteen-year-old activist who served as the president of the Panther Anti-Racist Union during the 2021–2022 school year. Edha, fellow officers, and advisors successfully protested a school board decision to ban more than three hundred books on diversity education throughout the Central York School District in Pennsylvania. In an article for Fandom Forward, Gupta wrote that the shame she felt and the mockery about her Indian background for twelve years "transformed into a healthy rage that made it my personal duty to combat this [book banning] decision in any way that I could.... I knew I had to take action. Not for me, but to save generations of students being schooled in this district."[3]

Viral Marketing: Ad Council PSAs

Viral marketing is a strategy that creates compelling content designed to quickly capture the audience's attention and encourage them to share it widely, leading to rapid and widespread distribution. Such engagement has great potential to raise public awareness and mobilize civic action against a myriad of injustices. This is especially true when there's a pending court case or piece of legislation. The underlying principle is that it's not only acceptable but necessary to bolster legal strategies with advocacy and messaging in the public sphere.

The national nonprofit Ad Council addresses up to forty social change issues each year. Collaborating with media outlets, tech companies, the marketing and advertising industry, government agencies, and other nonprofits, the Ad Council has long been a catalyst for impactful social justice campaigns.

In 2016, the Ad Council's "We Are America" video, featuring WWE super-star John Cena celebrating the nation's diversity on Independence Day, gar-nered significant attention.[4] The following year, their Fans of Love campaign used a stadium kiss cam to celebrate unbiased love. In 2020, the Ad Council launched two initiatives: Fight for Freedom addressed racial injustice by con-trasting privilege and simple freedoms that may be taken for granted in the face of systemic racism; Fight the Virus. Fight the Bias aimed at dispelling misconceptions, harassment, and hate directed at the Asian American and Pacific Islander community during and after the COVID pandemic.

One of the Ad Council's most successful campaigns, Love Has No Labels, launched in 2015, promoting acceptance and inclusion of all people regardless of sex, gender, race, religion, ability, or age. The campaign's debut video fea-tured skeletons dancing, embracing, and then emerging from behind an X-ray screen to reveal themselves as diverse couples, friends, and families. It was an immediate success. Within twenty-four hours of its Facebook debut, the video was viewed eleven million times, making it one of the most successful PSA campaigns in history. The audience engaged deeply with the video, shar-ing it widely and contributing to its success, according to Carolina Treviño, digital product manager at the Ad Council.

"We saw how people were connecting to the campaign and saw them-selves reflected in the real people featured in the video. They were organically sharing pictures of themselves and their diverse partners and friends with #LoveHasNoLabels," says Treviño.[5]

The video became the first public service announcement to win an Emmy for Outstanding Commercial. With more than 170 million views, it became the second most viewed social activism video of all time.[6]

Love Has No Labels received support from corporate partners such as Bank of America, Prudential Financial, and Walmart, which provided fund-ing and integrated the campaign into their social messaging, custom content creation, employee engagement, and events. Nonprofit partners provided re-sources and expertise, including AARP, Asian Americans Advancing Justice, Anti-Defamation League, American Immigration Council, Disability:IN (a network of hundreds of corporations for persons with disabilities), Human Rights Campaign, National Women's Law Center, Perception Institute, Story-Corps, the Asian American Foundation, and UnidosUS.

In 2022, Instagram reported that its most active users are those engaged in social justice advocacy.[7] More than half of the young people surveyed follow social justice accounts on social media platforms.[8] According to Instagram's

2022 *Trend Report*, Instagram and TikTok have emerged as significant channels for disseminating information related to activism. Instagram users were three times more likely (18 percent compared to 6 percent) than non-users to vote in local, state, and national elections. The report predicted that more young users tend to donate to social causes and follow and share activist information from even more social justice sites.[9]

Instagram has seen surges in activism in the past. In 2020, Instagram witnessed a flurry of so-called "PowerPoint Activism," the sharing of information through ten-slide posts. Activists told *NBC News* that Instagram—popular among teens for both entertainment and as a source of information and knowledge—provided an ideal platform for content sharing and organizing in-person events. The New York based anti-oppression group Warriors in the Garden, for example, used the platform to organize thousands of participants in citywide marches and demonstrations.[10]

As Terry Nguyen of *Vox* has pointed out: "The 10-image carousel, which Instagram launched in 2017, has been repurposed by activists, independent artists, advocacy groups, and well-meaning individuals as a means to educate and inform the masses, one slide at a time."[11] These activism slides frequently found their way onto Nguyen's Explore page or were shared on her friends' and followers' Instagram Stories. Nguyen likened some of the visually arresting slides to advertisements, blurring the line once again between public service announcements and aesthetic clickbait. Many accounts even include a slide of sources at the end of the carousel so users can fact-check and extend their research journey into the profiled issue.

One such example of the many activist-oriented accounts on social media is Slow Factory (@theslowfactory on Instagram)—a nonprofit organization working to promote climate justice and confront human rights crises through open education, narrative change, and regenerative design. One of its key strategies is community outreach, which includes hosting virtual teach-ins and lectures featuring activists, scientists, and professionals from diverse fields. By providing accessible educational resources via Instagram's carousel format and highlighting marginalized voices, Slow Factory encourages people to become active participants in the fight for climate justice and human rights.

Memes for Justice

Memes are cultural elements passed from one person to another by imitation. The term *meme* was coined by Richard Dawkins, a British evolutionary biologist, in his 1976 book *The Selfish Gene*.[12] Dawkins introduced the concept to explain how cultural information evolves much like genes, by replicating, mutating, and responding to selective pressures over time. He used the term to illustrate how ideas and cultural phenomena could propagate and evolve in society, much like biological traits do in a population through natural selection. On the internet, the concept evolved to fit the rapid nature of online culture, often images, videos, or text—usually humorous—copied, varied, shared rapidly.

The Center for Story-Based Strategy works with activist organizations to build their narrative capacity, skills, practice, and impact, from customized story-based strategy trainings to narrative coaching to campaign design and strategies. In 2020, the center recognized #DefundThePolice as the "Best Use of Making the Invisible Visible." The campaign, which emerged in the aftermath of police killings of Breonna Taylor, George Floyd, and others, was described by the center as "grounded, focused, and specific as #BlackLivesMatter is expansive, visionary and emergent," while highlighting the budgetary power often obfuscated by the undemocratic systems pervasive in our government.[13]

Research suggests that adding an image to a statement makes people more likely to believe it, even if the image is unrelated to the story idea. Attractive memes, shared and reposted, can persist in the public imagination, even if they are associated with false propositions.

Once created and unleashed, memes spread like molten lava across the internet, using humor, satire, and cultural commentary, and capturing public sentiment or reactions to current events, political figures, or social phenomena. The meme "I Am Once Again Asking You" originates from a 2019 fundraising video of Senator Bernie Sanders, in which he says, "I am once again asking for your financial support." The image of Sanders bundled up in a winter coat and mittens, with a sincere expression on his face, became widely used with the text altered to humorously represent various requests or complaints. The meme captures a sense of earnestness and repetition, making it relatable and easily adaptable for different contexts.

A Meme Come to Life

During Google CEO Sundar Pichai's testimony in December 2018 before the House Judiciary Committee about Google's data-collection practices, a distinctive figure donning a monocle, carrying cash, and sporting a mustache made a notable appearance. This character, reminiscent of the *Monopoly* game's Rich Uncle Pennybags, was none other than Ian Madrigal, formerly known as Amanda Werner. Madrigal, an activist and consultant on media and organizing campaigns, had previously made a similar appearance during an October 2017 Senate Committee on Banking, Housing, and Urban Affairs hearing with Equifax's CEO in the wake of its massive data breach.

Describing themselves as a "policy wonk," Madrigal's portrayal of Monopoly Man serves to underscore the urgency of implementing regulation and antitrust measures to curtail Google's monopolistic dominance. Madrigal's objectives include shedding light on Google's censored search engine Project Dragonfly, which poses risks to dissidents and human rights activists in China. Additionally, Madrigal aims to draw attention to the tech giant's internal challenges related to sexual harassment, racial discrimination, and wage disparities.

"All of these various controversies show that Google and other tech giants cannot be allowed to self-regulate. We need comprehensive legislation and agency oversight that we have in many areas of business outside of tech," Madrigal notes.[14]

Madrigal, with a law degree from UCLA and a background in music and improv, has inspired activists of all political bents. The *Washington Post* has said that Madrigal "makes the stunt look like a lark. But it is really an elaborate act of protest: a combination of entertainment and trolling that Madrigal calls 'cause-play.'"[15]

Their mission has involved rebranding "arbitration" in ways that the public can understand. Madrigal understands the power of multimedia and theater, having played audio of children crying in detention centers and dressed up as a Russian troll during congressional hearings. Because they wear costumes, friends reserve them a spot in the long waiting lines for public hearings to avoid alerting authorities to their presence. During their visits to Senate offices, Madrigal dropped off "Get Out of Jail Free" cards while dressed as Monopoly Man. On their X account, with nearly nineteen thousand followers as of late 2024, they describe themselves as a "Creative activist known for photobombing CEOs as the Monopoly Man & thread on Trump/Epstein."[16]

Madrigal offers two valuable lessons to defenders of democracy. The first is that clarity of message in an action is essential; it's the technique that right-wing think tanks like ALEC have used to transform our entire legal landscape over time, through slogans such as "limited government, free markets, and traditional values." Madrigal's second lesson is that the fusion of art and content is a powerful tool. Their actions vividly demonstrate how individuals can use creative elements like humor and performance to make serious subjects more engaging and accessible to the public.

"For me, one of the singular successes of the first Monopoly Man action was not just the attention it got, but the fact that every single article—from the *Washington Post* to the most clickbaity news site—talked about the reason I was there, which was to oppose Equifax's use of forced arbitration and specifically to oppose a bill that was pending in the Senate. Everyone who was writing and tweeting about it mentioned the bill," said Madrigal.[17]

They underscore the universal appeal of humor, which transcends partisan lines. Madrigal characterizes the Monopoly Man concept as a meme come to life. This kind of humor capitalizes on the novelty of internet culture—cartoonish, over-the-top, and resonant with people with diverse perspectives and backgrounds.

Madrigal emphasizes that humor alone is insufficient; the message must remain crystal clear. They point out that successful actions are those where individuals cannot be ignored when they step in front of cameras. In the context of a congressional hearing, the presence of Monopoly Man, twirling their mustache at the back of the room, becomes impossible to overlook.

Creative Challenges

Beyond simply delivering messages, many social media campaigns actively involve users in socially impactful projects. Take #TrashTag, for example. *TrashTag* is an internet challenge and hashtag campaign where people clean up a heavily littered area and post before and after photos with the hashtag #TrashTag.[18] The hashtag #TrashTag began when hikers Steve Jewett and Bill Willoughby decided to address the litter on their local trails. They started by picking up small debris that could fit in their pockets and then began carrying a bag for larger items. To handle undesirable items, Steve began using barbecue tongs. They made it a fun activity, with one spotting trash and the other picking it up. Wanting to encourage others to join their efforts, they created the nonprofit Clean Trails.

In 2017, Steve and Bill launched National CleanUp Day through Clean Trails, which has become the largest single-day cleanup event in the United States, with two million volunteers participating. Volunteers are encouraged to tag a before and after picture or video of their cleanup and share it online. Through strategic partnerships with organizations like World Cleanup Day and Earth Day, both recognized by the United Nations, National CleanUp Day has expanded its reach and impact.[19]

The #TrashTag challenge encourages participants to pledge to: (1) tag five pieces of litter at each stop on their next road trip; (2) tag one piece of litter they pick up every day for a week; (3) tag and bag litter collected along a busy street in their community; and (4) create a TikTok video, a popular way to gain more views, and post it on social media while having fun.

In another example, as the COVID-19 pandemic took hold in March 2020, William, a seventeen-year-old developer and designer near Oxford in the United Kingdom, created the Wash Your Lyrics website on March 8. The site "generates hand-washing instructions accompanied by lyrics from a song of your choice instantly," he tweeted.[20] Within a week, William reported that his site had grown to 1.2 million unique users.[21]

This initiative began when public health and social media experts, along with behavioral psychologists, encouraged people to think about everyone they are protecting from the coronavirus while spending twenty seconds washing their hands in the #20SecondChallenge. Wash Your Lyrics gained traction on March 14, when marketer Neil Hopkins tweeted, "Washing your hands properly for 20 seconds is a great way to stop #Coronavirus. Who are you doing it for? Tell the world in 20 seconds and share using #20Second-Challenge!" After listing the people he was protecting by washing his hands, Hopkins challenged a couple dozen others to do the same.[22]

Crowdsourcing

Crowdsourcing is a method of gathering input, ideas, services, or funding from a large group of people, typically through the internet. Leveraging the collective intelligence and efforts of diverse individuals often enables faster and more innovative solutions.

One crowdsourced project is Galaxy Zoo, part of the Zooniverse, a collection of citizen-science projects. *Citizen science* refers to a network of volunteers from the general public helping scientists with their research. While such projects have been ongoing for a century, advancements in technology have given rise to online citizen-science initiatives, greatly expanding the range of opportunities for involvement.

In Galaxy Zoo, volunteers assist in classifying a million galaxies, directly contributing to scientific research. Launched in 2007 by astronomers and astrophysicists in the United Kingdom and the United States, Galaxy Zoo reported that by January 2015, fifty-three scientific papers had been published as a result of the work of hundreds of thousands of volunteers.[23] Galaxy Zoo has enlisted the support of more than four hundred thousand volunteers, whose tasks have exceeded eleven million. Their work has resulted in an enriched database of galaxy classifications.[24]

Galaxy Zoo was the first citizen-science project on the Zooniverse platform, which has since expanded to encompass more than ninety projects in fields such as astronomy, ecology, archaeology, art history, and more.

One example of a Zooniverse project is the People's Contest, a digital-archiving initiative focused on the Civil War era. The project addresses two challenges: the relative lack of attention given to the Civil War's northern home front, especially Pennsylvania, compared to the Confederacy; and the presence of important yet unprocessed collections from 1851 to 1874.[25] This lack of processing hinders a comprehensive narrative of the Civil War era beyond the battlefield, particularly with respect to politics, race, ethnicity, and gender.

Members of the public actively engage with the digital archive by transcribing diaries and personal accounts at the Eberly Family Special Collections Library at Penn State, as well as from archives and museums across Pennsylvania. The project draws its name from Abraham Lincoln's July 4, 1861, address to Congress, in which he described the American Civil War as a people's contest.

Crowdsourcing has significantly transformed civic engagement by making it more accessible and adaptable to individual lifestyles. "Microdosing" activist efforts through online platforms has allowed people to participate in civic activities in small, manageable ways without committing to long-term or in-person involvement. Games like *Foldit*, a crowdsourced online puzzle game, enable thousands of people to contribute to scientific research on protein folding, collectively advancing medical science without requiring formal training or a significant time commitment from participants.

These models of crowdsourced engagement demonstrate how micro-volunteering enables a broader and more diverse group of individuals to participate in civic and scientific initiatives, fostering a sense of contribution and community without the traditional barriers related to time, location, or expertise. As a result, civic engagement has shifted toward more flexible, bite-sized participation opportunities, allowing people to integrate activism and volunteering into their daily routines.

The Kids Are All Right

Micro-volunteering and citizen-science methods, along with the increasing prevalence of social justice activism nationwide, help heighten awareness of social justice issues among young people, particularly students. A 2022 Best Colleges survey of undergraduate students revealed that nearly 60 percent of respondents supported one or more social justice initiatives, and another 30 percent said they were considering participation. Of those surveyed, 65 percent believed their involvement had made a significant impact in bringing about change.[26]

A few examples from 2023 show different forms of campus activism. At Stanford University, a #NoMoreExcuses campaign arose as students pushed for stronger university responses to sexual assault and misconduct cases. Activists utilized platforms such as Instagram and TikTok to share stories, rally support, and call for more transparent reporting and improved survivor support systems. The campaign's digital outreach successfully mobilized the student body and initiated critical dialogues with the university administration.

Since 2019, more than eighty multimillion-dollar police-training facilities have opened or are planned to open across the nation.[27] From 2023 on, students at Georgia State University, Emory University, and other campuses engaged in digital and in-person actions as part of the #StopCopCity movement. This campaign opposed the planned construction of a large police-training facility in Atlanta, highlighting broader social justice issues related to police funding and environmental impact. Digital strategies included coordinated hashtag activism and virtual teach-ins that spread awareness, gathered support, and organized protests.

In 2023, many universities witnessed significant student activism in response to the Israel-Hamas conflict. In Michigan, a coalition of over fifty student organizations, led by groups such as Students Allied for Freedom and Equality, participated in a series of demonstrations demanding that the university divest from companies involved in military activities in Gaza, like Lockheed Martin and Boeing. The activism drew attention to issues of student rights, policing on campus, and freedom of expression, amplified by digital campaigns and social media coordination. Similarly, New York, Columbia, and Emory Universities were particularly active. These actions were part of a larger mobilization across American campuses—the largest seen since the Vietnam War era—in which protests often relied on digital platforms to coordinate, share real-time updates, and amplify their message to broader audiences.

These innovative ways of garnering support for social justice causes reveal the deep potential of the internet to bring us together and make our lives better.

CHAPTER 14

Games for Democracy

In 2021, as US democracy faced significant challenges, the video game news site *GameRant* noted that the year provided some of the best "boss battles" in gaming history, predicting that "good boss fights are becoming more and more common in the industry."[1] Boss fights or battles occur at climax points in the game, when players face off with extremely powerful nonplayer characters.

Similarly, in the real world, the political and social sphere has seen an increase in dramatic, high-conflict encounters, akin to these digital showdowns. Small-business owners, tech startups, and advocates find themselves at pivotal moments resembling epic boss battles as they confront tech giants that surveil, exploit, and monetize personal data. Just as players strategize, persevere, and test their limits against imposing adversaries in games, real-world advocates rally resources and ingenuity to challenge the power and influence of tech conglomerates. These encounters often serve as climactic points in broader movements for accountability and privacy rights, highlighting parallels between high-stakes game confrontations and formidable struggles in contemporary politics.

Games provide hope for many, from players seeking a respite from the headaches of modern life to educators and social justice advocates using games as tools to model more equitable ways of living. In his elegant book *Death by Video Game: Danger, Pleasure, and Obsession on the Virtual Frontline*, British writer Simon Parkin explains:

> Even if players (and even perhaps the games designers) don't recognize it, many of the video games we play today have been built in a way that not only reflects the world and its systems, but also attempts to improve its balance. Video games may have morally neutral or ambiguous storylines, and they may distract humans from true progress through the illusion of accomplishment, but at least they provide

a place in which everyone who is able to view a screen and make inputs on a controller has a chance to triumph.[2]

Given our new reality, in which American politics resembles an action-packed game—emphasizing conflict, spectacle, rapid engagement, and the constant pursuit of victory, often at the expense of nuanced discussion and bipartisan cooperation—it stands to reason that the forces needed to save democracy must possess superhuman qualities akin to the heroes we train up in virtual worlds, online games, and the entertainment industry—heroes like Link from *Legend of Zelda* and Kratos from *God of War Ragnarök*.

How do we summon these heroes?

They're all around us. If you look for them, you will see them.

Leveraging gaming as a tool for engaging and connecting with younger audiences has shown significant potential for promoting civic involvement.

Casual Games

Casual games serve to motivate players to engage in altruistic actions in their real lives.

Unlike more episodic and narrative video games, these games target a broader audience, featuring simpler rules that demand less skill and a significantly shorter time commitment. They integrate easily with viral engagement strategies due to their straightforward mechanics, making them accessible even to non-seasoned gamers and playable in just a few minutes or longer if preferred.

A compelling example of a casual game with social significance is *Darfur Is Dying*, created in 2005 by University of Southern California graduate student Susan Ruiz as her master's thesis. Players assume the role of Darfurian refugees and must forage for water to harvest camp vegetable gardens and mix mud to build shelters. A threat meter monitors the number of days that players maintain camp survival, with a goal of reaching seven days. Players who die receive explanations of what happened to real-life people who perished.

Ruiz's motivation stemmed from concerns when her nephew revealed that his Holocaust class didn't draw connections to the Rwandan genocide. Sponsored by MTV and supported by celebrity endorsements, the game quickly gained traction.[3] In the eight months following its release, *Darfur Is Dying* garnered over two million plays, with as many as ten thousand players emailing their senators about the pressing issue. The game allows players to import contacts from their address book, inviting friends to play the game and to learn about Darfur, which also raises the overall health of the camp.[4] Ruiz aimed to involve more young people in activism around the issue.

The touch-screen mobile phone game *Get Water!*—available on iOS and Android devices—aims to raise awareness about water scarcity in India and South Asia, focusing on human rights and social justice, particularly the impact of water scarcity on girls' education. Developed by Decode Global Studio in Montreal, the game was launched on World Water Day in 2013. Its protagonist, Maya, is forced to abandon her education to fetch clean water due to frequent water pump breakdowns. Because boys aren't similarly burdened with this task, the game raises critical issues related to gender and education.

In a pilot study conducted to assess the game's effectiveness, participants responded positively, with one saying, "When I answered that survey before, I know I answered [that] gender inequality and access to water…weren't really alike.…Seeing how the game worked, I mean, you can kind of see where they're leading in that there is a correlation between them.…So it made me more aware of that."[5]

Itch.io is a platform for game developers to sell or host their games. Users have the opportunity to purchase independent games, and Itch.io takes a small percentage of the developers' profits. According to nerdschalk.com, Itch.io has amassed a library of over a million games since its establishment in 2013, with a substantial portion of these games being socially conscious.

One noteworthy example is the Social Justice Game Jam, featured on Itch. io from May 18 to May 26, 2020. A game jam is a time-limited event, typically lasting twenty-four to seventy-two hours, during which participants create video games from scratch, either individually or in teams. The annual Global Game Jam, which takes place in late January, is a collaborative event where developers and participants gather in more than eight hundred locations in over one hundred countries.

Social justice game jams are often organized to address specific causes or issues at particular times. These one-off jams are typically launched by nonprofits, advocacy groups, educational institutions, or collaborative partnerships focused on raising awareness or creating solutions through gaming. In February 2017, the Northwest Justice Project organized a game jam at the Living Computer Museum in Seattle, Washington.[6] This initiative aimed to tackle the issue of insufficient legal assistance for low-income households in the state. More than half of these households face legal challenges without any available help, spanning concerns such as home foreclosures, predatory lending, debt repayment, veterans' benefits, and more. Legal professionals were on hand to provide guidance to game developers, artists, writers, and programmers when they had questions.

Another social justice-oriented game jam was sponsored in 2021 by the Society of Asian Scientists and Engineers, partnering with Booz Allen and Unity.[7] Participants used diversity, equity, and inclusion issues to craft immersive experiences. Teams, composed of up to five students, were given seventy-two hours to complete submissions on one of two themes: raising awareness of and SWANA (Southwest Asian and North African) communities and the challenges they face, and how to become better allies.

Democracy Games

During the 2020 presidential election, Representative Alexandria Ocasio-Cortez (D-NY) displayed some "murderous" tendencies—virtually, that is. She "murdered" Imane "Pokimane" Anys, a video game streamer, while playing *Among Us with AOC*. AOC, along with Representative Ilhan Omar (D-MN) and other notable streamers, live streamed the game for an hour on Twitch.

The live video feed garnered more than 4.5 million viewers, growing to nearly 5 million within twenty-four hours as viewers watched it on demand.[8] During the stream, AOC encouraged viewers to register to vote and head to the polls on Election Day. While political commentary was limited, AOC did express her support for Joe Biden and urged viewers to cast their vote for him.

The Biden campaign had previously joined forces with the gaming news program *KindaFunnyGames*, organizing a tour of a Biden-themed island in Nintendo's *Animal Crossing: New Horizons*. The campaign even created virtual Biden yard signs for players to display in the game.[9]

Using gaming as a means to engage and reach new generations has proven to be an effective strategy for civic engagement. For example, in 2017, Louisa Hackett from the nonprofit Community Votes created and used *Civics Jeopardy* games for voter-registration trainings at the Jacob Riis public housing complex in New York City's East Village.[10]

Hackett wanted to make the process of conveying essential information about elections more engaging and interactive for a roomful of staff members. She achieved this by tweaking an online version of *Jeopardy!*, incorporating categories and questions related to politicians, definitions, and elections. To enhance the experience, she tailored the questions using district neighborhood voting profiles, making it a customized learning tool. As the game unfolded, competitive spirits were ignited, and participants were often surprised when they discovered gaps in their knowledge, such as not knowing their state-assembly representative or missing important voter-registration deadlines. Later, senior citizens at Jacob Riis adapted the questions into a game resembling *Wheel of Fortune*, using a spinning wheel on the table as part of their voter-registration activities. Hackett attributes her inspiration for this innovative approach to Josh A. Lerner's book *Making Democracy Fun: How Game Design Can Empower Citizens and Transform Politics*.[11]

Game developers are increasingly focusing on creating educational games designed to solve real-world problems. These games are crafted to be just as exciting and competitive as best-selling titles in the gaming industry.

It's a smart move. There is an abundance of enthusiasm and creativity ready to be harnessed, with thousands of gamers eager to take the next step in modifying open-source games or creating their own. One prominent example of this is Roblox, a highly popular online game platform and game-creation system that allows users to both program and play games created by fellow users. As of 2022, Roblox boasted 199 million monthly active users. The platform's mission, according to its website, "is to bring the world together through play. We enable anyone to imagine, create, and have fun with friends as they explore millions of immersive 3D experiences, all built by a global community of developers."[12]

Offering rewards can serve as a powerful incentive for fostering collaboration for the common good. When individuals work together to tackle challenges or solve puzzles, they could be eligible for various benefits, such as tax deductions or financial remuneration. This concept has gained traction in academia, where many students choose to study game design in college and later pursue careers across diverse gaming applications.

The popularity of these academic fields has grown to the extent that the Princeton Review introduced rankings for college video game design programs back in 2010. According to Purdue University's promotional information for academic concentrations, numerous fulfilling career options exist in this domain. "As the gaming industry expands into non-entertainment realms, be at the forefront of exploring how you can positively affect society."[13] Purdue touts undergraduate research projects that encompass the use of games in areas like sustainable energy, therapy and medicine, information visualization, and entertainment.

Elementary schools are increasingly adopting games to engage students more effectively than traditional curricula. The e-generation, having grown up in a digital world, require learning methods that resonate with their experiences and inspire them to acclimate to a growing electronically oriented society. It has been demonstrated that games can not only teach empathy but also alter attitudes and enhance the learning process.

Research has indicated that when lesson plans are transformed into narrative experiences and combined with challenges for students to conquer, learning outcomes significantly improve.[14] Games featuring educational components also promote learning beyond the classroom, as young individuals often devote substantial time to gameplay.

Some schools have integrated the online game *Minecraft* into their educational programs, as it can effectively teach students about engineering and coding. *Minecraft* places a strong emphasis on construction, and players have created intricate structures and even functional computers within the game. A feature called redstone circuits allows players to create simple machines and electrical systems within the game world. Redstone circuits are similar to electrical circuits in real life and can be used to build things like automatic doors, traps, and even basic computers. They help teach players about the basics of engineering and programming because they use logic gates, the building blocks of digital electronics. For example, players can learn how to create a circuit that turns on a light only when certain conditions are met, similar to how programming works in real life. By experimenting with redstone, students learn fundamental concepts like input and output, signal transmission, and conditional logic in a fun and interactive way.

The *American Democracy Game* is designed to impart knowledge about the workings of a representative democracy. This educational game received the 2021 Game of the Year award by the *Creative Child Magazine* Awards Program.[15] Originally created in 2011 for middle school students, the *American Democracy Game* underwent a redesign led by the National Conference of State Legislators (NCSL) in collaboration with the Entertainment Software Association.

In *The American Democracy Game*, players assume the role of a lawmaker and are tasked with navigating complex public-policy issues. The primary objective is to present both sides of various issues to explore the art of compromise.

Twelve-year-old Nicholas, the son of Holly South from NCSL's Legislative Staff Services Program, enthusiastically gave the game a five-star rating. According to Nicholas, "The game taught me about how bills are passed, which is interesting, and that you have to make compromises—a lot of compromises."[16]

The *Social Justice Game*, or "A Game About Cents and Sensibility," originated from the *Landlord Game*, created by Randal Harrison and initially created for a 2018 museum exhibit *Money Matters* at the University of Notre
Dame's Snite Museum of Art.[17] The game is a parody of the classic board
game *Monopoly* and serves as a tool for students to learn about social justice while aiding educators in examining the complexities of poverty. Players must balance their sense of fairness against the economic pressures they
encounter during gameplay. For instance, players discover the challenges of
avoiding bankruptcy as they shift roles from owner to manager or transition
from employed to unemployed.

From 2018 to 2019, the game was also introduced at academic gaming and
pedagogy conferences, including Teach, Play, Learn at Indiana University in
South Bend; at EDULEARN in Palma de Mallorca, Spain; and at the University of Michigan's 2019 Gameful Learning Institute.[18]

The game's website explains, "The Social Justice Game aims to stimulate
a frustration so comically absurd that gameplay evolves into a discussion
among the players around systemic inequity, and helps players complicate
the notion of economic success as a contest among equals."[19] The use of satire
and intentionally absurd scenarios in the game helps players experience frustration in a way that mirrors the unfairness of systemic inequalities in the real
world. This approach is effective: it disarms people, lowering their defenses
and making them more open to discussing difficult subjects. The exaggeration not only reveals the ridiculousness of certain societal structures but also
sparks curiosity and critical thinking. When players laugh at the game's ab-
surdity, they are simultaneously recognizing the flaws in our systems, which
naturally leads to deeper reflection and meaningful conversations about how
these inequities play out in everyday life.

Entering the Story

Utilizing gaming elements to address social problems is not a novel concept.
Many individuals are convinced that gaming can be a potent tool for driving
social good.

Alternate Reality Games (ARGs) offer a clue into how more Americans
might engage in the overarching contest to safeguard long-cherished freedoms. In ARGs, participants enter different universes through "rabbit holes,"
often found on social media platforms like X.

ARGs are typically used for marketing purposes, promoting albums, shows, and films. In these games, the real world serves as a canvas for players to interact with fictional characters.

An example is the ARG created for the 2008 film *The Dark Knight*, where select players aided the Joker in executing his bank-robbery escape using a school bus. In a pre-screening campaign, gamers even voted for Gotham City's district attorney, Harvey Dent. How? Players discovered a phone number concealed in the icing of real cakes reserved for "Robin Banks" at participating bakeries. Upon calling the number, a cell phone concealed inside the cake would ring.[20] Throughout the marketing campaign, players received text and voice messages directing them to dial specific numbers to access additional puzzles.

In ARGs, players collaborate to solve plot-based puzzles, engaging in both real-life and online activities through various communication channels like phone, email, or snail mail, all while relying on the internet as their central connection. When stumped, ARG websites serve as platforms where players can pool their collective skills to decipher puzzles.[21] This collaborative effort often prompts game makers to create even more thrilling and intricate riddles, drawing on a wide range of skills to solve a common problem.

Another example of applying civic-minded games for societal benefit can be found at the University of Chicago, where an alternate reality game was introduced in 2018. A team affiliated with the Weston Game Lab worked with the university to create the ARG *Terrarium* for first-year students. This game centered around the theme of climate change and used platforms such as Twitch and Open Broadcaster Software. It incorporated elements like live streaming, live-action performance, video game mechanics, and puzzles. Players engaged in sharing information and interacting with performers to navigate through "inverse escape rooms."[22] Faculty and staff members from several departments were involved, and it concluded with a session where students could share ideas on combating and mitigating climate change.[23]

If a significant number of the nearly four thousand degree-granting college-level institutions in the nation incorporated similar ARGs on socially relevant topics in their curricula, it would potentially motivate more students to remain actively involved in social justice efforts after graduation. Encouraging the continued use of altruistic gaming in more immersive iterations of social media has the potential to foster greater cohesiveness, a sense of purpose, and increased democratic participation to a wider swath of individuals. As we saw in the last chapter, one activist even found a creative way to adapt the persona of a game-born character to outwit some of society's most deceitful individuals.[24]

Games4Change

Games for Change (G4C) is a leader in recognizing the potential of games to address global challenges. Founded in 2004 by Benjamin Stokes, author of *Locally Played: Real World Games for Stronger Places and Communities*, G4C has helped foster a community of game developers, researchers, educators, and activists who are passionate about using games as a tool for social good.[25] It frequently collaborates with others to raise awareness about the potential of games to address pressing global challenges and encourage positive social impact, providing resources, funding opportunities, and mentorship to game developers who want to create socially responsible games. It also hosts an annual Games for Change Festival, which brings together game developers, educators, activists, and policymakers to discuss the potential of games for social change.

In collaboration with educators and schools, G4C develops and implements game-based curricula to enhance students' understanding of complex subjects and encourage critical thinking. The organization advocates for the positive impact of games and conducts research to understand how games can be used effectively in areas such as education, healthcare, and civic engagement.

In 2022, the team completed a project with *Minecraft* and the Nobel Peace Center. In this project, players assume the role of four Nobel Peace laureates who must make difficult decisions for the betterment of the world. Players can help share Pakistani education activist Malala Yousafzai's message of educational equality by retrieving segments of her journal while avoiding the Taliban.[26]

A few educational games explore the Underground Railroad, allowing players to help enslaved individuals find freedom by making strategic decisions about routes, safe houses, and trusted allies. These games teach about the courage, danger, and solidarity of this critical network in American history, highlighting the lengths people went to escape slavery and the risks taken by their helpers. *Flight to Freedom* by Mission US is an interactive online game where players take on the role of Lucy, a fourteen-year-old enslaved girl, navigating her escape. The National Geographic Society's *Underground Railroad: Journey to Freedom* also offers a journey through the challenges of escape, with decisions on routes and safe houses.

In another subject area, *Reconstructing After Natural Disasters*, by the United Nations Office for Disaster Risk Reduction, is a game in which players are responsible for rebuilding communities after natural disasters. In making decisions on allocating resources, prioritizing aid, and coordinating with local governments and organizations, they receive civics education, including knowledge of government officials at all levels, civil society, community dynamics, and volunteerism. It teaches the importance of community resilience and the challenges of equitable recovery efforts. Through gameplay, users learn how the location of a house and the materials used in its construction can affect its safety during disasters. They also discover the life-saving importance of early warning systems, evacuation plans, and disaster education.

NationStates is a free, browser-based online simulation game that allows players to create and manage their own fictional nation. The game was developed by Australian author Max Barry and launched in 2002 as a promotional tool for his novel *Jennifer Government*.[27] Players are responsible for shaping the political, economic, and social landscape of their nation by making decisions on various policy issues in a simple yet engaging game that combines political simulation with community interaction, allowing players to explore governance and nation-building in a fictional, low-pressure environment.

Another game, the award-winning *Bad News*, teaches players how to critically assess information and discern between reliable and deceptive sources.[28]

Games of diverse genres, along with activist actions that employ elements of fun, can help shape well-informed and responsible citizens who are better equipped to participate in and strengthen democratic systems.

Create Your Own Family Game

Parents can be creative in teaching their kids about civics and activism by making their own game related to a local issue that resonates with all family members. For those without coding skills, the game need not be digital; families can design their own tabletop or role-playing game, making it as simple or complex as desired. For example, they could create a game called *Save Our Corner Park!* to teach the importance of civic engagement in protecting public spaces.

The goal of the game is to prevent developers from demolishing a local park in a largely residential neighborhood to make way for a new shopping mall. Players must work together to organize a community campaign, gather support, and present their case to the city council.

How to Play

1. **Set the scene.** The game begins with a story: Our beloved corner park where we bring the family dog each morning to run is under threat from a greedy developer who wants to build a shopping mall. The players (parents and kids) take on roles as community members who love the park and want to save it.

2. **Gather support.** Players must collect "support cards" by performing activities that educate the community about the importance of the park. For instance, parents and kids could role-play writing and delivering a speech, creating a petition for neighbors to sign, or designing posters to raise awareness about the issue.

3. **Organize a protest.** The game could include a mini-challenge where players simulate organizing a peaceful protest. They must decide on the date, create signs with catchy slogans, and practice chanting messages that emphasize the park's value to the community.

4. **Engage with local government.** Players can then take on the role of different city council members to simulate a meeting. Parents can help their kids prepare arguments about why the park should be saved, teaching them about public speaking and the importance of presenting a well-thought-out case.

5. **Make decisions.** During the city council meeting, parents can introduce scenarios where the council members propose compromises, such as reducing the park's size or creating a new green space elsewhere. Kids must decide whether to accept these compromises or push for more, teaching them negotiation and decision-making skills.

6. **Reflect and discuss.** After the game, parents can discuss with their children what strategies worked best and why some decisions were more effective than others. They can also relate these strategies to real-world examples of activism and civic engagement, like actual campaigns to save parks or public spaces in their community.

Through games like this, kids learn how to organize, advocate, and engage in civic action creatively. They gain a hands-on understanding of activism, the democratic process, and the importance of community involvement in addressing social issues. This approach makes learning about civics and activism interactive and memorable, fostering a sense of empowerment and responsibility.

To engage more deeply with educational games that promote civics and activism, start by watching coverage of events like the Games for Change Festival, which showcases a variety of games designed to drive social impact and foster civic engagement. Many events are streamed online, offering panels, workshops, and gameplay sessions where developers and educators discuss how their games teach about social justice, activism, and civic responsibility.

The Games for Change website helps you find local chapters or communities in your area that focus on using games for education and activism. These chapters often host meetups, game jams, and workshops, providing opportunities to connect with like-minded individuals, learn from experts, and participate in discussions on leveraging games for social change. By staying connected with these communities, you can discover new games, share experiences, and collaborate on initiatives that promote civics education through interactive and innovative methods.

Cyber Sparks:
Inspiring Informed Action

Democracy, both digital and real-world, requires a less polarized ecosystem. With extreme polarization, society suffers in the relentless race for power and influence. As online conflicts continue unabated, users have a moral imperative to develop the skills necessary for informed and reparative action.

Digitally literate individuals and communities are fighting to reclaim the free and democratic nature of the internet, now overshadowed by dominant tech players. These information-era activists—cyber citizens—advocate for privacy and data protection while ensuring the internet remains an open and inclusive space, free of alternative facts and hateful propaganda. Their efforts inspire others who feel out of control or in the dark as power-mongers exploit personal data to manipulate and distract us from full citizen engagement. Frontline "digital literati" are counteracting the forces destroying free speech, a free press, full civic participation, and other fundamental democratic principles.

The New Paul Reveres

A glance back in history is instructive when considering how we might spread the message widely about the need for community action to ensure digital democracy.

More than two centuries ago, the secret organization the Sons of Liberty formed in the American colonies in the mid-1760s to oppose British policies and assert colonial rights. This group played a crucial role in mobilizing colonial resistance to the British Crown, especially in response to oppressive legislation like the Stamp Act and the Townshend Acts. Composed of tradesmen, artisans, merchants, and other patriots, the Sons of Liberty utilized a network of local chapters to coordinate actions and spread revolutionary sentiment across the colonies. They organized protests, disseminated pamphlets, and led acts of defiance such as the Boston Tea Party, which became a symbolic event in the build-up to the American Revolution. The network's decentralized nature allowed it to effectively communicate and coordinate efforts, fostering a sense of unity and shared purpose among the colonists.

Paul Revere was a key figure within this network, particularly known for his role in the events leading up to the battles of Lexington and Concord in April 1775. Revere was part of an intricate web of riders and informants tasked with warning colonial militias of British troop movements. On the night of April 18, 1775, Revere, along with William Dawes and Dr. Samuel Prescott, set out on horseback to alert the countryside that British forces were advancing to seize colonial arms stored in Concord. Revere's famous ride was not a solitary act but rather a part of a broader alarm system designed by the Sons of Liberty to ensure that the colonial militias were ready to resist British aggression. This effective use of intelligence and communication exemplified the organizational skills and resourcefulness of the Sons of Liberty, setting the stage for the first armed confrontations of the American Revolution.

Today, we see a parallel in the way digital activists, technologists, and whistleblowers act as modern-day Paul Reveres, raising alarms in a vastly more complex, digitized world. Just as Revere's ride was part of an organized response to oppression, these individuals work within digital networks to warn the public about threats to our privacy, democracy, and security.

Because the internet and advancements like the iPhone emerged at breakneck speed, commercialization has exploited the internet's democratic promise. In this context, pioneering figures—hackers, early engineers, creators, and whistleblowers—act as sentinels of our era, defending digital rights and freedoms against forces that would otherwise exploit them. Just fifteen years before the 2013 revelations by Edward Snowden, computer experts raised concerns about internet security. A group of hackers warned lawmakers in person about critical vulnerabilities of the internet and computer infrastructure. In landmark testimony, members of the Boston-based hacker group L0pht Heavy Industries, including Twitter whistleblower Peiter Zatko, went to Capitol Hill in 1988 to caution members of the US Senate Committee on Governmental Affairs. The experts' famous claim that they could take down the internet in thirty minutes highlighted significant cybersecurity risks.

Senator Joe Lieberman praised the hackers for "performing an act of very good citizenship," comparing them to modern-day Paul Reveres. He invoked the then-recent Oklahoma City bombing and admitted, "If we looked at it, we would've understood as some did that there was real vulnerability. But we didn't do anything about it and I think that's what you're telling us and I hope we can continue to work with you to try to raise our guard."[1]

Unfortunately, that never happened. It took Snowden's 2013 leak to publicly sound the alarm about the surveillance state and the need for legislative democratization in the online arena. Following his revelations that the NSA had been spying on American citizens, foreign leaders and governments, including close allies like Germany, Brazil, and France, led more Americans to pay attention and call for regulation.

Another modern Paul Revere is former Facebook employee and whistleblower Frances Haugen. She gained international attention by disclosing tens of thousands of pages of internal Facebook documents to Congress and the Securities and Exchange Commission, revealing the company knew its harmful effects on users, especially regarding mental health. Her 2021 testimony before the US Congress highlighted Facebook's prioritization of profit over public safety.[2] Both Zatko and Haugen have sparked important ongoing discussions about social media regulation and corporate accountability.

Power in Numbers

These modern Paul Reveres provide inspiration, but they can't transform our digital ecosystem alone. Movements model digital citizenship.

One inspiring net-neutrality campaign in 2017 attracted a mass movement. After the FCC voted to repeal net-neutrality protections, the nonprofit advocacy organization Fight for the Future, founded in 2011, mobilized millions to contact their representatives, submit comments to the FCC, and participate in protests and online actions. Net neutrality ensures that all internet traffic is treated equally, preventing service providers from discriminating against or favoring certain content. The widespread public engagement catalyzed by Fight for the Future prompted several states to implement their own net-neutrality laws, demonstrating the power of collective digital action to influence policy, even in the face of significant opposition. But despite this mass organizing, the Trump administration's FCC rolled back net-neutrality rules in 2017. On April 25, 2024, the FCC restored net neutrality with an effective date of July 22, 2024, bringing back a national standard for broadband reliability, security, and consumer protection.

Numerous other community-driven initiatives offer hope. Local tech cooperatives provide alternatives to the monopolistic practices of Big Tech companies. The Detroit Community Technology Project (DCTP) is recognized as a leader in digital equity, focusing on building community-owned internet infrastructure. Their Equitable Internet Initiative, founded in 2016, created internet networks in three Detroit neighborhoods. Starting with a forty-five-household pilot, the network grew to include over five hundred households and small businesses.[3]

DCTP also developed a Digital Steward curriculum that trained three hundred people to build the community networks. This curriculum has been implemented and recognized both in the US and abroad, with replications in Seattle and New York City.[4] Similar initiatives exist in the UK, with the network CoTech (Co-operative Technologists). Germany's Technologiestiftung Berlin advances digital transformation in city administration, education, culture, and commerce. In New Zealand, Enspiral is a collaborative network of social enterprises and technology cooperatives.

Philanthropic gifts to advocacy groups are as essential as the work they do. For Americans who want to improve the technology infrastructure but lack hands-on experience, this is an excellent way to contribute. Pierre Omidyar, founder of eBay and the Omidyar Network, exemplifies positive leadership in the tech field by funding many digital-rights organizations, including the Electronic Frontier Foundation (EFF), enabling organizations like the EFF to respond nimbly to emerging crises requiring urgent action or litigation.[5] While Omidyar Network's support is important, individual gifts committed to an egalitarian internet make up two-thirds of EFF's budget, a reliance common among most US nonprofits.

Financial contributions enable these organizations to continue their essential work, from launching lawsuits and policy initiatives to developing tools and resources that help individuals protect their digital rights. By donating, cyber citizens can ensure these frontline groups have the necessary resources to promote a fair and secure digital environment for all.

Training Cyber Citizens

Without understanding the dangers that a corporate-owned internet poses to democracy, citizens are unlikely to prioritize digital hygiene. However, when people recognize the stakes—such as the commodification of personal data to control lives and erode freedoms—they are more likely to practice sound digital hygiene. For those unaware of its broader significance, digital hygiene may seem like a nuisance. But negligence not only impacts the individual; it also weakens the entire digital system supporting the nation's critical infrastructure.

Many organizations work to combat this apathetic mindset by combining digital media literacy, cybersecurity, and civics in various ways to educate users on best practices in our interconnected world. Please refer to the list in the end matter for details.

Regulation Revolution

State laws such as California's Consumer Privacy Act, Virginia's Consumer Data Protection Act, and Colorado's Privacy Act set a precedent, pushing for higher privacy standards and prompting other states to consider similar legislation. This growing patchwork of laws sends a message to the federal government to establish a nationwide privacy standard.

Awareness is growing among parents, teachers, and legislators about the aggressive targeting of children by marketers. In 2024, Maryland passed the Age-Appropriate Design Code, or the "Kid's Code," which requires online products and services likely to be accessed by minors under eighteen to be designed with their best interests and age-appropriateness in mind.[6] It emphasizes privacy by design and default to ensure that young users' personal information is protected from the start.

Catalyzing a profound shift in how both corporations and consumers think about data privacy is the GDPR. By enforcing strict standards and penalties for mishandling user data, it has effectively drawn a line that even American companies can't afford to ignore, setting a powerful precedent. This policy has led companies like Microsoft to extend GDPR-style rights to all customers worldwide—a striking example of how European regulation has permeated global business practices.

In many ways, the GDPR has become a double-edged sword. It has raised the bar for privacy protections but has also highlighted the vast influence American tech giants wield over global data. This paradox calls into question how much meaningful autonomy individuals actually have in the face of such colossal, boundary-spanning corporations. It raises a more philosophical query: If a regulation like the GDPR is needed to safeguard our privacy, are we really the ones in control of our personal information? The GDPR may be a step toward a more privacy-conscious world, but it also exposes the vast and uneasy power dynamics between nations, corporations, and individuals in the digital age.

In countries like Estonia, Finland, and Germany, children are learning to navigate the digital world with intelligence, safety, and confidence. They grow up with privacy rights that protect them, digital literacy skills that empower them, and systems that entrust them with secure access to information. These countries are showing us that when a nation prioritizes its young people, it builds a generation capable of meeting the future with resilience and insight. Yet here in the United States, our children enter the same world unprepared, with only patchwork programs and half-measures to guide them. We tell them to be wary of their online surroundings, but we don't give them the tools or knowledge to make that possible.

Imagine an America where every child grows up knowing their right to privacy, understands how their data is used, and can discern truth from manipulation online. An America where digital literacy is not a luxury but a right for every student, from rural communities to city centers. This concept isn't only about giving kids better access to technology; it's also about instilling in them a sense of agency, a belief that their personal information belongs to them, and a trust that their country stands with them. If we look to nations that have already taken these steps, we see a clear path forward—one that puts young people's safety, rights, and knowledge at the heart of our national agenda.

So, we must ask ourselves: What does it say about our priorities that we're willing to let commercial interests define the digital lives of future generations? Are we content to let them face a complex world without the tools to fully understand it? Or will we rise to the challenge, knowing that when we invest in everyone's digital future, we invest in the very resilience of our democracy? The choice is ours to make.

The next section offers a few basic tips that, if widely practiced, can help make the internet a safer place for all users.

A USER'S GUIDE FOR THE DIGITAL AGE

With creativity and fun, all members of the family can practice safe internet navigation. Importantly, this can happen without policing children's activities.

Your "Digital Tattoo"

How do we teach the importance of maintaining a positive digital footprint and the potential long-term impacts of our online behavior? One university has a novel approach.

The Digital Tattoo Project at the University of British Columbia collaborates with several libraries and with local high schools using a creative approach to teaching kids about the long-term consequences of social media.[1] Its goal is to raise questions, encourage students to think about their presence online, navigate the issues involved in forming and re-forming one's digital identity, and learn digital citizens' rights and responsibilities. Students are asked to think of their online presence as a "digital tattoo" that is permanent and can impact their future opportunities. They participate in activities like creating hypothetical social media profiles and then examining how those profiles might affect their lives in ten years, such as when applying for college or jobs.

Educational topics are varied and cover issues like cyberbullying, collaborative learning online, privacy, copyright, and digital identity as they may affect career and post-graduation opportunities. For example, one of the project's short videos covers the topic of "clickjacking," a malicious technique where an attacker tricks a user to click on something different from what the user perceives, often by overlaying an invisible element or button over a legitimate web page. This manipulation can lead the user to unintentionally perform actions like sharing sensitive information, changing settings, or initiating unwanted transactions. After the four-minute video, watchers can take a short multiple-question quiz followed by an informational analysis of their responses.

Another initiative is the Internet Keep Safe Coalition (iKeepSafe), established in 2005 as a nonprofit alliance of more than one hundred policy leaders, including governors, attorneys general, educators, law enforcement members, technology experts, and public health professionals. iKeepSafe tracks global trends and issues surrounding digitally connected products and their effect on children and shares research with parents, educators, and policymakers to teach children how to use safely use new technologies and the internet.

Further Reading

For parents seeking resources on how to keep kids' online identities safe, check out Diana Graber's *Raising Humans in a Digital World: Helping Kids Build a Healthy Relationship with Technology*, which contains practical advice on guiding children in navigating the digital world safely, from online privacy to digital citizenship and managing screen time.

The Tech-Wise Family: Everyday Steps for Putting Technology in Its Proper Place by Andy Crouch includes tips on protecting children's online identities and ensuring a balanced relationship with technology.

Screen-Smart Parenting: How to Find Balance and Benefit in Your Child's Use of Social Media, Apps, and Digital Devices by Jodi Gold provides age-specific strategies to help parents guide their children in making responsible choices online.

The Big Disconnect: Protecting Childhood and Family Relationships in the Digital Age by Catherine Steiner-Adair offers guidance on how to protect children's digital footprints while fostering healthy relationships both online and offline.

Parenting in the Digital World: A Step-by-Step Guide to Keeping Your Kids Safe Online by Clayton Cranford provides actionable steps for parents to protect their kids' online identities, understand social media platforms, and navigate cyberbullying and online predators.

Know Your Marketers

Social media companies generated over $11 billion in ad revenue in 2022, as reported by a 2023 study from the Harvard T.H. Chan School of Public Health. Platforms aimed at children, such as YouTube Kids, Google Kids, and TikTok, afford marketers with direct access to young audiences.[2] Educate your children about online advertising, including how ads function, how search history influences ad targeting, the nature of pop-up ads, and how to manage them. Additionally, children should be informed about social media influencers and their role in advertising. For further resources on this topic, Erica Fyvie's 2021 book, *Mad for Ads: How Advertising Gets (and Stays) in Our Heads*, tailored for ten- to twelve-year-olds, is just one example of the literature available addressing advertising aimed at kids. The Boston-based nonprofit organization Fairplay (formerly known as the Campaign for a Commercial-Free Childhood) is committed to safeguarding the welfare of children in a society inundated with advertising. They emphasize that their advocacy efforts are grounded in evidence demonstrating that marketing directed at children leads to excessive screen time and hampers their healthy development.

Family Activities

Collaborate to create a "Digital Privacy Toolkit." This could include homemade "Do Not Track" cards, privacy stickers to cover webcams, and simple digital encryption tools (like password managers or privacy-focused browsers). This helps kids understand practical tools for protecting their privacy online and makes the concept of digital security tangible and interactive.

Host a family privacy audit party. Dedicate a day to conduct a fun "Privacy Audit" at home. Review privacy settings on all family devices, apps, and online accounts together. Discuss why certain settings might be more secure and the importance of limiting data sharing. This strengthens privacy awareness and teaches kids to critically analyze how their data is collected and used by corporations.

Play the "Who Owns This Data?" game. Turn data ownership into an educational game. Ask questions like, "Who owns the photos we post online?" or "What happens to the information we enter on websites?" Kids can earn points by correctly identifying who has access to different types of data and the implications. This can teach kids about data ownership and the often-hidden terms of service agreements, increasing their awareness of how corporations use personal data.

Design a privacy-focused app or website. Encourage kids to brainstorm and design a mock app or website that prioritizes user privacy. Discuss features like no tracking, minimal data collection, and transparency in user agreements. This creative exercise helps kids think critically about user-centric design and the importance of privacy in digital products, fostering an understanding of ethical considerations in tech.

Engage in "privacy role-play" scenarios. Set up role-playing scenarios where kids have to decide how to handle different privacy situations, such as receiving a suspicious email or being asked for personal information online. Parents can play the role of companies, hackers, or peers to simulate different privacy challenges. Role-playing helps kids practice making privacy-conscious decisions in a safe environment, reinforcing proactive thinking about personal-data security and corporate intent.

Follow the data trail challenge. Pick a common household product and research the companies involved in its production, distribution, and marketing. Discuss the data these companies might collect about their customers and how they might use it. Kids learn about corporate power structures, supply chains, and how consumer data can be a valuable asset for companies, promoting a deeper understanding of corporate dynamics and data economics.

Develop a family manifesto on digital rights. Create a Family Manifesto on Digital Rights that outlines values and rules about data privacy and corporate transparency. Include pledges like supporting companies with ethical data practices and regularly discussing digital-privacy issues. This shared document helps cement a family culture of privacy awareness and conscientious consumerism, encouraging kids to think about their digital rights and the impacts of their choices.

Use storytelling with characters and adventures. Write a story or create a comic with your child where characters go on adventures that involve privacy challenges, like protecting a secret code from data thieves or navigating a city where corporations control all personal information. Storytelling makes abstract concepts relatable and memorable, helping kids internalize lessons about privacy and corporate power in a fun and engaging way.

AI Cleverness

The *MIT Technology Review* offers six tips for parents to teach children about interacting with artificial intelligence.[3]

1. Don't forget: AI is not your friend. While chatbots may sound like caring humans, they are only mimicking human speech from data scraped off the internet. Tell kids not to give personal data to systems like ChatGPT because once it's in their database, it's virtually impossible to remove. Companies can profit off it and it's vulnerable to hackers.

2. **AI models are not replacements for search engines.** While chatbots confidently answer questions with text that seems reasonable, not all the information is accurate. AI language models are also known to present falsehoods as facts; depending on what sources that data was collected, they can often reinforce bias or stereotypes. Students should fact-check everything large language models say.

3. **Teachers might falsely accuse you of using AI.** While several companies have introduced products aimed at identifying whether text was written by a human or a machine, these tools are unreliable and easy to fool. In many cases, teachers assume an essay is AI-generated when it was not. Learn your child's school's AI policies or AI disclosure processes (if any) and remind students of the importance of abiding by them. If your child is wrongly accused of using AI, challenge the decision and ask how it was made. ChatGPT keeps records of individual users' conversations if you need proof.

4. **Recommended systems are designed to get you hooked and might show bad stuff.** Explain to kids how recommendation algorithms work. Tech platforms make money when people watch ads; their AI algorithms recommend content, such as videos on YouTube or TikTok, so people will remain on their platform. The algorithms track and closely measure the kinds of videos people watch, then recommend similar ones. Such services tend to steer users to harmful content like misinformation, given humans' tendency to linger on shocking or odd content, such as misinformation about health or extreme political ideologies. Don't believe everything you read online and always check information from reliable sources.

5. **Use AI safely and responsibly.** A host of free deepfake apps and web programs can easily superimpose someone's face onto someone else's body. Students should be wary of uploading friends' faces into risqué apps. Courts have found teens guilty of spreading child pornography for sending explicit material about other teens or themselves. Pointing out articles about platforms being hacked will likely make a greater impression on kids than general "be careful" warnings. Save any data-breach letters you receive (they're on the uptick!) and discuss with the family.

6. **Don't miss out on AI's benefits.** When used intelligently, AI is a useful tool. Students struggling to understand a tricky topic can ask ChatGPT to explain it step by step, or to take on the persona of an expert

biology teacher to allow them to test their own knowledge. It can efficiently present comparisons, for example, of the pros and cons of an issue that might otherwise take hours of research and can be helpful in evaluating student drafts.

Hate Group Recruiting Symbols and Tactics

Hate groups often use specific signs and images to recruit teens online by tapping into youth culture and employing symbols that may initially seem harmless or appealing. Look for:

Innocuous elements appropriated into icons of the alt-right, such as:

- "Okay" index-to-thumb hand gesture, used by some as a "sincere expression of white supremacy." New Zealand white supremacist shooter Brenton Tarrant flashed the sign to reporters at a court hearing.
- triple parentheses ((( ))) to brand users as Jewish
- 1980s vaporwave art style and synthwave music (which the alt-right calls "fashwave")

Numerics, on tattoos and in other images, to represent insider variations on the hate theme, including:

- "14 words" slogan: "We must secure the existence of our people and a future for white children," coined by David Lane, from the white supremacist terrorist group known as The Order
- 1488, also written as 14/88, or 14–88, combining popular white supremacist numeric symbols 14, for the 14 words slogan and 88 for "Heil Hitler" (H being the alphabet's 8th letter), signaling an endorsement of white supremacy
- H8, to mean "hate"

Memes and humor containing hateful messages are disguised as jokes to make hate seem more palatable and normalize bigoted viewpoints. Flags and emblems like the Confederate flag or the Nordic rune symbols (e.g., the "odal rune" used by some white supremacist groups) are often displayed to signal alignment with certain ideologies.

For adults, these measures of digital literacy and cyber hygiene are increasingly important:

Browse safely

When browsing the web, ensure that the URL of the website you're visiting starts with "https," as the *s* indicates it's secure. Verify the presence of a lock symbol on the left side of the web address, and be cautious if you see an exclamation point, because it signifies that the site isn't secure.

Don't dismiss cookie banners

In our haste to read a website, who among us hasn't quickly dismissed a cookie banner without reading the options? Cookie banners are a notification that appears on websites to inform visitors about the use of cookies and to obtain their consent. When you encounter a cookie banner, the primary goal is to protect your privacy by limiting the data that websites can collect about you. First, look for an option to reject or decline all non-essential cookies, which are often used for tracking and advertising purposes. Essential cookies, necessary for the website's basic functionality, usually can't be disabled. Some banners have a "Manage Preferences" or "Customize Settings" button, where you can selectively disable cookies related to advertising, analytics, and social media. Choosing to reject or customize cookies reduces the amount of data shared and limits your exposure to targeted ads.

Second, consider using browser settings and extensions to further enhance your privacy. Most modern browsers offer built-in tools to block third-party cookies by default or to notify you about cookie usage. Privacy-focused browser extensions, such as ad blockers or anti-tracking tools, can provide additional protective layers by automatically blocking trackers and unwanted cookies. Regularly clearing your browser's cookies and cache can also help minimize the amount of stored data. By combining these steps with prudent choices on cookie banners, you can better control your online privacy and reduce the risk of data misuse.

Encrypt, encrypt, encrypt

Many devices offer the option to encrypt their hard drives, safeguarding the full operating system, programs, and personal data stored on them. Develop the habit of meticulously reviewing the settings of each service you use to ensure you're utilizing the strongest privacy options available. Encrypting messages before sharing or sending them over the internet is a crucial privacy measure. For email, GnuPG (often referred to as GPG) serves as the Free/Libre Open Source Software (FLOSS) alternative to the proprietary PGP encryption. This "end-to-end encryption" is currently the most robust encryption method available for email and certain messaging apps.

Encryption on emails and apps is essential for privacy because it ensures that only the intended recipients can access the content, protecting sensitive information from unauthorized parties, including hackers and surveillance entities. By scrambling data into unreadable formats during transmission, encryption safeguards personal and confidential communications against interception and misuse.

Don't forget to FLOSS (Free and Libre Open Source Software)

FLOSS (also known simply as Free and Open Source, or FOSS) software refers to software projects that embody a collaborative ethos, where developers from around the world contribute to building and refining code that is freely available to all. The "libre" in FLOSS refers to the freedom it affords users to study, modify, and distribute the software according to specific criteria outlined in the license. A key advantage of FLOSS is its transparency. Since the code is open and accessible to anyone, it undergoes continuous scrutiny by a diverse community of developers. This collective effort acts as a safeguard against malicious code or hidden vulnerabilities. With so many privacy-minded individuals examining the code base, potential issues are often identified and addressed swiftly.

Show me the money

The axiom "If it's free, then you are the product" serves as a useful reminder that the proliferation of "free" apps, games, memes, and other services often serves as a means for corporations and bad actors to harvest personal data to sell to third parties, or to aid in password guessing. While FLOSS software itself is free, corporations frequently use it as a foundation, adding their own proprietary data-gathering elements when packaging and branding it for sale. By embracing platforms that are purely FLOSS, and by being vigilant about those that have been altered and repackaged to collect data, users not only benefit from robust and secure software but also contribute to the preservation of their digital privacy and autonomy.

Choose better software tools

In addition to FLOSS products, many tools are available that prioritize maximizing privacy. Signal, developed by WhisperSystems, stands out as the most secure texting app as of 2024. DuckDuckGo offers a search engine alternative that doesn't track users in the intrusive way that Google does. The Mozilla Foundation offers several widely used FLOSS programs, including the Firefox browser and the Thunderbird email client. Another notable option is the Tor browser, which is widely trusted for its innovative technology that ensures secure internet communication.

Step up your password game (no birthdays or pet names)

Avoid the common trap of reusing simple passwords that are easily remembered. Strengthen your passwords by using full sentences, adding capitalization, spaces between words, and punctuation. Password-manager tools like KeePassXC and Bitwarden can help generate and manage strong, random passwords for enhanced security. Computer OS and browser-based password managers are generally safe to use, as they offer a convenient way to store and autofill passwords securely, often incorporating encryption and other security measures. However, third-party password managers might offer additional features such as cross-platform compatibility, advanced encryption, secure password sharing, and more robust protection against breaches, making them a preferable choice for users seeking enhanced security and flexibility.

No knowledge is good knowledge

An effective approach to safeguarding your personal information is to adopt a "no knowledge" principle, which entails only gathering, storing, or retaining information that is absolutely necessary. By designing systems that don't require the service to retain any of your information, you minimize the risk of compromise. Remember, if they don't have it, they can't contribute it to its potential compromise.

Party!

One of the most effective ways to address privacy threats, navigate the ever-changing landscape of technology, and accommodate varying levels of expertise is through mutual assistance. "Crypto parties" are gatherings where people bring their devices, such as cell phones and computers, and collaborate with each other to implement privacy-enhancing changes. This could involve helping someone locate encryption settings on their phone or assisting them with changing their computer's default search engine. Privacy advocates frequently organize crypto parties that are open to members of their communities. If you possess a certain level of skill and comfort with these technologies, you can also take the initiative to organize one yourself. Remember, friends support friends by ensuring they have access to basic, freely available privacy tools.

Improve your digital literacy

Numerous online resources are available to help individuals improve their digital literacy. Look for reputable websites, tutorials, and online courses that cover topics such as basic computer skills, internet safety, digital communication, and critical thinking in the digital age. One example is DigitalLearn.org, a program of the Public Library Association. Its website offers simple tutorials on basic computer skills, including how to use email, internet browsers, and online safety tips. It's designed to be especially accessible for beginners. *Coursera* features a range of courses from reputable universities and institutions on basic computer skills, such as navigating operating systems, internet safety, and introductory programming. Many courses are free to audit, with an option to pay for a certificate.

In 2017, the University of Michigan launched the Fake News Teach-Out, an online series of twenty interactive online modules allowing participants worldwide to engage with the content at their own pace. Experts from various disciplines, including journalists, scholars, and media professionals, provide insights into how fake news spreads and its impact on democracy and society.[4] One participant is Will Potter, an award-winning investigative journalist known for his work on environmental issues and civil liberties. Potter shares strategies on how to identify false information and critically assess news sources. This initiative underscores the role of educational institutions in fostering informed and critical citizens capable of discerning truth from misinformation.

Keep learning. Technology is constantly evolving, so it's essential to commit to lifelong learning. Stay updated on the latest trends, tools, and best practices in digital technology through online courses, webinars, podcasts, and industry publications.

Attend a "Lunch and Learn" session. Many organizations across various sectors offer these sessions for IT topics, including corporations, educational institutions, nonprofits, and government agencies. Tech companies and IT departments within businesses frequently host these gatherings to keep employees updated on the latest technology trends, software tools, and cybersecurity practices. Professional associations, tech-training providers, and coworking spaces may also offer these events. And as noted above, crypto parties are an excellent way to foster community-based learning.

Practice regularly. Put your digital literacy skills into practice by incorporating technology into your daily life. Whether it's using social media, managing online accounts, or learning to code, regular practice will help reinforce your skills and build confidence.

Seek support and collaboration. Don't be afraid to seek help and support from friends, family members, colleagues or online communities. Collaborating with others can provide valuable insights, feedback, and encouragement as you work to improve your digital literacy skills.

Develop critical-thinking skills. Digital literacy goes beyond technical proficiency; it also involves critical thinking, information literacy, and media literacy. Learn to critically evaluate online information, identify credible sources, and recognize misinformation and digital threats.

Explore digital creativity. Embrace your creativity and explore digital tools and platforms for creating, sharing, and collaborating. Whether it's blogging, podcasting, digital art, or video editing, digital literacy opens endless opportunities for expression and creativity, whether for sharing publicly or enjoying privately. Use ad-free open-source options to create a website and safely surf the web. Neocities is a free web hosting platform that allows users to create and share their own websites with creativity and individuality. In its simple, community-driven environment, people can learn HTML, CSS, and JavaScript, encouraging a hands-on approach to web development and fostering a DIY ethos.

Promote digital inclusion. Advocate for designing interfaces that are accessible and usable for all, regardless of ability, age, background, or device, promoting digital inclusion and access to technology for all members of society. This means implementing principles of universal design to ensure that platforms are intuitive and easy to navigate for everyone; key practices include using high-contrast colors and readable fonts for visually impaired users, ensuring compatibility with screen readers and other assistive technologies, and offering keyboard navigability for those who cannot use a mouse. Providing text alternatives for images, videos, and other non-text content can help users with auditory or visual challenges access the same information as others, fostering a more inclusive digital environment.

In addition to connecting with and learning from groups like these, consider giving financial support to these and other initiatives that aim to bridge the digital divide and ensure that everyone can participate fully in the digital world.

Don't forget civic participation. Stay up to date on local, state, and federal elections by reviewing news coverage from multiple sources or subscribe to alerts from your government's elections division. Two sites for short-term volunteering opportunities are VolunteerMatch and Points of Light Engage. VolunteerMatch connects individuals with local and virtual volunteer opportunities based on their interests, skills, and availability. Formerly All for Good, Points of Light Engage aggregates volunteer listings from various organizations. Local city and community websites also often post listings of local nonprofits and events looking for volunteers.

If all this seems like a lot to do at once, start gradually. Here are a few steps you can take right now:

1. Identify and follow five reputable news outlets on social media that prioritize unbiased news and cover that mainstream outlets may overlook.

2. Bookmark key sites for easy access or add them to your homepage feed.

3. Review and update your browser privacy settings to enhance tracking preferences.

4. Bookmark a reliable independent fact-checker or install a fact-checking browser extension. This tool will help you quickly assess the credibility of news articles and identify potential biases and misinformation in real time.

5. Follow Mozilla's newsletter for updates on the latest privacy violations and disputes in Big Tech.

By committing to most of these lifelong practices, Americans can strive to improve their digital literacy and better navigate the complexities of the digital age with confidence, competence, and resilience.

Armed with the will to learn new habits, and the resolve to implement them, cyber citizens possess a formidable ability to uphold democracy in the digital age.

ORGANIZATIONS SUPPORTING DIGITAL LITERACY, PRIVACY, CIVICS, AND ACTIVISM

Access Now: New York, NY, with regional offices globally. Provides real-time assistance and training on digital security and privacy, including a 24/7 Digital Security Helpline.

AI Now Institute: New York University, New York, NY. Produces policy research on the social implications of AI, focusing on ethics, accountability, and fairness.

Algorithmic Justice League: Cambridge, MA. Advocates for accountability in AI to prevent algorithmic discrimination.

American Civil Liberties Union: National office in New York, NY, with affiliates across the nation. Advocates and litigates to protect civil liberties, focusing on privacy and surveillance issues.

Black Girls Code: Oakland, CA, with chapters nationwide. Empowers girls of color through coding education and technology workshops. Partners with schools, local organizations, and businesses to offer in-person and virtual educational events.

Brennan Center for Justice: New York University School of Law, New York, NY. Focuses on democracy, justice, and privacy rights through education, advocacy, and litigation.

Center for Applied Special Technology: Lynnfield, MA. Develops inclusive educational technology and promotes a universal design for learning framework.

Center for Civic Education: Calabasas, CA. Provides instructional materials and learning for teachers, and advocates for more robust civics education.

Center for Cyber Safety and Education: Clearwater, FL. Provides cybersecurity education for all age groups, raises awareness of cyber career options, and provides scholarships and support in pursuing careers in the field. It also helps small organizations safeguard against cyber threats.

Center for Democracy & Technology: Washington, DC. Advocates for privacy, free speech, and net neutrality. Advocates to policymakers and the courts in the US and Europe, works with companies to improve policies and product designs, and produces scholarship.

Center for Digital Democracy: Washington, DC. Advocates for digital privacy, consumer protection, and data justice.

Center for Humane Technology: San Francisco, CA. Founded by design ethicist Tristan Harris. Works to realign tech with humane values. Produces educational media, partners with organizations to craft cross-sector solutions, and provides trainings and resources.

Center for Media and Democracy: Madison, WI. Investigates corporate influence on democracy and advocates for transparency. Hosts the wiki Source-Watch, a directory of think tanks, industry funded organizations, and PR firms.

Center for Media Literacy: Los Angeles, CA. Promotes critical thinking and informed media choices. Provides leadership, public education, and educational resources. Promotes and supports media literacy education, particularly for young people.

Center for News Literacy: Stony Brook University, Stony Brook, NY. Develops news literacy curricula to teach students to use critical-thinking skills to navigate online information.

Citizen Lab: University of Toronto, Canada. An interdisciplinary laboratory that conducts research on cybersecurity, surveillance, and digital rights.

Close Up Foundation: Alexandria, VA. Provides experiential civic education programs for students so they can exercise the rights and responsibilities of citizens in a democracy.

Code.org: Seattle, WA. Dedicated to the premise that every student has the chance to learn computer science and AI as part of their core K-12 education. Promotes computer science education with free resources for schools.

Common Sense Media: San Francisco, CA. Reviews and rates media and technology to assist parents in determining their suitability for children. It funds research on the role of media in young people's lives and advocates for youth-friendly media laws and policies.

Consumer Financial Protection Bureau: Washington, DC. Protects consumers by enforcing fair practices in finance.

Data & Society: New York, NY. Conducts research on the social implications of data-centric technologies, including privacy and ethics.

Detroit Community Technology Project: Detroit, MI. Provides digital literacy training with an emphasis on using and creating technology within the community, while also expanding digital literacy.

Digital Public Library of America: Boston, MA. Makes millions of digital resources and historical archives accessible to the public through a library-controlled marketplace and platforms to purchase, organize, and deliver ebooks and other content to patrons.

Digital Responsibility: Santa Monica, CA. Offers an educational website about online safety and responsible tech use for youth. Provides scholarships to high school students.

Electronic Frontier Foundation: San Francisco, CA. Premier organization defending digital rights, focusing on privacy, free expression, and innovation. EFF conducts impact litigation, policy analysis, activism, and technology development.

Fairplay: Boston, MA. Helps children thrive in a commercialized, screen-obsessed culture and advocates to end marketing to children. They work to end exploitative and harmful business practices of Big Tech and marketers.

Fandom Forward: Binghamton, NY. Mobilizes fans of popular culture to engage in social and political activism, using creative campaigns inspired by fictional worlds to drive awareness and community action.

Fight for the Future: Worcester, MA. Campaigns for digital rights, including net neutrality and privacy. They have organized some of the most successful online protests in history.

Future of Privacy Forum: Washington, DC. Promotes responsible data practices and research on privacy. They conduct research, issue publications, hold educational meetings, and provide expert testimony.

Games for Change: New York, NY. Supports the development of games for social impact and learning. They hold an annual Games for Change Festival where innovators brainstorm, network, and work to create immersive media and social justice games.

Generation Citizen: Headquarters in New York, NY, with chapters across the US. Empowers students with action-based civics education. Their mission is to transform how civics is taught by working with school districts to provide community-based civics education.

Georgetown Law School, Center for Privacy and Technology: Washington, DC. With a focus on the intersection of privacy, surveillance, and civil rights, the center conducts research, advocacy, and education to address privacy challenges, particularly focusing on the impact of surveillance and technology on marginalized communities.

Girls Who Code: New York, NY. Provides tech education to close the gender gap in computing.

iCivics: Boston, MA. Dedicated to advancing civic learning by equipping teachers and students with the knowledge, skills, and resources to engage in civic life.

iKeepSafe: Salt Lake City, UT. Provides data-privacy certifications to technology companies, educational resources to schools, and information to the community. The organization certifies digital products as compliant with state and federal requirements for handling personal information.

International Association of Privacy Professionals: Portsmouth, NH. Dedicated to promoting and improving professions in privacy, AI governance, and digital responsibility around the world. Educates and certifies privacy professionals.

Internet Society: Reston, VA, with global chapters. Advocates for an open, globally connected, secure, and stronger internet. Committed to closing the digital divide for the one-third of the global population that is not connected.

Library Freedom Project: US-based. Recognizing that libraries are essential to democracy, the Library Freedom Project provides library workers and their communities with trainings on digital privacy, intellectual freedom, security, and information democracy.

Media Education Lab: University of Rhode Island, Kingston, RI. An online-learning community focused on leadership development to develop media literacy programs, provide research and scholarship, and promote an inclusive community of scholars, advocates, and practitioners.

Media Literacy Now: Boston, MA. Advances media literacy education through policy advocacy at the local, state, and national levels in the US to ensure all K–12 students can become competent media consumers and creators.

Mikva Challenge: Chicago, IL. Develops youth to be informed and active citizens who will promote an equitable society.

Mozilla Foundation: Mountain View, CA. Promotes a healthy internet through digital literacy, privacy, inclusion, and decentralization through open-source tools. Its duty is to ensure the internet remains a force for good.

New America's Open Technology Institute (OTI): Washington, DC. Supports free expression and open technologies and is dedicated to supporting engaged, self-sufficient communities by promoting safe and affordable access to connectivity.

Privacy International: London, UK. Challenges corporate and government surveillance practices globally. Protects democracy, defends people's dignity, and seeks accountability from institutions who breach public trust.

Project Censored: Petaluma, CA. Promotes critical media literacy, investigative journalism, and democracy. Educates students and the public about the importance of a free press and exposes underreported issues.

Public Knowledge: Washington, DC. Advocates for digital rights, including free expression and open internet policies. Promotes access to affordable communications tools and creative works.

Signal Foundation: Mountain View, CA. Supports secure global messaging through open-source privacy technology.

Stay Safe Online (National Security Alliance Initiative): Washington, DC. Advocates for the safe use of all technology and provides education on digital safety and cybersecurity.

StopBullying.gov: A comprehensive online resource offering information, prevention strategies, and support for addressing and preventing bullying among children and teenagers.

Surveillance Technology Oversight Project: New York, NY. Litigates and advocates for privacy, working to end local government systems of mass surveillance.

TechGirlz: Philadelphia, PA, and in several other states. Works to help middle school girls excel in technology by providing hands-on digital learning.

We the People: The Citizen and the Constitution: Program under the Center for Civic Education, based in Calabasas, CA. A curriculum for elementary, middle, and high school students about the history and principles of constitutional democracy.

World Wide Web Consortium: Headquarters in Cambridge, MA, with offices worldwide. Develops web standards and guidelines to ensure the open web remains accessible, private, internationalized, and secure.

ACKNOWLEDGMENTS

Without the marvelous Nicole-Anne Keyton at Beacon Press this book would not exist. Her generosity of time, clarity of thought, and tremendous wisdom helped to restore focus, structure, and a relevant angle to more than one draft. I owe her a debt of gratitude for her patience, vision, and enthusiasm over the past two years. Her exacting ethos reflects the care that Beacon Press brings to all its projects.

A special thanks to Molly Woodward for her precise eye and thoughtful assistance.

Over the years I have relied on Arthur Nersesian, Frances Levy, Joseph Silver, Tomasso Fiacchino, Henry Alcalay, Jeff Turboff, and Michael Avery for ongoing feedback. They are faithful readers and astute commenters. My equally talented friends—Lesley Alderman, Devon Kearney, Julie Erickson, Louisa Hackett—have provided a critical gaze when needed. Johanna Fernandez devoted significant time to read, comment, and question, and to remind me not to get lost in the weeds when so much is at stake in the world. Mischa Geracoulis shared her expertise in critical digital media literacy and also introduced me to the epic team at Project Censored. It's been a treat to make new friends with a shared interest in improving daily digital experiences for all.

Rounding out the support is my dear friend "Jim," an expert in data aggregation. He patiently slogged through an earlier draft, leaving dryly humorous comments throughout and sending me PDFs of *Wall Street Journal* articles. "Jim," an unabashed capitalist and devotee of Milton Friedman, requested anonymity. Despite our divergent political views, he has been eager to help his differently oriented friend since college.

I also thank Professor Andries (Andy) van Dam—the film *Toy Story*'s Andy is named in his honor—for the opportunity, years ago, to be part of his pioneering Hypertext educational experiment in the English and computer science departments at Brown University. The class taught poetry, in what van Dam likened to "creative graffiti" between professors and students. Decades later, he reflected, "I really believe that we built the world's first online scholarly community. It foreshadowed wikis, blogs, and communal documents of all kinds." That was the first time I used a computer, an IMLAC PDS-1D display console and minicomputer.

Those were the days when computers were seen as tools that could democratize access to information, empowering individuals and fostering greater transparency in governance. That era heralded the potential of technology to break down barriers, promote social equality, and enhance collective intelligence. Let's hope we can revive those ideals and use them to restore a nation where cyber citizens vanquish autocratic tendencies, allowing democracy to thrive.

NOTES

INTRODUCTION

1. "One Year Later: September 11 and the Internet," Pew Research Center, Sept. 5, 2002, https://www.pewresearch.org/internet/2002/09/05/one-year-later-september-11-and-the-internet/.

2. "One Year Later: September 11 and the Internet"; Alex Halavais, "Part 3. The Rise of Do-It-Yourself Journalism After September 11," Pew Research Center, Sept. 4, 2002, https://www.pewresearch.org/internet/2002/09/05/part-3-the-rise-of-do-it-yourself-journalism-after-september-11/#fn-97325-44.

3. Tim Berners-Lee with Mark Fischetti, *Weaving the Web: The Original Design and Ultimate Destiny of the World Wide Web* (New York: Harper Collins, 2000).

4. "Information Overload Is a Personal and Societal Danger," *Science Daily*, Rensselaer Polytechnic Institute, Mar. 14, 2024, https://www.sciencedaily.com/releases/2024/03/240314122208.htm.

5. Joel Supan, "Data Report: How Americans Use the Internet," allconnect.com, Mar. 15, 2023, https://www.allconnect.com/blog/data-report-how-americans-use-the-internet.

6. Paul Gilster, *Digital Literacy* (New York: John Wiley & Sons, 1998).

7. Timothy C. May, *Crypto Anarchist Manifesto*, 1988, available at https://perma.cc/7U4C-RMUB.

CHAPTER 1: FLUNKING CIVICS 101

1. Nicole Higgins DeSmet, "Vermont Named the Only State to Pass a U.S. History Civics Test," *Burlington Free Press*, Feb. 15, 2019, https://www.burlingtonfreepress.com/story/news/2019/02/15/vermont-named-only-state-u-s-pass-civics-test-exception-after-all/2868373002/.

2. National Center for Education Statistics, "Lower Average Civics Score for Eighth Graders Than in 2018," 2022, https://www.nationsreportcard.gov/civics/results/scores/.

3. "New Study Finds Alarming Lack of Civic Literacy Among Americans," US Chamber of Commerce Foundation, Feb. 12, 2024, https://www.uschamberfoundation.org/civics/new-study-finds-alarming-lack-of-civic-literacy-among-americans.

4. American Council of Trustees and Alumni, *A Crisis in Civics Education*, Jan.

2016, https://www.goacta.org/wp-content/uploads/ee/download/A_Crisis_in_Civic _Education.pdf.

5. Amanda Litvinov, "Forgotten Purpose: Civics Education in Public Schools," *NEA Today*, Mar. 16, 2017, https://www.nea.org/nea-today/all-news-articles/forgotten -purpose-civics-education-public-schools.

6. Elizabeth M. Ross, "Rebuilding Civic Education," Harvard Graduate School of Education, May 30, 2023, https://www.gse.harvard.edu/ideas/usable-knowledge/23/05 /rebuilding-civic-education.

7. "Test Preparation Market Size, Share, Growth, and Industry Analysis, by Type (University Exams, Certification Exams, High School Exams, and Elementary Exams), by Application (K–12, and Higher Education), Regional Insights, and Forecast from 2023 to 2030," *Business Research Insights*, Aug. 2023, https://www .businessresearchinsights.com/market-reports/test-preparation-market-107427.

8. Open Society Foundations, "Generational Shift: New Global Poll Reveals Large Minorities of Young People Lack Faith in Democracy to Deliver on Their Priorities," press release, Sept. 11, 2023, https://www.opensocietyfoundations.org/newsroom /generational-shift-new-global-poll-reveals-large-minorities-of-young-people-lack -faith-in-democracy-to-deliver-on-their-priorities.

9. Laura Silver and Janell Fetterolf, "Who Likes Authoritarianism and How Do They Want to Change Their Government?" Pew Research Center, Feb. 28, 2024, https:// www.pewresearch.org/short-reads/2024/02/28/who-likes-authoritarianism-and-how -do-they-want-to-change-their-government/.

10. Stephen Sawchuk, "Could Requiring Students to Take the Citizenship Test Do More Harm Than Good?" *Education Week*, Apr. 9, 2018, https://www.edweek.org /teaching-learning/could-requiring-students-to-take-the-citizenship-test-do-more -harm-than-good/2018/04.

11. "Joe Foss Institute Joins Center," Center for American Civics, press release, https://civics.asu.edu/JFI_Joins_CPTL, accessed Nov. 12, 2024.

12. *A Crisis in Education, A Report by the American Council of Trustees and Alumni*, January 2016, available at https://www.goacta.org/wp-content/uploads/ee/download /A_Crisis_in_Civic_Education.pdf.

13. Jilli Jung and Maithreyi Gopalan, "The Stubborn Unresponsiveness of Youth Voter Turnout to Civic Education: Quasi-Experimental Evidence from State-Mandated Civics Tests," Educational Evaluation and Policy Analysis (2023), https://doi.org/10.3102 /01623737231195887.

14. "Arizona Becomes First State to Require Students to Pass Civics Test," *NBC News*, Jan. 15, 2015, https://www.nbcnews.com/news/us-news/arizona-becomes-first -state-require-students-pass-civics-test-n287251.

15. Johanna Alonso, "Making Students 'Angry and Proud,'" *Inside Higher Ed*, Feb. 19, 2023, https://www.insidehighered.com/news/2023/02/20/new-civics-requirement-tests -arizonas-public-universities.

16. International Civic and Citizenship Education Study 2022, International Asso-

ciation for the Evaluation of Educational Achievement, https://www.iea.nl/studies/iea/iccs/2022.

17. Junior ROTC website, https://armyrotc.army.mil/jrotc/.

18. Junior ROTC website.

19. Mike Baker, Nichola Bogel-Burroughs, and Ilana Marcus, "Thousands of Teens Are Being Pushed into Military's Junior R.O.T.C.," *New York Times*, Dec. 11, 2022, https://www.nytimes.com/2022/12/11/us/jrotc-schools-mandatory-automatic-enrollment.html.

20. Author interview with Rick Jankhow, *Law and Disorder Radio*, May 29, 2023.

21. *Leadership and Training 1* (Pearson Custom Publishing, 2005). For more details, see 2020 *JROTC Textbook Review Report*, Project YANO, July 6, 2021, https://www.projectyano.org/pdf/2020_JROTC_Textbook_Review_2.pdf.

22. *Cultural Studies: An Introduction to Global Awareness* (Jones and Bartlett Publishers, 2010). For more details, see 2020 *JROTC Textbook Review Report*, Project YANO, July 6, 2021, https://www.projectyano.org/pdf/2020_JROTC_Textbook_Review_2.pdf.

23. *Leadership and Ethics Naval Science 4: Selected Readings for NJROTC Students* (no publisher or date listed; textbook in use in 2021). For more details, see 2020 *JROTC Textbook Review Report*, Project YANO, July 6, 2021, https://www.projectyano.org/pdf/2020_JROTC_Textbook_Review_2.pdf.

24. *Leadership and Ethics Naval Science 4.*

25. Cook v. Raimondo, Case 1:18-cv-00645-WES-PAS, Document 42, Filed Oct. 13, 2020.

26. GoLocalProv News Team, "Musah Sesay & Student Activists: 18 Who Made a Difference in 2018," GoLocalProv.com, Dec. 29, 2018.

27. Martha Minnow's amicus brief is available at http://www.cookvmckee.info/media/microsites/cook-v-raimondo/Amicus-Brief-Martha-Minow.pdf.

28. *San Antonio Independent School District v. Rodriguez*, 411 U.S. 1 (1973).

29. Yvonne Lau, "Finland's 'Visionary' Fight Against Disinformation Teaches Citizens to Questions What They See Online," *Canada's National Observer*, May 16, 2023, https://www.nationalobserver.com/2023/05/16/news/finland-visionary-fight-disinformation-teaches-citizens-question-online.

30. Patricia Lamiell, "Rhode Island Lawsuit, Filed by the Center for Educational Equity at TC, Ends with Agreement to Improve Civic Education," Teachers College, Columbia University, June 10, 2022, https://www.tc.columbia.edu/articles/2022/june/rhode-island-lawsuit-ends-with-agreement-to-improve-civics-education/.

31. Jon Henley, "How Finland Starts Its Fight Against Fake News in Primary Schools," *The Guardian*, Jan. 29, 2020, https://www.theguardian.com/world/2020/jan/28/fact-from-fiction-finlands-new-lessons-in-combating-fake-news.

32. Henley, "How Finland Starts Its Fight Against Fake News in Primary Schools."

33. Rosalind KennyBirch, "How Finland Shuts Down Fake News," Apolitical, Dec. 3, 2019, https://apolitical.co/solution-articles/en/how-finland-shuts-down-fake-news.

34. Henley, "How Finland Starts Its Fight Against Fake News in Primary Schools."

35. Henley, "How Finland Starts Its Fight Against Fake News in Primary Schools."

CHAPTER 2: FAILING DIGITAL LITERACY

1. Matthew Mettler and Jeffery Mondak, "Fact-Opinion Differentiation," *Harvard Kennedy School (HKS) Misinformation Review* 5, no. 2 (2024).

2. Jennifer Kavanagh and Michael D. Rich, "Truth Decay: An Initial Exploration of the Diminishing Role of Facts and Analysis in American Public Life," RAND Corporation 2014, https://www.rand.org/content/dam/rand/pubs/research_reports/RR2300 /RR2314/.

3. Kellyanne Conway, interview with Chuck Todd, *Meet the Press*, Jan. 22, 2017, https://www.nbcnews.com/meet-the-press/meet-press-01-22-17-n710491.

4. American Library Association, "Digital Literacy," https://literacy.ala.org/digital -literacy/, accessed Oct. 8, 2024.

5. "Internet, Social Media Use and Device Ownership in U.S. Have Plateaued After Years of Growth," Pew Research Center, Sept. 28, 2018, https://www.pewresearch.org /short-reads/2018/09/28/internet-social-media-use-and-device-ownership-in-u-s-have -plateaued-after-years-of-growth/.

6. US Department of Education, National Center for Education Statistics, Highlights of the 2017 U.S. PIAAC Results Web Report (NCES 2020-777) and PIAAC International Highlights Web Report (NCES 2020-127), 2019, https://nces.ed.gov/fastfacts /display.asp?id=683&utm_source=chatgpt.com.

7. Lauren Frias, "A Pro-Trump Youth Activist Group Paid Teenagers to Push Conservative Talking Points on Social Media, Including Misleading Claims and Disinformation," *Business Insider*, Sept. 16, 2020, https://www.businessinsider.com/turning -point-action-conservative-talking-points-social-media-report2020–9.

8. Desmond Butler, Stephen Braun, and Ryan Nakashima, "How to Disrupt an Election: Fake IDS, Fraud and Facebook," Associated Press, Feb. 17, 2018.

9. Charles M. Blow, "Attacking the 'Woke' Black Vote," editorial, *New York Times*, Feb. 18, 2018, https://www.nytimes.com/2018/02/18/opinion/black-vote-russia.html.

10. William J. Bray, Killian McLoughlin, Tuan N. Doan, and Molly J. Crockett, "How Social Learning Amplifies Moral Outrage Expression in Online Social Networks," *Science Advances* 7, no. 33 (Aug. 13, 2021), https://www.science.org/doi/10.1126 /sciadv.abe5641.

11. Mike Isaac and Daisuke Wakabayashi, "Russian Influence Reached 126 Million Through Facebook Alone," *New York Times*, Oct. 30, 2017, https://www.nytimes.com /2017/10/30/technology/facebook-google-russia.html.

12. Mike Gooding, "Jan. 6 Capitol Riot: Law Enforcement Didn't Share Critical Information, Report Says," *13 News Now*, July 25, 2023, https://www.13newsnow.com /article/news/crime/cost-of-capitol-riot-january-6/291–6fb5117e-dea1–4631-a76a -76e87b268bfd.

13. "Conspiracy Theory Claims Parkland Survivor a 'Crisis Actor,'" *NBC Nightly News*, Feb. 21, 2018, available at https://www.youtube.com/watch?v=RvKGmzEt4hM.

14. Southern Poverty Law Center, "Alex Jones," https://www.splcenter.org/fighting -hate/extremist-files/individual/alex-jones, accessed Oct. 8, 2024.

15. Katie Malafronte, "NRA Official Reached Out to Sandy Hook Truther About Parkland Shooting," *Campus Safety*, Mar. 29, 2019, https://www.campussafetymagazine .com/safety/nra-official-question-parkland-shooting/.

16. "Twitter, YouTube and Facebook Removed 'Abhorrent' Content and Threats," *ABC News*, Feb. 21, 2018, https://abcnews.go.com/Politics/social-media-blocks-abuse -parkland-shooting-survivors-online/story?id=53250460.

17. Olivia Sidoti and Jeffrey Gottfried, "About 1 in 5 U.S. Teens Who've Heard of ChatGPT Have Used It for Schoolwork," Pew Research, Nov. 16, 2023, https://www .pewresearch.org/short-reads/2023/11/16/about-1-in-5-us-teens-whove-heard-of -chatgpt-have-used-it-for-schoolwork/.

18. "What Are AI Hallucinations?" IBM, https://www.ibm.com/topics/ai -hallucinations, accessed Oct. 8, 2024.

19. Ian Sample, "What Are Deepfakes—and How Can You Spot Them?" *The Guard-ian*, Jan. 13, 2020, https://www.theguardian.com/technology/2020/jan/13/what-are -deepfakes-and-how-can-you-spot-them.

20. Jared Gans, "FBI Warns of 'Deepfakes' in Sextortion Schemes," The Hill, June 6, 2023, https://thehill.com/policy/cybersecurity/4037204-fbi-warns-of-deepfakes-in -sextortion-schemes/.

21. H.R. 5586—118th Congress (2023–24), https://www.congress.gov/bill/118th -congress/house-bill/5586/text.

22. Society of Professional Journalists, Code of Ethics, revised Sept. 6, 2014, https:// www.spj.org/ethicscode.asp.

23. Sara Fischer, "'Unreliable' News Sources Got More Traction in 2020," *Axios*, Dec. 22, 2020, https://www.axios.com/2020/12/22/unreliable-news-sources-social -media-engagement.

24. Newsguard's advisory board available at https://www.newsguardtech.com/our -advisory-board/.

25. Accesswire, "Consortium News Sues Canadian TV Network for Defamation over Report CN Was 'Directed' by Russia," Oct. 13, 2020, available at https://finance .yahoo.com/news/consortium-news-sues-canadian-tv-234000618.html?fr=sycsrp _catchall&guccounter=1.

26. Small Business: Instruments and Casualties of the Censorship-Industrial Com-plex, The House Committee on Small Business Interim Staff Report 2024, referencing an email from Gordon Crovitz, NewsGuard, Co-CEO, to Matt Taibbi, RacketNews, Investigative Journalist (Mar. 10, 2023), https://smallbusiness.house.gov/uploadedfiles /house_committee_on_small_business_-_cic_report_september_2024.pdf.

27. Amended Complaint, Consortium for Independent Journalism, Inc. v. The

United States of America and Newsguard Technologies, Docket No: 23-cv-07088, filed Oct. 23, 2023.

28. "Press Advisory: Surgeon General Issues New Advisory About Effects Social Media Use Has on Youth Mental Health," US Department of Health and Human Services, May 23, 2023, https://www.hhs.gov/about/news/2023/05/23/surgeon-general -issues-new-advisory-about-effects-social-media-use-has-youth-mental-health.html.

29. Lory Hough, "Truce Be Told," Harvard Graduate School of Education, *Ed Magazine*, Sept. 9, 2011, https://www.gse.harvard.edu/ideas/ed-magazine/11/09/truce -be-told.

CHAPTER 3: BAD DIGITAL HYGIENE

1. Jack Evans, "Someone Tried to Poison Oldsmar's Water Supply During Hack, Sheriff Says," *Tampa Bay Times*, Feb. 9, 2021, https://www.tampabay.com/news/pinellas /2021/02/08/someone-tried-to-poison-oldsmars-water-supply-during-hack-sheriff -says/.

2. About Team Viewer: "A Global Leader in Innovative Remote Connectivity and Support Solutions," https://www.teamviewer.com/en-us/global/company/about -teamviewer/, accessed Jan. 24, 2025.

3. "Compromise of U.S. Water Treatment Facility," Joint Cybersecurity Advisory, Feb. 11, 2021, https://www.cisa.gov/sites/default/files/2023-04/AA21-042A_Joint _Cybersecurity_Advisory_Cyber_Actors_Compromise_U.S._Water_Treatment _Facility.pdf.

4. Peter Chawaga, "Former Official Claims Oldsmar Drinking Water Hack Was Really Operator Error," Wateronline.com, Mar. 29, 2023, https://www.wateronline.com /doc/former-official-claims-oldsmar-drinking-water-hack-was-really-operator-error -0001.

5. "Psychology of Human Error Could Help Businesses Prevent Security Breaches," *Ciso Mag*, Sept. 12, 2020, https://cisomag.com/psychology-of-human-error-could-help -businesses-prevent-security-breaches/.

6. IBM, *Half of Breached Organizations Unwilling to Increase Security Spend Despite Soaring Breach Costs*, July 24, 2023, https://newsroom.ibm.com/2023-07-24-IBM -Report-Half-of-Breached-Organizations-Unwilling-to-Increase-Security-Spend -Despite-Soaring-Breach-Costs.

7. Christopher Krebs, "How to Stop Handing Our Cybersecurity Keys to Hackers," *The Hill*, Feb. 10, 2021.

8. US Government Accountability Office, "Critical Infrastructure: Actions Needed to Better Secure Internet-Connected Devices," GAO-23–105337, Dec. 1, 2022, https:// www.gao.gov/products/gao-23-105327.

9. Cybersecurity and Infrastructure Security Agency, "Critical Infrastructure Sectors," https://www.cisa.gov/topics/critical-infrastructure-security-and-resilience /critical-infrastructure-sectors, accessed Oct. 8, 2024.

10. US Department of Justice, Office of Justice Programs, "In 2021, 1 in 10 Persons Had Been Victims of Identity Theft in the Past 12 Months," press release, Oct. 12, 2023, bjs.ojp.gov//document/vit21_pr.pdf.

11. Federal Trade Commission, "New Data Shows FTC Received 2.8 Million Fraud Reports from Consumers in 2021," press release, Feb. 22, 2022, https://www.ftc.gov /news-events/news/press-releases/2022/02/new-data-shows-ftc-received-28-million -fraud-reports-consumers-2021–0.

12. Brian Roche, "Remote Access Scams Are Costing Victims Thousands of Dollars," WGAL (Lancaster, PA), Apr. 29, 2022, https://www.wgal.com/article/remote -access-scams-are-costing-victims-thousands-of-dollars/39853236.

13. FBI, "Internet Crime Complaint Center Releases 2022 Statistics," Mar. 22, 2023, https://www.fbi.gov/contact-us/field-offices/springfield/news/internet-crime -complaint-center-releases-2022-statistics.

14. Lana Harris, "Woman Shares Warning After Being the Target of Romance Scammers," WCNC, Feb. 14, 2022, https://www.wcnc.com/article/money/warnings -signs-online-romance-scam/275-778d9ddc-789d-4ef0-8e59-43c6be33d78c.

15. Harris, "Woman Shares Warning After Being the Target of Romance Scammers."

16. Federal Bureau of Investigation, Internet Crime Complaint Center (IC3), https://www.ic3.gov/, accessed Oct. 8, 2024.

17. Emma Fletcher, "Social Media: A Golden Goose for Scammers," Federal Trade Commission, Oct. 6, 2023, https://www.ftc.gov/news-events/data-visualizations/data -spotlight/2023/10/social-media-golden-goose-scammers.

18. Anne D'Innocenzio and Haleluya Hadero, "Small Businesses Grapple with Global Tech Outages Created by CrowdStrike," Associated Press, July 21, 2024, https:// apnews.com/article/microsoft-crowdstrike-small-businesses-ad1e4f964d1560d50d085 64cce9513d7.

19. The White House, *Back to the Building Blocks: A Path Toward Secure and Measurable Software*, Feb. 2024.

20. *Cost of a Data Breach Report 2024*, IBM, https://www.ibm.com/reports/data -breach.

21. IBM, *Escalating Data Breach Disruption Pushes Costs to New Highs*, July 30, 2024, https://newsroom.ibm.com/2024-07-30-ibm-report-escalating-data-breach -disruption-pushes-costs-to-new-highs#.

22. Keman Huang, Xiaoqing Wang, William Wei, and Stuart Madnick, "The Devastating Business Impacts of a Cyber Breach," *Harvard Business Review*, May 4, 2023, https://hbr.org/2023/05/the-devastating-business-impacts-of-a-cyber-breach.

23. Tara Siegel Bernard, Tiffany Hsu, Nicole Pertroth, and Ron Lieber, "Equifax Says Cyberattack May Have Affected 143 Million in the U.S.," *New York Times*, Sept. 7, 2017, https://www.nytimes.com/2017/09/07/business/equifax-cyberattack.html.

24. Garrett M. Graf, "China's Hacking Spree Will Have a Decades' Long Fallout," *Wired*, Feb. 11, 2020, https://www.wired.com/story/china-equifax-anthem-marriott -opm-hacks-data/.

25. Department of Homeland Security, "Privacy Incident Involving DHS Office of Inspector General Case Management System (Update)," press release, Jan. 18, 2018, original release date, Jan. 3, 2018, https://www.dhs.gov/archive/news/2018/01/18/privacy-incident-involving-dhs-oig-case-management-system-update.

26. Noah Shachtman, "Communication with 50 Nuke Missiles Dropped in ICBM Snafu," *Wired*, Oct. 26, 2010, https://www.wired.com/2010/10/communications-dropped-to-50-nuke-missiles-in-icbm-snafu/.

27. *Task Force Report: Resilient Military Systems and the Advanced Cyber Threat*, Department of Defense, Defense Science Board, Jan. 2013, https://nsarchive2.gwu.edu/NSAEBB/NSAEBB424/docs/Cyber-081.pdf.

28. "Inside America's Missile Fields," *60 Minutes*, Apr. 25, 2014.

29. Brian Naylor, "U.S. Chief Information Officer Seeks to Upgrade Government's Computers," *All Things Considered*, NPR, Oct. 31, 2016.

30. Ricardo Alonso-Zaldivar, Associated Press, "Government Wastes Billions of Dollars on Old Computers, Report Says," *NewsHour*, PBS, May 25, 2016, https://www.pbs.org/newshour/nation/government-wastes-billions-of-dollars-on-old-computers-report-says.

31. Alonso-Zaldivar, Associated Press, "Government Wastes Billions of Dollars on Old Computers."

32. *Information Technology: Additional Actions and Oversight Urgently Needed to Reduce Waste and Improve Performance in Acquisitions and Operations*, Testimony Before the Subcommittee on Government Operations and Information Technology, Committee on Oversight and Government Reform, House of Representatives, US Government Accountability Office (statement of David A. Powner, director of Information Technology Management Issues), https://oversight.house.gov/wp-content/uploads/2015/06/Powner-GAO-Statement-6-10-FITARA.pdf.

33. *Information Technology: Additional Actions and Oversight Urgently Needed.*

34. London Homer-Wambeam, "F. E. Warren Air Force Base to Modernize ICBM Systems," Wyoming Public Radio, Sept. 13, 2018, https://www.wyomingpublicmedia.org/business/2018-09-13/f-e-warren-air-force-base-to-modernize-icbm-systems; Airman 1st Class Sarah Post, "Minuteman III Modernization Effort Kicks Off at F. E. Warren," 90th Missile Wing Public Affairs, Dec. 6, 2022, https://www.warren.af.mil/News/Article/3237273/minuteman-iii-modernization-effort-kicks-off-at-fe-warren/.

35. Roger Cressey, "Legacy IT Companies Continue to Put the Government at Risk," *Government Technology Insider*, Sept. 27, 2023, https://governmenttechnologyinsider.com/legacy-it-companies-continue-to-put-the-government-at-risk/.

36. Molly Weisner, "Data Breaches Led by USPS, OPM, Cost Governments $26 Billion," *Federal Times*, Dec. 20, 2022, https://tinyurl.com/FederalTimesDataBreaches.

37. Computer and Communications Industry Association, "New Study Shows Microsoft Holds 85% Market Share in U.S. Public Sector Productivity Software," Sept. 21, 2021, https://ccianet.org/news/2021/09/new-study-shows-microsoft-holds-85-market-share-in-u-s-public-sector-productivity-software/.

38. America's Cyber Defense Agency, *Known Exploited Vulnerabilities Catalog*, Critical Infrastructure Security and Resilience, updated June 25, 2024, https://www.cisa.gov/known-exploited-vulnerabilities-catalog.

39. Michael Garland, *Vendor-Lock: And Lack of Competition in the Government's Software Estate*, data through 2022, Net Choice, https://netchoice.org/wp-content/uploads/2023/01/NetChoice_Garland_The-Pernicious-Consequences-of-Vendor-Lock.pdf.

40. Cressey, "Legacy IT Companies Continue to Put the Government at Risk."

41. Ron Wyden to Jen Easterly, director CISA; Attorney General Merrick Garland; and Lina Khan, chair FTC, July 27, 2023, https://www.wyden.senate.gov/imo/media/doc/wyden_letter_to_cisa_doj_ftc_re_2023_microsoft_breach.pdf; Cressey, "Legacy IT Companies Continue to Put the Government at Risk."

42. Marybeth Gasman, "How a Cyberattack Led to Innovation at Stillman College," Forbes, Nov. 3, 2023, https://www.forbes.com/sites/marybethgasman/2023/11/03/how-a-cyberattack-led-to-innovation-at-stillman-college/.

43. "Number of K-12 Students," IBISWorld, May 9, 2024, https://www.ibisworld.com/us/bed/number-of-k-12-students/4251/.

44. Ash-har Quraishi, Ari Sen, Scott Pham, Amy Corral, Taylor Johnston, "Ransomware: Attacks on Schools Threaten Student Data Nationwide," CBS News, Aug. 26, 2024, https://www.cbsnews.com/news/school-ransomware-attacks-threaten-student-data/.

45. Ilya Smith and John F. Howard, "Cyberthreats and K-12: EdTech Third Party Risk Management Checklist," Clark Hill, June 27, 2023, https://www.clarkhill.com/news-events/news/cyberthreats-and-k-12-edtech-third-party-risk-management-checklist/.

46. Heidi Boghosian, "Op-Ed: The Cyberattack on Los Angeles Schools Could Happen Anywhere," *Los Angeles Times*, Oct. 11, 2022, https://www.latimes.com/opinion/story/2022-10-11/cybersecurity-ransomware-schools-los-angeles.

47. *Evaluating Information: The Cornerstone of Civic Online Reasoning*, Stanford History Education Group, Nov. 22, 2016, https://stacks.stanford.edu/file/druid:fv751yt5934/SHEG%20Evaluating%20Information%20Online.pdf.

CHAPTER 4: MEET MEGA THINK TANKS

1. Charles L. Heatherly, ed., *Mandate for Leadership: Policy Management in a Conservative Administration* (The Heritage Society, Jan. 1, 1981).

2. Jason Stahl, *Conservatives in a Marketplace of Ideas: Think Tanks, Interests, and Expertise in the 1970s* (Washington, DC: Library of Congress, 2009), video available at https://loc.gov/item/2021688286.

3. Eugene F. Smith, "The Influence of Conservative Think Tanks: 1970s Capitalism and the Rise of Conservative Think Tanks," master's thesis, Graduate School Newark Rutgers, State University of New Jersey, May 2014.

4. Larry Luxner, "DC-Based Organizations Dominate 2020 List of World's Top

Think Tanks," *Washington Diplomat*, Feb. 5, 2021, https://washdiplomat.com/dc-based -organizations-dominate-2020-list-of-worlds-top-think-tanks/.

5. Tom Flynn, "What's Wrong with Megachurches?" op-ed, *Secular Humanism* 26, no. 5 (Aug./Sept. 2006), https://secularhumanism.org/2006/08/whats-wrong-with -megachurches/.

6. Scott Newman, "Megachurches Are Getting Even Bigger as Churches Close Across the Country," NPR, July 14, 2023, https://www.npr.org/2023/07/14/1187460517 /megachurches-growing-liquid-church.

7. Carrie Levine, "New Tax Documents Show Crossroads GPS Poured Millions into 2014 Senate Race: Group Supplied Nearly All Funds to North Carolina 'Dark Money' Group," Center for Public Integrity, Nov. 17, 2015, https://publicintegrity.org/politics /new-tax-documents-show-crossroads-gps-poured-millions-into-2014-senate-race/.

8. Jing Zhao and Xufeng Zhu, "Spreading Expertise: Think Tanks as Digital Advocators in the Social Media Era," *Policy and Society* 42, no. 3 (Sept. 8, 2023): 359–77, https://doi.org/10.1093/polsoc/puad025.

9. Chris Welch and Sara Ganim, "White Supremacist Richard Spencer: 'We Reached Tens of Millions of People' with Video," CNN, Dec. 6, 2016, https://www.cnn .com/2016/12/06/politics/richard-spencer-interview-texas-am-speech/index.html.

10. Bill Morlin, "White Supremacist Group Loses Tax Exempt Status," Southern Poverty Law Center, Mar. 15, 2017, https://www.splcenter.org/hatewatch/2017/03/15 /white-nationalist-group-loses-tax-exempt-status.

11. Barry Bowen, "Churches Have Little to Fear from the IRS: Scare Tactics Don't Match the Reality: List of 2023 Disciplinary Actions," Trinity Foundation, Dec. 20, 2023, https://trinityfi.org/investigations/churches-have-little-to-fear-from-the-irs-scare -tactics-dont-match-the-reality-list-of-2023-disciplinary-actions/.

12. Reposted on Republican Accountability (@AccountableGOP), X, Feb. 22, 2024, https://x.com/AccountableGOP/status/1760761957437599856.

13. Katherine Stewart, "The Claremont Institute: The Anti-Democracy Think Tank," *New Republic*, Aug. 10, 2023, https://newrepublic.com/article/174656/claremont -institute-think-tank-trump.

14. Cameron Joseph, "Meet the Obscure Think Tank Powering Trump's Biggest Lies," *Vice*, Nov. 4, 2021, https://www.vice.com/en/article/qjb4y3/john-eastman -claremont-institute-supporting-jan-6-trumpism.

15. Elisabeth Zerofsky, "How the Claremont Institute Became a Nerve Center of the American Right," *New York Times*, Aug. 3, 2022, https://www.nytimes.com/2022/08/03 /magazine/claremont-institute-conservative.html.

16. Maggie Astor, "Trump Declines to Back Away From 'You Don't Have to Vote Again' Line," *New York Times*, July 30, 2024, https://www.nytimes.com/2024/07/30/us /politics/trump-christians-vote-ingraham.html.

17. Alejandro Antonio Chafuen, "The 2023 Ranking of Free-Market Think Tanks and Organizations Measured by Social Media Impact," *Forbes*, https://www.forbes.com

/sites/alejandrochafuen/2023/06/07/the-2023-ranking-of-free-market-think-tanks-and
-organizations-measured-by-social-media-impact/.

18. Chafuen, "The 2023 Ranking of Free-Market Think Tanks and Organizations
Measured by Social Media Impact."

19. Kyle Spencer, *Raising Them Right: The Untold Story of America's Ultraconservative Youth Movement and Its Plot for Power* (New York: Harper Collins, 2022), 200.

20. Emma Grey Ellis, "Fake Think Tanks Fuel Fake News—and the President's
Tweets," *Wired*, Jan. 24, 2017, https://www.wired.com/2017/01/fake-think-tanks-fuel
-fake-news-presidents-tweets/.

21. Southern Poverty Law Center, "SPLC Designated Hate Group: American
Renaissance," https://www.splcenter.org/fighting-hate/extremist-files/group/american
-renaissance, accessed Oct. 8, 2024.

22. "The Press: The Hot Middle," *Time*, May 16, 1955, https://content.time.com/time
/subscriber/article/0,33009,866355,00.html.

23. Earl P. Holt III, "Monkeys and Typewriters," reposted by Council of Conservative Citizens, "Conservative Headlines," Feb. 19, 2024, https://conservative-headlines
.org/monkeys-typewriters/.

24. Amanda Seitz (Associated Press), "White Supremacists Are Riling Up Thousands on Social Media," PBS, June 10, 2022, https://www.pbs.org/newshour/politics
/white-supremacists-are-riling-up-thousands-on-social-media; Kaya Yurieff,
"YouTube Removes Richard Spencer and David Duke a Year After Saying It Would Ban
Supremacists," CNN Business, June 29, 2020, https://www.cnn.com/2020/06/29/tech
/white-supremacists-youtube/index.html.

25. "Protecting Civil Rights," Atlas Network, https://www.atlasnetwork.org/stories
/topic/protecting-civil-rights.

26. Atlas Network, "Freedom Worldwide with Tom G. Palmer: Helping Americans
Free Themselves from Welfare," June 28, 2024, available at https://www.youtube.com
/watch?v=NMwphvgOhtg.

27. Dominic Renfrey, interview with *Law and Disorder Radio*, Dec. 16, 2019.

28. Robert G. Kaiser and Ira Chinoy, "Scaife: Funding Father of the Right," *Washington Post*, May 2, 1999, https://www.washingtonpost.com/wp-srv/politics/special
/clinton/stories/scaifemain050299.htm.

29. Robert G. Kaiser and Ira Chinoy, "Scaife: Funding Father of the Right," *Washington Post*, May 2, 1999.

30. James D'Angelo and Brent Ranalli, "The Dark Side of Sunlight," *Foreign Affairs*
(May/June 2019).

31. American Legislative Exchange Council (ALEC), "Join Us," membership application, https://alec.org/wp-content/uploads/2015/12/ALEC-Membership-Brochure
-1.pdf, accessed Oct. 8, 2024.

32. Yvonne Wingett Sanchez and Rob O'Dell, "What Is ALEC? 'The Most Effective
Organization' for Conservatives, Says Newt Gingrich," *USA Today*, Apr. 3, 2019, https://

www.usatoday.com/story/news/investigations/2019/04/03/alec-american-legislative
-exchange-council-model-bills-republican-conservative-devos-gingrich/3162357002/.

33. "Stand Your Ground Laws: 50-State Survey," Justia, https://www.justia.com
/criminal/defenses/stand-your-ground-laws-50-state-survey/; "US Protest Law
Tracker," ICNL, https://www.icnl.org/usprotestlawtracker/?location=&status=enacted
&issue=&date=&type=legislative#.

34. Tim Marcin, "Republican Politician's 'Biblical Basis for War' Called for Killing All Non-Christian Men Who Don't 'Yield,'" *Newsweek*, Nov. 1, 2018, https://
www.newsweek.com/republican-politicians-biblical-basis-war-kill-non-christians
-washington-1197703

35. Jason Wilson, "Revealed: Republican Lawmaker Aided Group Training Young
Men for 'Biblical Warfare,'" *The Guardian*, Aug. 14, 2019, https://www.theguardian.com
/world/2019/aug/13/matt-shea-biblical-war-washington-team-rugged.

36. Alex Kotch, "Leading Free Market Policy Network Enabling Anti-LGBTQ
Hate," Southern Poverty Law Center, Dec. 7, 2021, https://www.splcenter.org/hatewatch
/2021/12/07/leading-free-market-policy-network-enabling-anti-lgbtq-hate.

37. Plessy v. Ferguson, 163 U.S. 537, 550 (1896).

38. Center for Constitutional Rights, *ALEC Attacks*, 2019, https://www.alecattacks
.org/.

39. State Policy Network, *SPN News*, May 8, 2006.

40. State Policy Network FAQS, https://spn.org/spn-faqs/, accessed Nov. 12, 2024.

41. Janus v. American Federation of State, County, and Municipal Employees,
Council 31, No. 16-1466, 585 U.S. ___ (2018), abbreviated *Janus v. AFSCME*.

CHAPTER 5: HATE MIGRATES ONLINE

1. Nick Statt, "Amazon Pulls White Supremacist Novel *The Turner Diaries* Alongside Qanon Purge," *The Verge*, Jan. 12, 2021, https://www.theverge.com/2021/1/12
/22227049/amazon-the-turner-diaries-q-anon-purge-removal-capitol-attack.

2. William Luther Pierce (writing as Andrew Macdonald), *The Turner Diaries*
(Hillsboro, WV: National Vanguard Press, 1978).

3. Booksellers Alibris and Thriftbooks had copies available for sale as of August
2024, and the San Diego Public Library and the Carnegie Library of Pittsburgh had
copies available for borrowing.

4. Jean Raspail, *The Camp of the Saints*, 4th American ed. (Social Contract Press,
1987); "The Camp of the Saints," *Kirkus Reviews*, July 28, 2015; Alexandra Alter, "How
'The Turner Diaries' Incites White Supremacists," *New York Times*, Jan. 12, 2021, https://
www.nytimes.com/2021/01/12/books/turner-diaries-white-supremacists.html.

5. Alter, "How 'The Turner Diaries' Incites White Supremacists."

6. J. M. Berger, "The Turner Legacy: The Storied Origins and Enduring Impact of
White Nationalism's Bible," International Centre for Counter Terrorism, The Hague,

7, no. 8 (2016), https://www.icct.nl/sites/default/files/import/publication/ICCT-Berger
-The-Turner-Legacy-September2016-2.pdf.

7. Berger, "The Turner Legacy."

8. "Staten Island Man Arrested in Connection with Threats to Kill Protesters, Politicians and Members of Law Enforcement," press release, US Attorney's Office, Eastern
District of New York, Nov. 10, 2020, https://www.justice.gov/usao-edny/pr/staten
-island-man-arrested-connection-threats-kill-protesters-politicians-and-members.

9. Associated Press, "Supremacists Hope for Boost from Obama Win," NBC News,
Aug. 8, 2008, https://www.nbcnews.com/id/wbna26087413.

10. "The Truth About Christian Nationalism," Evangelicals for Democracy, https://
www.evangelicalsfordemocracy.org/issues/blog-post-title-two-ek6ws.

11. The landmark cases are Dobbs v. Jackson Women's Health Organization, 597 U.S.
215 (2022); Roe v. Wade, 410 U.S. 113 (1973); Caron v. Makin, 596 U.S. 767 (2022); and
West Virginia v. Environmental Protection Agency, 597 U.S. 697.

12. Brian Fishman, "Dual-Use Regulation: Managing Hate and Terrorism Online
Before and After Section 230 Reform," *Brookings*, Mar. 14, 2023, https://www.brookings
.edu/articles/dual-use-regulation-managing-hate-and-terrorism-online-before-and
-after-section-230-reform/.

13. Pete Simi and Robert Futrell, *American Swastika: Inside the White Power Movement's Hidden Spaces of Hate* (Rowman & Littlefield, 2010).

14. Christina Schori Liang, "Far-Right Contagion: The Global Challenge of
Transnational Extremist Networks," in *Handbook of Security Science*, ed. A. J. Masys
(Springer, 2022), https://doi.org/10.1007/978-3-319-91875-4_81.

15. "The Changing Threat Landscape of Terrorism and Violent Extremism: Implications for Research and Policy," video, National Institute of Justice, Jan. 18, 2022, https://
nij.ojp.gov/media/video/27866#o-od.

16. Dennis Arp, "Testimony of Chapman Sociologist Pete Simi Leads to Judgment
Against Organizers of Charlottesville Rally," *Chapman University*, Jan. 25, 2022.

17. Andrew Marantz, "Inside the Daily Stormer's Style Guide," *New Yorker*, Jan. 8,
2018, https://www.newyorker.com/magazine/2018/01/15/inside-the-daily-stormers
-style-guide.

18. Marantz, "Inside the Daily Stormer's Style Guide."

19. "Leaders of Transnational Terrorist Group Charged with Soliciting the Murder
of Federal Officials, and Conspiring to Provide Material Support to Terrorists," press
release, US Department of Justice, Sept. 9, 2024, https://www.justice.gov/opa/pr/leaders
-transnational-terrorist-group-charged-soliciting-hate-crimes-soliciting-murder.

20. Morgan Meaker, "'Hate Is Way More Interesting Than That': Why Algorithms
Can't Stop Toxic Speech Online," *Pacific Standard*, Feb. 28, 2019, https://psmag.com
/ideas/neo-nazi-hate-speech-foiling-algorithms.

21. Written Testimony of Heidi L. Beirich, cofounder/executive vice president,
Global Project Against Hate and Extremism, Before the Congress of the United States
House of Representatives Committee on Homeland Security, Intelligence and Coun-

terterrorism Subcommittee, Regarding "Assessing the Threat from Accelerationists and Far-Right Militia Extremists," July 16, 2020, https://democrats-homeland.house.gov/imo/media/doc/Testimony%20-%20Beirich.pdf.

22. Christina Schori Liang and Matthew John Cross, "White Crusade: How to Prevent Right-Wing Extremists from Exploiting the Internet," Geneva Centre for Security Policy, *Strategic Security Analyses* 11 (July 10, 2020).

23. "Pepe the Frog," ADL, https://www.adl.org/resources/hate-symbol/pepe-frog, accessed Oct. 8, 2024.

24. Liang and Cross, "White Crusade."

25. Eli Saslow, "The White Flight of Derek Black," *Washington Post*, Oct. 15, 2016, https://www.washingtonpost.com/national/the-white-flight-of-derek-black/2016/10/15/ed5f906a-8f3b-11e6-a6a3-d50061aa9fae_story.html.

26. Terry Gross, "How Twitter Helped Change the Mind of a Westboro Baptist Church Member," *Fresh Air*, NPR, Oct. 10, 2019, https://www.npr.org/2019/10/10/768894901/how-twitter-helped-change-the-mind-of-a-westboro-baptist-church-member.

27. "The Awakening of a Former White Nationalist," *Fresh Air*, NPR, Sept. 24, 2018, https://www.npr.org/2018/09/24/651172700/the-awakening-of-a-former-white-nationalist.

28. US Department of Homeland Security, *Reference Aid: US Violent White Supremacist Extremists*, Sept. 2017, https://www.dhs.gov/sites/default/files/publications/US%20White%20Supremacist%20Extremists_CVE%20Task%20Force_Final.pdf.

29. American Progress, "Christian Nationalism Is 'Single Biggest Threat' to America's Religious Freedom," Apr. 13, 2022, https://www.americanprogress.org/article/christian-nationalism-is-single-biggest-threat-to-americas-religious-freedom/.

30. German Lopez, "Survey: White Evangelicals Think Christians Face More Discrimination Than Muslims," *Vox*, Mar. 10, 2017, https://www.vox.com/identities/2017/3/10/14881446/prri-survey-muslims-christians-discrimination.

31. "Wild Video Claims God Made Trump," YouTube @TheProjectTV, Jan. 8, 2024, https://www.youtube.com/watch?v=zttm3HcPQdo.

32. Miles T. Armaly, David T. Buckley, and Adam M. Enders, "Christian Nationalism and Political Violence: Victimhood, Racial Identity, Conspiracy, and Support for the Capitol Attacks," *Political Behavior* 44, no. 2 (2022): 937–60, https://www.ncbi.nlm.nih.gov/pmc/articles/PMC8724742/.

33. Gillian Brockell, "The Father of 'Great Replacement:' An Ex-Socialist French Writer," *Washington Post*, May 17, 2022, https://www.washingtonpost.com/history/2022/05/17/renaud-camus-great-replacement-history/.

34. "Hate Is No Game: Hate and Harassment in Online Games 2020," ADL/Center for Technology and Society, Dec. 2022, https://www.adl.org/sites/default/files/documents/2022-12/Hate-and-Harassment-in-Online-Games-120622-v2.pdf.

35. Dan Hall, "Mind Games: Inside the Call of Duty Games Hosted by British Far-Right Group to 'Recruit Young People' into Twisted White Nationalism," *The Sun*,

Feb. 16, 2021, https://www.thesun.co.uk/news/13986628/call-duty-warzone-far-right
-patriotic-alternative-mark-collett/.

36. Senator Margaret Wood Hassan to Gabe Newell, Dec. 15, 2022, https://www
.hassan.senate.gov/imo/media/doc/senators_hassan_calls_on_largest_gaming
_company_to_address_onliine_extremism.pdf.

37. Steam Online Conduct, store.steampowered.com/online_conduct, accessed
Nov. 12, 2024.

38. "Primed to Kill: Video Games Are Simulating Real-World Terror Tactics," Kids-
onlineworld, 2023, https://www.kidsonlineworld.com/primed-to-kill---article.html.

39. UN Office of Counter-Terrorism, Expert Roundtable Event on Video Games
and Violent Extremism, Dec. 6, 2021, https://www.un.org/counterterrorism/events
/expert-roundtable-event-video-games-and-violent-extremism.

40. Cited in Jeremy Bauer-Wolf, "White Supremacy Activity Spreads on Campuses,"
Inside Higher Ed, June 26, 2019, https://www.insidehighered.com/news/2019/06/27
/white-nationalist-propaganda-rise-college-campuses.

41. Kristin Lam, "Recruiting Hate: White Supremacist Propaganda Rises for Third
Straight Year on College Campuses, ADL Says," *USA Today*, June 28, 2019, https://
www.usatoday.com/story/news/nation/2019/06/27/white-supremacist-recruiting-rise
-college-campuses-report/1590886001/.

42. Sarah Emerson, "Trump Supporters Flock to 'Free Speech' Platforms After
Facebook Ban," *Medium*, Nov. 10, 2020, https://onezero.medium.com/trump
-supporters-flock-to-free-speech-platforms-after-facebook-ban-bf3e6ab1a70d.

43. Siladitya Ray, "The Far-Right Is Flocking to These Alternate Social Media
Apps—Not All of Them Are Thrilled," Forbes, Jan. 14, 2021, https://www.forbes.com
/sites/siladityaray/2021/01/14/the-far-right-is-flocking-to-these-alternate-social-media
-apps---not-all-of-them-are-thrilled/.

44. Ray, "The Far Right Is Flocking to These Alternate Social Media Apps."

45. Corinne Segal, "What Supremacists Once Wore Hoods. Now, an Internet Mob
Won't Let Them Stay Anonymous," *PBS News Weekend*, Aug. 20, 2017, https://www.pbs
.org/newshour/nation/white-supremacists-wore-hoods-now-internet-mob-wont-let
-stay-anonymous.

46. Author interview with Daryle Lamont Jenkins, Feb. 9, 2024.

47. "Why Turning Point USA's AmFest Is Integral to the Conservative Movement,"
Dec. 20, 2023, https://www.tpusa.com/live/why-turning-point-usas-amfest-is-integral
-to-the-conservative-movement.

48. Bridge Initiative Team, "Factsheet: Young America's Foundation," Georgetown
University, Mar. 14, 2018, https://bridge.georgetown.edu/research/factsheet-young
-americas-foundation/.

49. Nick Bauman, "Top Conservatives Run PAC That Funded White Nationalists," *Mother Jones*, Jan. 19, 2013, https://www.motherjones.com/politics/2013/01/ron
-robinson-james-b-taylor-young-americas-foundation-white-nationalists/.

CHAPTER 6: AD TECH

1. Dave Chaffey, "2024 Email Marketing Statistics Compilation Including Open Rates, Clickthrough Rates and Click-to-Open Rates," *Smart Insights*, Jan. 2, 2023, https://www.smartinsights.com/email-marketing/email-communications-strategy /statistics-sources-for-email-marketing/.

2. Joe McCambley, "The First Ever Banner Ad: Why Did It Work So Well?" *The Guardian*, Dec. 12, 2013.

3. "The Secret History of Advertising on the Internet," *Paleo Ad Tech*, Dec. 10, 2023, https://paleoadtech.com/2023/12/10/46-jay-schwedelson-was-webconnect-the-first-ad -network/.

4. Nick Stat, "The Rise, Disappearance, and Retirement of Google Cofounders Larry Page and Sergey Brin," *The Verge*, Dec. 4, 2019, https://www.theverge.com/2019 /12/4/20994361/google-alphabet-larry-page-sergey-brin-sundar-pichai-co-founders -ceo-timeline.

5. Founders' IPO Letter from S-1 Securities and Exchange Commission Registration Statement, Google, Inc., filed Aug. 18, 2004, https://abc.xyz/investor/founders-letters /ipo-letter/.

6. Ryan Redding, "A Brief History of Google Ad Strategy (and Why You Should Care)," Levergy Marketing, Dec. 11, 2019, https://www.levergy.io/a-brief-history-of -google-ad-strategy-and-why-you-should-care.

7. Karina Montoya, "How Three Mergers Buttressed Google's Ad Tech Monopoly, Per DOJ," *Tech Policy Press*, Mar. 9, 2023, https://www.techpolicy.press/how-three -mergers-buttressed-googles-ad-tech-monopoly-per-doj/. See also Jason Kincaid, "Google Acquires AdMob for $750 Million," *TechCrunch*, Nov. 9, 2009, https:// techcrunch.com/2009/11/09/google-acquires-admob/.

8. US Securities and Exchange Commission, Form 10-K, *Alphabet, Inc., Annual Report for fiscal year ended December 31, 2023*, Commission file number: 001–37580.

9. Sapna Maheshwari and Daisuke Wakabayashi, "AT&T and Johnson & Johnson Pull Ads from YouTube," *New York Times*, Mar. 22, 2017, https://www.nytimes.com/2017 /03/22/business/atampt-and-johnson-amp-johnson-pull-ads-from-youtube-amid-hate -speech-concerns.html.

10. Carole Cadwalladr, "Google, Democracy and the Truth About Internet Search," *The Guardian*, Dec. 4, 2016, https://www.theguardian.com/technology/2016/dec/04 /google-democracy-truth-internet-search-facebook.

11. Cadwalladr, "Google, Democracy and the Truth About Internet Search."

12. Adalytics, *Did Google Mislead Advertisers About Trueview Skippable In-Stream Ads for the Past Three Years?* May 2023, https://adalytics.io/blog/invalid-google-video -partner-trueview-ads, accessed Nov. 12, 2024.

13. Marvin Renaud, "Transparency and Brand Safety on Google Video Partners," Google Ads and Commerce Blog, June 27, 2023, https://blog.google/products/ads -commerce/transparency-and-brand-safety-on-google-video-partners/.

14. See Nandini and Claire, "Thanks, Google: We're Still Seeing Major Brands Funding Toxic Sites Weeks After Adalytics' Exposé," Check My Ads, Dec. 8, 2023, https://checkmyads.org/thanks-google-were-still-seeing-major-brands-funding-toxic -sites-weeks-after-adalytics-expose/.

15. American Economic Liberties Project, "The Truth About Google, Facebook, and Small Businesses," May 3, 2021, https://www.economicliberties.us/our-work/the-truth -about-google-facebook-and-small-businesses/.

16. USA et al. v. Google, LLC, Complaint, Jan. 24, 2023, https://storage.courtlistener .com/recap/gov.uscourts.vaed.533508/gov.uscourts.vaed.533508.1.0_2.pdf.

17. Congresswoman Anna G. Eshoo, "Schakowsky, Eshoo, Wyden, Booker Introduce Bill to Ban Surveillance Advertising," press release, Sept. 18, 2023, https:// schakowsky.house.gov/media/press-releases/schakowsky-eshoo-wyden-booker -introduce-bill-ban-surveillance-advertising.

18. IAB, "IAB Slams Bill That Would Eliminate Data-Driven Advertising," Jan. 20, 2022, https://www.iab.com/news/iab-slams-bill-that-would-eliminate-data-driven -advertising/.

19. Justin Hendrix, "Reactions to the Banning Surveillance Advertising Act," *Tech Policy Press*, Jan. 22, 2022, https://www.techpolicy.press/reactions-to-the-banning -surveillance-advertising-act/.

20. Eshoo, "Schakowsky, Eshoo, Wyden, Booker Introduce Bill to Ban Surveillance Advertising."

21. Elisabeth Bumiller, "Bush Aides Set Strategy to Sell Policy on Iraq," *New York Times*, Sept. 7, 2002.

22. Susannah Fox and Deborah Fallows, The Internet and the Iraq War, Pew Internet & American Life Project and Pew Research Center for the People & the Press, Apr. 1, 2003, https://www.pewresearch.org/internet/2003/04/01/the-internet-and-the-iraq -war/.

23. Michael R. Gordon and Judith Miller, "Threats and Responses: The Iraqis; U.S. Says Hussein Intensifies Quest for A-Bomb Parts," *New York Times*, Sept. 8, 2002.

24. Interview with Scott Bonn, *Law and Disorder Radio*, Feb. 1, 2011.

25. Colin Moynihan, "Trump Supporter Convicted in 2016 Scheme to Suppress Votes for Clinton," *New York Times*, Mar. 31, 2023, https://www.nytimes.com/2023/03/31 /nyregion/douglass-mackey-trial-twitter-misinformation.html.

26. US Department of Justice, "Social Media Influencer Sentenced for Election Interference in 2016 Presidential Race," press release, Oct. 18, 2023, https://www.justice .gov/opa/pr/social-media-influencer-sentenced-election-interference-2016-presidential -race.

27. Olivia Solon, "Cambridge Analytica Whistleblower Says Bannon Wanted to Suppress Votes," *The Guardian*, May 16, 2018, https://www.theguardian.com/uk-news /2018/may/16/steve-bannon-cambridge-analytica-whistleblower-suppress-voters -testimony.

28. Cecilia Kang and Sheera Frenkel, "Facebook Says Cambridge Analytica Har-

vested Data of Up to 87 Million Users," *New York Times*, Apr. 4, 2018, https://www
.nytimes.com/2018/04/04/technology/mark-zuckerberg-testify-congress.html.

29. Jeremy B. Merrill and Olivia Goldhill, "These Are the Political Ads Cambridge
Analytica Designed for You," *Quartz*, Jan. 10, 2020, https://qz.com/1782348/cambridge
-analytica-used-these-5-political-ads-to-target-voters.

30. Lakshmi Gopal, "Facebook's Oversight Board & the Rule of Law: The Importance of Being Earnest," American Bar Association, Oct. 12, 2021, https://www
.americanbar.org/groups/business_law/resources/business-law-today/2021-october
/facebooks-oversight-board-and-rule-of-law/.

31. Gopal, "Facebook's Oversight Board and the Rule of Law."

32. Office of the Privacy Commissioner of Canada, *Report of Findings*, Joint
Investigation of Facebook, Inc. by the Privacy Commissioner of Canada and the Information and Privacy Commissioner for British Columbia, Apr. 25, 2019, https://www
.priv.gc.ca/en/opc-actions-and-decisions/investigations/investigations-into-businesses
/2019/pipeda-2019-002/.

33. *The Economic Impact of Advertising on the US Economy 2018–2026*, prepared for the Advertising Coalition, IHS Market, Nov. 2021, https://aro36532638-my
.sharepoint.com/personal/amelendez_capitolcounsel_com/_layouts/15/onedrive.aspx
?id=%2Fpersonal%2Famelendez%5Fcapitolcounsel%5Fcom%2FDocuments%2FThe
%20Advertising%20Coalition%20EIA%20Final%20Report%20%2D%20November
%202021%2D1%2Epdf&parent=%2Fpersonal%2Famelendez%5Fcapitolcounsel%5Fcom
%2FDocuments&ga=1.

34. Tabitha Whiting, "When Did We Stop Being 'Citizens' and Become 'Consumers'?" *Medium*, May 8, 2019, https://tabitha-whiting.medium.com/when-did-we-stop
-being-citizens-and-become-consumers-6176f3424ddo.

35. "Industry Conditions: Shopping Centers: Where Americans Buy, Socialize,
Play," International Association of Shopping Centers, May 19, 2016, available at https://
www.icsc.com/news-and-views/icsc-exchange/industry-conditions-shopping-centers
-where-americans-buy-socialize-play-and.

36. "Online vs. In-Store Shopping Statistics," Capital One Shopping, Dec. 10, 2024,
https://capitaloneshopping.com/research/online-vs-in-store-shopping-statistics/.

37. Pew Research Center, "Political Engagement, Knowledge, and the Mid-
terms," Apr. 26, 2018, https://www.pewresearch.org/politics/2018/04/26/10-political
-engagement-knowledge-and-the-midterms/.

CHAPTER 7: TRILLIONAIRE TECH OVERLORDS

1. DataHorizzon Research, Chatbot Market Size to Reach USD 32.4 Billion by 2032
CAGR: Yahoo Finance, Sept. 24, 2023, https://finance.yahoo.com/news/chatbot-market
-size-reach-usd-235000000.html.

2. Stefan Wojcik, Solomon Messing, Aaron Smith, Lee Rainie, and Paul Hit-

lin, "Bots in the Twittersphere," Pew Research Center, Apr. 9, 2018, https://www.pewresearch.org/internet/2018/04/09/bots-in-the-twittersphere.

3. L'Oreal Thompson Payton, "Americans Check Their Phones 144 Times a Day. Here's How to Cut Back," *YahooFinance*, July 19, 2023, https://finance.yahoo.com/news/americans-check-phones-144-times-183345369.html.

4. Michael Winnick, "Putting a Finger on Our Phone Obsession," dscout, https://dscout.com/people-nerds/mobile-touches, accessed Nov. 12, 2024.

5. Michael Bennet, "Bennet Calls on Tech Companies to Protect Kids as They Deploy AI Chatbots," press release, Mar. 21, 2013, https://www.bennet.senate.gov/public/index.cfm/2023/3/bennet-calls-on-tech-companies-to-protect-kids-as-they-deploy-ai-chatbots.

6. "Snapchat Evokes Stronger Emotions than Biggest Platforms," Snap, Sept. 29, 2022, https://forbusiness.snapchat.com/blog/happy-emotions-drive-deeper-engagements.

7. Snapchat, "Snapchat Evokes Stronger Emotions than Biggest Platforms," Business, Sept. 29, 2022, https://forbusiness.snapchat.com/blog/happy-emotions-drive-deeper-engagements.

8. Sasha Labadze, Maya Grigolia, and Lela Machaidze, "Role of AI Chatbots in Education: Systematic Literature Review," *International Journal of Educational Technology in Higher Education*, Oct. 31, 2023, https://educationaltechnologyjournal.springeropen.com/articles/10.1186/s41239-023-00426-1.

9. Eric S. Hintz, "Remembering Apple's '1984' Super Bowl Ad," Lemelson Center for the Study of Invention and Innovation, Smithsonian Institute, Jan. 22, 2014, https://invention.si.edu/remembering-apple-s-1984-super-bowl-ad.

10. Bradley Johnson, "Ten Years After Apple's '1984': The Commercial and Product That Changed Advertising," *AdAge*, Jan. 10, 1994, https://adage.com/article/news/ten-years-apple-s-1984-commercial-product-changed-advertising/88772.

11. Martin Watzinger and Monika Schnitzer, "The Breakup of the Bell System and Its Impact on US Innovation," Center for Economic Policy Research, Nov. 2, 2022, https://cepr.org/publications/dp17635.

12. Alexander Eser, "Essential Apple Customer Loyalty Statistics 2024," ZipDo, June 8, 2023, https://zipdo.co/statistics/apple-customer-loyalty/.

13. Adam Hayes, "Why Do People Love Apple SO Much?" *Wyzowl*, Sept. 28, 2023, https://www.wyzowl.com/why-do-people-love-apple-so-much/. (This article is no longer available.)

14. Sarah Perez, "Apple Faces New Lawsuit over Its Data Collection Practices in First-Party Apps, Like the App Store," *TechCrunch*, Nov. 14, 2022, https://techcrunch.com/2022/11/14/apple-faces-new-lawsuit-over-its-data-collection-practices-in-first-party-apps-like-the-app-store/.

15. Libman v. Apple, Inc. 5:22-cv-07069, US District Court for the Northern District of California, filed Nov. 10, 2022.

16. Johana Bhuiyan, "Apple Says It Prioritizes Privacy. Experts Say Gaps Remain," *The Guardian*, Sept. 23, 2022, https://www.theguardian.com/technology/2022/sep/23/apple-user-data-law-enforcement-falling-short.

17. Ben Wolford, "Apple Can See Much of What You Store in iCloud," Proton, June 8, 2023, https://proton.me/blog/apple-icloud-privacy.

18. Robert Scammell, "Last JEDI Appeal for Oracles Fails at Supreme Court," *Verdict*, Oct. 2021, https://www.verdict.co.uk/oracle-jedi-appeal/?cf-view.

19. Wilneida Negrón and Morgan Hargrave, "Why You Should Care About Bots If You Care About Social Justice," Ford Foundation, May 30, 2017, https://www.fordfoundation.org/news-and-stories/stories/why-you-should-care-about-bots-if-you-care-about-social-justice/.

20. Open Secrets, Client Profile: Amazon.com, 2023, https://www.opensecrets.org/federal-lobbying/clients/summary?cycle=2023&id=D000023883.

21. European Commission, "Antitrust: Commission Fines Google €2.42 Billion for Abusing Dominance as Search Engine by Giving Illegal Advantage to Own Comparison Shopping Service," press release, June 26, 2017, https://ec.europa.eu/commission/presscorner/detail/es/memo_17_1785.

22. Foo Yun Chee, "Google Loses Fight Against 42.7 Billion EU Antitrust Fine," Reuters, Sept. 10, 2024, https://www.reuters.com/technology/eu-court-upholds-googles-27-bln-eu-antitrust-fine-2024-09-10/.

23. Court of Justice of the European Union, "The Court of Justice Upholds the Fine of €2.4 Billion Imposed on Google for Abuse of Its Dominant Position by Favouring Its Own Comparison Shopping Service," press release, Sept. 10, 2024, https://curia.europa.eu/jcms/upload/docs/application/pdf/2024-09/cp240135en.pdf.

24. Abhinar Kaustubh, "Epic vs Google: The Big $147 Billion That Was Refused," *Times of India*, Nov. 9, 2023, http://timesofindia.indiatimes.com/articleshow/105100600.cms.

25. Maxwell Zeff, "Google Denies That Its 'Project Hug' Bribed 20 Developers," Gizmodo, Nov. 9, 2023, https://gizmodo.com/google-denies-its-project-hug-bribed-20-developers-1851009202.

26. Zeff, "Google Denies That Its 'Project Hug' Bribed 20 Developers."

27. Epic, "Epic v. Google Trial Verdict, a Win for All Developers," Dec. 11, 2023, https://www.epicgames.com/site/en-US/news/epic-v-google-trial-verdict-a-win-for-all-developers.

28. Adi Robertson, "Supreme Court Rejects Epic v. Apple Antitrust Case," *The Verge*, Jan. 16, 2024, https://www.theverge.com/2024/1/16/24039983/supreme-court-epic-apple-antitrust-case-rejected.

29. Lauren Feiner, "Apple Buys a Company Every Few Weeks, Says CEO Tim Cook," CNBC, May 6, 2019, https://www.cnbc.com/2019/05/06/apple-buys-a-company-every-few-weeks-says-ceo-tim-cook.html.

30. Rebecca Solnit, "Poison Apples," *Harper's Magazine*, Dec. 2014.

31. Joe Hindy, "Google Pays $18 Billion Per Year to Be the Default Search Engine

on Apple Devices," *PC Magazine*, Oct. 27, 2023, https://www.pcmag.com/news/google
-pays-18-billion-per-year-to-be-the-default-search-engine-on-apple.

32. United States of America v. Google LLC (1:20-cv-03010), District Court, District
of Columbia, filed Oct. 20, 2020.

33. Cecilia D'Anastasio, "Epic Leaves a Big Crack in Apple's Walled Garden," Wired,
Sept. 10, 2021, https://www.wired.com/story/epic-leaves-big-crack-in-apple-walled
-garden/.

34. Tristan Harris, "The Slot Machine in Your Pocket," *Speigel*, July 27, 2016, https://
www.spiegel.de/international/zeitgeist/smartphone-addiction-is-part-of-the-design
-a-1104237.html.

CHAPTER 8: SURVEILLANCE

1. H. Keith Melton and Robert Wallace, *The Official CIA Manual of Trickery and
Deception* (Boston: Mariner Books, 2010).

2. Noah Shachtman, "CIA's Lost Magic Manual Resurfaces," *Wired*, Nov. 24, 2009,
https://www.wired.com/2009/11/cias-lost-magic-manual-resurfaces/.

3. Frank J. Donner, *The Age of Surveillance: The Aims and Methods of America's
Political Intelligence System* (New York: Knopf, 1980), 452–53.

4. Author's email correspondence with former 9/11 Museum staff member (name
withheld), July 2, 2023.

5. Sanya Mansoor, "*The Outsider* Unpacks the Controversy Behind the National
September 11 Memorial & Museum," *Time*, https://time.com/6091193/the-outsider
-explainer-september-11-documentary/.

6. Mansoor, "*The Outsider* Unpacks the Controversy Behind the National September 11 Memorial & Museum."

7. Abby Phillip, "Families Infuriated by 'Crass Commercialism' of 9/11 Museum Gift
Shop," *Washington Post*, May 19, 2014, families-infuriated-by-crass-commercialism-of-
911-museum-gift-shop.

8. Megan Willett-Wei, "A Controversial Cheese Plate Has Been Removed from
the 9/11 Memorial Museum Shop," *Business Insider*, May 29, 2014, https://www
.businessinsider.com/cheese-plate-removed-from-911-memorial-museum-2014-5.

9. Mark Hosenball, "Exclusive: House Republican Staffer Introduced Alleged NSA
Leaker to Reporter," *Newsweek*, Apr. 16, 2010, https://www.newsweek.com/exclusive
-house-republican-staffer-introduced-alleged-nsa-leaker-reporter-217060.

10. Gray News Staff, "Sheriff: Father, Son Shoot at Innocent Woman While Looking for Nonexistent Burglar," TV6, Oct. 19, 2022, https://www.uppermichiganssource
.com/2022/10/19/sheriff-father-son-shoot-innocent-woman-while-looking-nonexistent
-burglar/.

11. Caroline Haskins, "Amazon's Home Security Company Is Turning Everyone
into Cops," *Vice*, Feb. 7, 2019, https://www.vice.com/en/article/qvyvzd/amazons-home
-security-company-is-turning-everyone-into-cops.

12. Charles Pulliam-Moore, "Dozens of Civil Rights Groups Are Calling on Amazon and MGM to Cancel Ring Nation Reality Show," *The Verge*, Sept. 20, 2022, https://www.theverge.com/2022/9/20/23362010/ring-nation-mgm-amazon-mark-burnett-barry-poznick-civil-rights-cancel.

13. Zeke J. Miller, "Former NSA Chief Was Worried About 'Enemy of the State' Reputation," *Time*, June 7, 2013, https://swampland.time.com/2013/06/07/former-nsa-chief-was-worried-about-enemy-of-the-state-reputation/.

14. Natasha Singer, "How Google Took Over the Classroom," *New York Times*, May 13, 2017, https://www.nytimes.com/2017/05/13/technology/google-education-chromebooks-schools.html.

15. "Capturing the Classroom: How Google Sidestepped School Authorities to Push its Products into Schools," Tech Transparency Project, Jan. 2019, https://techtransparencyproject.cdn.prismic.io/techtransparencyproject/b6fb2036-0917-46d2-87a3-632d45653616_Capturing-the-Classroom-January-2019.pdf.

16. Author interview with Michael Vakian, August 19, 2024, via email.

17. Jessa Crispin, "US Schools Gave Kids Laptops During the Pandemic. Then They Spied on Them," *The Guardian*, Oct. 11, 2021, https://tinyurl.com/GuardianSchoolLaptops.

18. Jason Kelley, "A Long Overdue Reckoning for Online Proctoring Companies May Finally Be Here," Electronic Frontier Foundation, June 22, 2021, https://www.eff.org/deeplinks/2021/06/long-overdue-reckoning-online-proctoring-companies-may-finally-be-here.

19. Sarah Silverman et al., "What Happens When You Close the Door on Remote Proctoring? Moving Toward Authentic Assessments with a People-Centered Approach," *Educational Development in the Time of Crises* 39, no. 3 (Spring 2021).

20. Vakian interview.

21. Robert L. Linn and Norman E. Gronlund, *Measurement and Assessment in Teaching*, 8th ed. (Des Moines, IA: Prentice-Hall, 2020).

22. Sean Michael Morris and Jesse Stommel, "A Guide for Resisting Edtech: The Case Against Turnitin," *Hybrid Pedagogy*, June 15, 2017, https://hybridpedagogy.org/resisting-edtech/.

23. Ed Markey, "Senators Markey, Warren Investigation Finds That EdTech Student Surveillance Platforms Need Urgent Federal Action to Protect Students," press release, Mar. 30, 2022, https://www.markey.senate.gov/news/press-releases/senators-markey-warren-investigation-finds-that-edtech-student-surveillance-platforms-need-urgent-federal-action-to-protect-students.

24. Vakian interview.

25. American Consortium for Equity in Education, "School Districts Partnering with Gaggle Saved More than 700 Students from Suicide in 2018–19," https://www.ace-ed.org/school-districts-partnering-with-gaggle-saved-more-than-700-students-from-suicide-in-2018–19/.

26. Lois Beckett, "Under Digital Surveillance: How American Schools Spy on Millions of Kids," *The Guardian*, Oct. 22, 2019, https://www.theguardian.com/world/2019/oct/22/school-student-surveillance-bark-gaggle.

27. Todd Feathers, "After Dobbs, Advocates Fear School Surveillance Tools Could Put Teens at Risk," *The MarkUp*, July 8, 2022, https://themarkup.org/privacy/2022/07/08/after-dobbs-advocates-fear-school-surveillance-tools-could-put-teens-at-risk.

28. Human Rights Watch, "Human Rights Crisis: Abortion in the United States After *Dobbs*," Apr. 18, 2023, https://www.hrw.org/news/2023/04/18/human-rights-crisis-abortion-united-states-after-dobbs.

29. Human Rights Watch, "Human Rights Crisis."

30. Ron Wyden et al. to Sundar Pichai, CEO of Google, LLC, May 24, 2022, https://www.wyden.senate.gov/imo/media/doc/Wyden-led%20letter%20to%20Google%20on%20geofence%20data%20and%20abortion-related%20surveillance%205.24.22.pdf.

31. Zack Whittaker, "Google Says Geofence Warrants Make Up One-Quarter of All US Demands," *Tech Crunch*, Aug. 19, 2021, https://techcrunch.com/2021/08/19/google-geofence-warrants/.

32. Emily Bazelon, "Purvi Patel Could Be Just the Beginning," *New York Times*, Apr. 1, 2015, https://www.nytimes.com/2015/04/01/magazine/purvi-patel-could-be-just-the-beginning.html.

33. Patricia Hurtado, Francesca Maglione, and Bloomberg, "In a Post-Roe World, More Miscarriage and Stillbirth Prosecutions Await Women," *Fortune*, July 5, 2022, https://fortune.com/2022/07/05/roe-v-wade-miscarriage-abortion-prosecution-charge/.

34. Geoffrey A. Fowler, "It's the Middle of the Night. Do You Know Who Your iPhone Is Talking To?," *Washington Post*, May 28, 2019, https://www.washingtonpost.com/technology/2019/05/28/its-middle-night-do-you-know-who-your-iphone-is-talking/.

35. "Popular Apps on Your Smartphone Are Selling Your Location Data," opinion, *Washington Post*, Feb. 9, 2020, https://www.washingtonpost.com/opinions/apps-are-selling-your-location-data-the-us-government-is-buying/2020/02/09/9d09475e-49e2-11ea-b4d9-29cc419287eb_story.html.

36. Lee Matthews, "70% of Mobile Apps Share Your Data with Third Parties," *Forbes*, June 13, 2017, https://www.forbes.com/sites/leemathews/2017/06/13/70-percent-of-mobile-apps-share-your-data-with-third-parties/.

37. Consumer Financial Protection Bureau, "CFPB Launches Inquiry into the Business Practices of Data Brokers," Mar. 15, 2023, https://www.consumerfinance.gov/about-us/newsroom/cfpb-launches-inquiry-into-the-business-practices-of-data-brokers/.

38. Odia Kagan, "The Consumer Financial Protection Bureau Is Coming to a Data Broker Near You," Fox Rothschild, Aug. 15, 2023, https://dataprivacy.foxrothschild.com/2023/08/articles/artificial-intelligence/the-consumer-financial-protection-bureau-is-coming-to-a-data-broker-near-you/.

PART THREE: PRACTICES FOR THE PEOPLE

1. Elizabeth Schulze, "The Inventor of the Web Says the Internet Is Broken—but He Has a Plan to Fix It," CNBC, Nov. 5, 2018, https://www.cnbc.com/2018/11/05/inventor -of-the-web-says-the-internet-is-at-a-tipping-point-and-reveals-a-new-plan-to-fix-it .html.

CHAPTER 9: DISRUPTERS FOR DEMOCRACY

1. Brian McCullough, "20 Years On: Why Netscape's IPO Was the 'Big Bang' of the Internet Era," Internet History Podcast blog, Aug. 7, 2015, https://www .internethistorypodcast.com/2015/08/20-years-on-why-netscapes-ipo-was-the-big -bang-of-the-internet-era/.

2. "Browser Wars," episode 1 of Download: The True Story of the Internet, aired on the Discovery Channel, June 9, 2022, accessed via YouTube.

3. Download: The True Story of the Internet.

4. Wired Staff, "May 26, 1995."

5. Steven Vaughn-Nichols, "How Internet Explorer Really Beat Netscape," ZDNET, Aug. 18, 2021, https://www.zdnet.com/home-and-office/networking/how-ie-really-beat -netscape/.

6. United States of America v. Microsoft Corporation, 253 F.3d 34 (D.C. Cir. 2001). The government accused Microsoft of unlawfully maintaining a monopoly over the personal computer market, largely through legal and technical restrictions it placed on the PC manufacturers and users to uninstall Internet Explorer and use other programs such as Netscape.

7. Godzilla, Ishirō Honda, dir., Toho Co., Ltd., 1954.

8. Natalie Gagliordi, "Mozilla Pulls Facebook Advertising After Cambridge Ana-lytica Scandal," ZDNET, Mar. 22, 2018, https://www.zdnet.com/article/mozilla-pulls -facebook-advertising-after-cambridge-analytica-scandal/.

9. Branka, "Linux Statistics," True List, Feb. 17, 2024, https://truelist.co/blog/linux -statistics/.

10. WPExplorer, "History of WordPress: The Good, The Bad & The Ugly," updated Dec. 11, 2019, https://www.wpexplorer.com/history-wordpress/.

11. Indesign Web, "How Many Websites Use WordPress in 2024?" Apr. 17, 2024, https://www.indesignweb.com/news/how-many-websites-use-wordpress-in-2024/.

12. Satoshi Nakamoto, "Bitcoin: A Peer-to-Peer Electronic Cash System," https:// bitcoin.org/bitcoin.pdf.

13. David Chaum, "Computer Systems Established, Maintained, and Trusted by Mutually Suspicious Groups," Satoshi Nakamoto Institute, June 1982, PhD diss. for University of California, Berkeley, 1982, available at https://nakamotoinstitute.org/library /computer-systems-by-mutually-suspicious-groups/.

14. Rohit Khare and Ian Jacobs, "W3C Recommendations Rescue 'World Wild Wait,'" W3C, https://www.w3.org/Protocols/NL-PerfNote, accessed Oct. 8, 2024.

15. Walter Isaacson, *The Innovators: How a Group of Hackers, Geniuses, and Geeks Created the Digital Revolution* (New York: Simon & Schuster, 2014), 381.

CHAPTER 10: BENDING TO THE GDPR

1. Tim Cook's speech at the International Conference of Data Protection and Privacy Commissioners, Oct. 2018; Sundar Pichai's op-ed in the *New York Times*, May 2019; Mark Zuckerberg's Facebook post, Mar. 2019; Satya Nadella's talk at the Microsoft Build Conference, May 2019; and Jeff Bezos's annual letter to shareholders, Apr. 2018.

2. Sam Shead, "Amazon Hit with $887 Million Fine by European Privacy Watchdog," CNBC, July 30, 2021, https://www.cnbc.com/2021/07/30/amazon-hit-with-fine-by -eu-privacy-watchdog-.html.

3. Ryan Browne, "Top EU Regulator Defends Mega $1.3 Billion Privacy Fine on Meta: 'I Have to Enforce the Law,'" CNBC, May 24, 2023, https://www.cnbc.com/2023 /05/24/irish-data-regulator-defends-1point3-billion-meta-fine.html.

4. Natasha Lomas, "France Slaps Google with $166M Antitrust Fine for Opaque and Inconsistent Ad Rules," *Tech Crunch*, Dec. 20, 2019, https://techcrunch.com/2019 /12/20/france-slaps-google-with-166m-antitrust-fine-for-opaque-and-inconsistent-ad -rules/.

5. F. Paul Pittman, Hope Anderson, and Abdul M. Hafix, "US Data Privacy Guide," White & Case newsletter, June 4, 2024, https://www.whitecase.com/insight-our -thinking/us-data-privacy-guide.

6. Lauren Rubenstein, "Zimmeck Spearheads Launch of Important Online Privacy Tool," *The Wesleyan Connection*, Oct. 11, 2020, https://newsletter.blogs.wesleyan.edu /2020/10/11/zimmeck-spearheads-launch-of-important-online-privacy-tool/.

7. Rubenstein, "Zimmeck Spearheads Launch of Important Online Privacy Tool."

8. Dylan Walsh, "GDPR Reduced Firms' Data and Computation Use," MIT Sloan School of Management, Sept. 10, 2024, https://mitsloan.mit.edu/ideas-made-to-matter /gdpr-reduced-firms-data-and-computation-use.

9. Ash Johnson and Daniel Castro, "Maintaining a Light-Touch Approach to Data Protection in the United States," Information Technology and Innovation Foundation, Aug. 8, 2022, https://itif.org/publications/2022/08/08/maintaining-a-light-touch -approach-to-data-protection-in-the-united-states/.

10. Boston Women's Workforce Council, "Data Privacy: Ensuring Secure and Private Data Analysis," https://thebwwc.org/mpc, accessed Oct. 18, 2024.

11. Arjun Kharpal, "Signal and Telegram downloads Surge After Whatsapp Says It Will Share Data with Facebook," CNBC, Jan. 12, 2021, https://www.cnbc.com/2021/01/12 /signal-telegram-downloads-surge-after-update-to-whatsapp-data-policy.html.

12. Mike Sweeney and Paulina Zawiślak, "The Demise of Third-Party Cookies in AdTech: Why Are They Being Phased Out?" May 15, 2024, *The Clearcode Blog*, https:// clearcode.cc/blog/third-party-cookies-demise/.

13. See Mastodon, https://mastodon-analytics.com/, last accessed Nov. 15, 2024.

14. Colleen McClain, Michelle Faverio, Monica Anderson, and Eugenie Park, "How Americans Protect Their Online Data," Pew Research Center, Oct. 18, 2023, https://www.pewresearch.org/internet/2023/10/18/how-americans-protect-their-online-data/.

15. Ryan Chiavetta, "Study Finds 93% of US Citizens Would Switch to Privacy-Conscious Organizations," International Association of Privacy Professionals, Aug. 19, 2020, https://iapp.org/news/a/study-finds-93-of-americans-would-switch-to-privacy-conscious-organizations.

16. McClain, Faverio, Anderson, and Park, "How Americans Protect Their Online Data."

CHAPTER 11: BECOMING DIGITALLY LITERATE CITIZENS

1. Sandra Day O'Connor Institute for American Democracy, "The Legacy of Sandra Day O'Connor," https://oconnorinstitute.org/civic-programs/oconnor-history/sandra-day-oconnor-policy-archives-research-library/legacy/, accessed Oct. 8, 2024.

2. Kei Kawashima-Ginsberg and Peter Levine, "Diversity in Classrooms: The Relationship Between Deliberative and Associative Opportunities in School and Later Electoral Engagement," Society for the Psychological Study of Social Issues 14, no. 1 (Jan. 2014), https://spssi.onlinelibrary.wiley.com/doi/abs/10.1111/asap.12038.

3. Justine Petrone, "A Roadmap for Life," Republic of Estonia E-Residency, Jan. 24, 2024, https://www.e-resident.gov.ee/blog/posts/a-roadmap-for-life/.

4. Petrone, "A Social Network for People and Their Pets."

5. Ben Bovington, Allison T. Butler, Nolan Higdon, Mickey Huff, and Andy Lee Roth, *The Media and Me: A Guide to Critical Media Literacy for Young People* (New York: Triangle Square, 2022).

6. Author interview, Andy Lee Roth, *Law and Disorder Radio,* Nov. 14, 2022, https://lawanddisorder.org/?s=andy+lee+roth.

7. Media Literacy Now, *U.S. Media Literacy Policy Report 2023: A State-by-State Status of Media Literacy Education Laws for K–12 Schools,* https://medialiteracynow.org/wp-content/uploads/2024/02/MediaLiteracyNowPolicyReport2023_publishedFeb2024b.pdf.

8. "Gov. Phil Murphy Signs First in the Nation K–12 Information Literacy Education Legislation," New Jersey School Boards Association, Jan. 10, 2023, https://www.njsba.org/news-publications/school-board-notes/january-10–2023-vol-xl-no-21/gov-phil-murphy-signs-first-in-the-nation-k-12-information-literacy-education-legislation/.

9. National Association of State Boards of Education, "States Increase Focus on Critical Media Literacy Skills," press release, https://www.nasbe.org/states-increase-focus-on-critical-media-literacy-skills/, accessed Jan. 24, 2025.

10. National Association for Media Literacy Education, *Snapshot 2024: State of Media Literacy Education in the U.S.,* 2024, https://namle.org/wp-content/uploads/2024/01/Snapshot-2024-State-of-Media-Literacy-FINAL.pdf.

11. Koret Foundation, "Common Sense Media: Providing Media Literacy for All," https://koret.org/grantees/common-sense-media-media-literacy/, accessed Jan. 24, 2025.

12. Olivia Sidoti and Emily A. Vogels, "What Americans Know About AI, Cybersecurity and Big Tech," Pew Research Center, Aug. 17, 2023, https://www.pewresearch.org/internet/2023/08/17/what-americans-know-about-ai-cybersecurity-and-big-tech/.

13. Kelly Field, "Teaching 'Action Civics' Engages Kids and Ignites Controversy," *Hechinger Report*, Aug. 1, 2021, https://hechingerreport.org/teaching-action-civics-engages-kids-and-ignites-controversy/.

14. See Mikva Challenge, mikvachallenge.org, accessed Oct. 8, 2024.

15. An Act to Promote and Enhance Civic Engagement, Massachusetts, https://malegislature.gov/Laws/SessionLaws/Acts/2018/Chapter296, accessed Oct. 8, 2024.

16. Field, "Teaching 'Action Civics' Engages Kids and Ignites Controversy."

17. Generation Citizen, *Democracy's Rising Generation*, 2023 annual report, https://cms.generationcitizen.org/wp-content/uploads/2023/11/2023-GC-Annual-Report-Democracys-Rising-Generation-1.pdf.

18. Generation Citizen, *Democracy's Rising Generation*.

19. Civics Alliance, National Association of Scholars, "Our Vision," https://civicsalliance.org/our-vision/, accessed Oct. 8, 2024.

20. Pierce Gillen and Alex Khammar, "The Problem with Action Civics," Texas Public Policy Foundation, Dec. 1, 2021, https://www.texaspolicy.com/the-problem-with-action-civics/.

21. Sandra Day O'Connor Public Letter, Oct. 23, 2018, https://oconnorinstitute.org/wp-content/uploads/Public-Letter-from-Sandra-Day-OConnor-10-23-16.pdf.

22. CivxNow, "Civics Leaders Call for Greater Investment in Civic Education Following Release of National Assessment of Educational Progress (NAEP) on Civics," press release, May 3, 2023, https://civxnow.org/press-release-civics-leaders-call-for-greater-investment-in-civic-education-following-release-of-national-assessment-of-educational-progress-naep-on-civics/.

23. iCivics, "New Poll Shows Strong Support for Civic Education Across Party Lines," press release, Oct. 27, 2022, https://www.prnewswire.com/news-releases/new-poll-shows-strong-support-for-civic-education-across-party-lines-301660642.html.

24. Karen Walker, "Team Earns Top Prize in Adversarial Artificial Intelligence Machine Learning Challenge," University of Virginia, Engineering, Mar. 31, 2021, https://engineering.virginia.edu/news/2021/03/uva-undergrads-offer-new-approach-detecting-deepfakes.

25. Karen Walker, "UVA Undergrads Offer New Approach to Detecting 'Deepfake' Videos," *UVA Today*, June 2, 2021, https://news.virginia.edu/content/uva-undergrads-offer-new-approach-detecting-deepfake-videos.

26. Chantal Tattoli, "Inside Snopes: The Rise, Fall, and Rebirth of an Internet Icon," *Fast Company*, June 2, 2023, https://www.fastcompany.com/90901113/inside-snopes-the-rise-fall-and-rebirth-of-an-internet-icon.

27. Sian Lee, Dongon Lee, Aiping Xiong, and Haeseung Seo, "'Fact-Checking' Fact Checkers: A Data-Driven Approach," *MisInformation Review*, Harvard Kennedy School, Oct. 26, 2023, https://misinforeview.hks.harvard.edu/article/fact-checking-fact -checkers-a-data-driven-approach/.

28. Sevana Wenn, "How Meta, TikTok, Twitter and YouTube Plan to Address 2024 Election Misinformation," Poynter Institute, July 6, 2023, https://www.poynter.org/fact -checking/2023/how-meta-tiktok-twitter-and-youtube-plan-to-address-2024-election -misinformation/. On June 2, 2023, YouTube said it will no longer remove videos that include false information about the 2020 presidential election. Some advocates warn that the policy change could have ripple effects across social media platforms and allow misinformation to spread more easily.

29. Madison Czopek, "2 Weeks, 450+ Posts: How Elon Musk Uses His X Profile to Push FEMA, Immigration, Voting Falsehoods," PolitiFact, Oct. 23, 2024, https:// www.politifact.com/article/2024/oct/23/2-weeks-450-posts-how-elon-musk-uses-his -x-profile/.

30. *Exploring Legal Mechanisms for Data Stewardship*, a joint publication of the Ada Lovelace Institute and the AI Council, Mar. 4, 2021, https://www.adalovelaceinstitute .org/report/legal-mechanisms-data-stewardship/.

31. Algorithmic Justice League, https://www.ajl.org/, accessed Oct. 8, 2024.

32. Amba Oak and Sarah Myers West, "Confronting Tech Power," AI Now Institute, https://ainowinstitute.org/2023-landscape.

33. Author interview with Carrie Goldberg, *Law and Disorder Radio*, Aug. 19, 2019.

34. Carrie Goldberg, *Nobody's Victim: Fighting Psychos, Stalkers, Pervs, and Trolls* (New York: Plume, 2019).

35. Unlawful Dissemination or Publication of an Intimate Image: NY Penal Law 245.15.

36. Gabrielle Fonrouge, "Inside the Twisted Revenge Porn Site That's Ruining Women's Lives," *New York Post*, Sept. 22, 2017, https://nypost.com/2017/09/22/revenge -porn-site-leaves-trail-of-innocent-victims/.

37. Lee Fang, "In the Name of 'Fake News,' Newsguard Extorts Sites to Follow the Government Narrative," *New York Post*, Dec. 10, 2023, https://nypost.com/2023/12/10 /opinion/newsguard-extorts-sites-to-follow-the-government-narrative/.

CHAPTER 12: A SAFER DIGITAL WORLD

1. SETDA, "Education and Library Coalition Urges FCC to Strengthen Cybersecurity in Schools and Libraries," press release, Jan. 31, 2024, https://www.setda.org/news /press-releases/press-release-2024/ed-coalition-urges-fcc-to-strengthen-cybersecurity/.

2. H.R. 3138, State and Local Cybersecurity Improvement Act 117th Congress (2021–2022), https://www.congress.gov/bill/117th-congress/house-bill/3138.

3. University of South Florida, Corporate Training and Professional Education,

Innovative Education, https://www.usf.edu/continuing-education/explore-programs/education/for-parents/cybersecurity-7-12.aspx, accessed Oct. 8, 2024.

4. Francesca Lockhart, "How University Cybersecurity Clinics Can Help Cities Fight Ransomware," *CyberScoop*, June 2, 2023, https://cyberscoop.com/cybersecurity-clinics-ransomware/.

5. "Congressman Veasey Introduces the Cybersecurity Clinics Grant Program Act," press release, Oct. 4, 2022, https://veasey.house.gov/media-center/press-releases/congressman-veasey-introduces-the-cybersecurity-clinics-grant-program-0.

6. Center for Long-Term Cyber Security, "National Security," University of California, Berkeley, Jan. 2024, https://cltc.berkeley.edu/news-events/.

7. UNICEF, "More Than 175,000 Children Go Online for the First Time Every Day, Tapping into Great Opportunities, but Facing Grave Risks," press release, Feb. 6, 2018, https://www.unicef.org/eca/press-releases/more-175000-children-go-online-first-time-every-day-tapping-great-opportunities.

8. Protected & Sensitive Whistleblower Disclosure, Further Redacted for Congress, Whistleblower Aid, filed by lawyers representing Peter "Mudge" Zatko, July 6, 2022, available at https://cdn.sanity.io/files/3tzzh18d/production/be635f31797f4ec18a47271998ff2785b52ed7d3.pdf.

9. Craig Timberg, "A Disaster Foretold—and Ignored," *Washington Post*, June 22, 2015, https://www.washingtonpost.com/sf/business/2015/06/22/net-of-insecurity-part-3/.

10. Cat Zakrzewski, Joseph Menn, Faiz Siddiqui, Cristiano Lima-Strong, and Rachel Lerman, "Twitter Whistleblower Says Security Holes Cause Real Harm to Real People," *Washington Post*, Sept. 13, 2022, https://www.washingtonpost.com/technology/2022/09/13/twitter-whistleblower-peiter-zatko-testifies/.

11. Kara Alaimo, "Social Media Companies Like Twitter Can't Be Trusted to Regulate Themselves," *CNN Business Perspectives*, Aug. 29, 2022, https://www.cnn.com/2022/08/29/perspectives/social-media-twitter-peiter-zatko/index.html.

12. Laura Dobberstein, "Twitter Whistleblower Peiter 'Mudge' Zatko Lands New Gig at Rapid7," *The Register*, Jan. 5, 2023, https://www.theregister.com/2023/01/05/zatko_rapid7/.

13. Matthew Decker v. Pennsylvania State University, 22-cv-03895-PD, Eastern District of Pennsylvania (Oct. 5, 2022).

14. Protecting Controlled Unclassified Information in Nonfederal Systems and Organizations, Computer Security Resource Center, NIST SP 800-171 Rev. 2, Jan. 28, 2021, available at https://csrc.nist.gov/pubs/sp/800/171/r2/upd1/final.

15. US Attorney's Office, Eastern District of Pennsylvania, "Penn State Agrees to Pay $1.25 Million to Resolve False Claims Act Allegations Relating to Non-Compliance with Contractual Cybersecurity Requirements," press release, Oct. 22, 2024, https://www.justice.gov/usao-edpa/pr/penn-state-agrees-pay-125-million-resolve-false-claims-act-allegations-relating-non.

16. US Department of Justice, "Medical Services Contractor Pays $930,000 to Settle

False Claims Act Allegations Relating to Medical Services Contracts at State Department and Air Force Facilities in Iraq and Afghanistan," press release, Mar. 8, 2022, https://www.justice.gov/opa/pr/medical-services-contractor-pays-930000-settle-false -claims-act-allegations-relating-medical.

17. US Department of Justice, "Jelly Bean Communications Design and Its Manager Settle False Claims Act Liability for Cybersecurity Failures on Florida Medicaid Enrollment Website," press release, Mar. 14, 2023, https://www.justice.gov/opa/pr/jelly-bean -communications-design-and-its-manager-settle-false-claims-act-liability.

18. Lauren Feiner, "Meta Sued by 33 State AGs for Addictive Features Targeting Kids," NBC News, Oct. 24, 2023, https://www.nbcnews.com/tech/tech-news/meta-sued -33-state-ags-addictive-features-targeting-kids-rcna121927.

19. Alexai Alexis, "Lessons from SEC's $3M Blackbaud Cyber Penalty," CFODive, Mar. 21, 2023, https://www.cfodive.com/news/lessons-secs-3m-blackbaud-cyber -penalty/645522/.

20. Ogletree v. Cleveland State, No. 1:21-cv-00500, 2022 WL 3581569, at 2 (N.D. Ohio Aug. 22, 2022).

21. Ogletree v. Cleveland State Univ., 647 F. Supp. 3d 602 (N.D. Ohio 2022).

22. Illinois Biometric Information Privacy Act (BIPA) of 2008, 740 ILCS 14, https:// www.ilga.gov/legislation/ilcs/ilcs3.asp?ActID=3004&ChapterID=57.

23. Thakkar v. ProctorU Inc., 571 F. Supp. 3d 927 (C.D. Ill. 2021).

24. ProctorU, Support Page, support.proctoru.com.

25. Jason Kelley, "A Long Overdue Reckoning for Online Proctoring Companies May Finally Be Here," Electronic Frontier Foundation, June 22, 2021, https://www.eff .org/deeplinks/2021/06/long-overdue-reckoning-online-proctoring-companies-may -finally-be-here.

26. "Respondus Online Exam BIPA $6.25M Class Action Lawsuit Settlement," *Top Class Actions*, June 22, 2023, https://topclassactions.com/lawsuit-settlements/closed -settlements/respondus-online-exam-bipa-6-25m-class-action-lawsuit-settlement/.

27. CISA, "CISA Releases 2023 Year in Review Showcasing Efforts to Protect Critical Infrastructure," press release, Jan. 17, 2024, https://www.cisa.gov/news-events/news/cisa -releases-2023-year-review-showcasing-efforts-protect-critical-infrastructure.

28. Cybersecurity and Infrastructure Security Agency, Facebook, https://www .facebook.com/reel/1926679417848115, accessed Jan. 24, 2025.

29. US Government Accountability Office, "Cybersecurity: DOD Needs to Take Decisive Actions to Improve Cyber Hygiene," GAO-20–241, Apr. 13, 2020, https://www .gao.gov/products/gao-20-241.

30. Federal Trade Commission, "FTC Releases 2023 Privacy and Data Security Update," press release, Mar. 28, 2024, https://www.ftc.gov/news-events/news/press -releases/2024/03/ftc-releases-2023-privacy-data-security-update; Federal Trade Commission, "FTC Amends Safeguards Rule to Require Non-Banking Financial Institutions to Report Data Security Breaches," press release, Oct. 27, 2023, https://www.ftc.gov

/news-events/news/press-releases/2023/10/ftc-amends-safeguards-rule-require-non
-banking-financial-institutions-report-data-security-breaches.

31. UNICEF, "More Than 175,000 Children Go Online for the First Time Every
Day," press release, Feb. 2018, https://www.unicef.org/eap/press-releases/more-175000
-children-go-online-first-time-every-day-tapping-great-opportunities.

CHAPTER 13: CORRECTING THE TILT

1. Author interview with Sarah Mortensen, July 10, 2023.

2. Fandom Forward Campaigns, https://fandomforward.org
/educationlibrarystories.

3. Edha Gupta, "How Book Ban Silencing Led to Finding My Student Voice,"
Medium, Sept. 19, 2023, https://fandomforward.medium.com/how-book-ban-silencing
-led-to-finding-my-student-voice-199e2a9c8f44.

4. "Love Leads :60 | Love Has No Labels – Unlisted," Ad Council, https://c212.net
/c/link/?t=0&l=en&o=3576307-1&h=3194007976&u=https%3A%2F%2Fwww.youtube
.com%2Fwatch%3Fv%3D0MdK8hBkR3s%26list%3DPLdSSKSOSBh4mknah4uWyiZ2ls
lUv_UTSD%26t%3D0s%26index%3D3&a=We+Are+America, accessed Nov. 12, 2024.

5. Nosto, "Ad Council Powers Emmy-Winning #LoveHasNoLabels Campaign
with User-Generated Content," Sept. 12, 2016. https://www.nosto.com/case-studies/ad
-council-love-has-no-labels/.

6. Lisa Sherman, "Lisa Sherman on 'Love Has No Labels' and Beyond," *Ad Age*,
June 19, 2023, https://adage.com/article/creativity/lisa-sherman-love-has-no-labels-and
-beyond/2500426.

7. Instagram, "The 2022 Instagram Trend Report," https://about.instagram.com
/blog/announcements/instagram-trends-2022.

8. Morgan Gerald, "Instagram Activism: Using Slideshows to Promote Social Justice," Action Teaching, https://www.actionteaching.org/award/instagram-activism.

9. *The 2022 Instagram Trend Report*, Dec. 13, 2021, https://about.instagram.com
/blog/announcements/instagram-trends-2022.

10. Shannon Ho and Phil McCausland, "How Instagram Became a Destination for
the Protest Movement," *NBC News*, June 28, 2020, https://www.nbcnews.com/tech/tech
-news/how-instagram-became-destination-protest-movement-n1232342.

11. Terry Nguyen, "How Social Justice Slideshows Took Over Instagram," *Vox*,
Aug. 12, 2020, https://www.vox.com/the-goods/21359098/social-justice-slideshows
-instagram-activism.

12. Richard Dawkins, *The Selfish Gene* (Oxford: Oxford University Press, 1990).

13. Center for Story-Based Strategy, "Top Memes 2020: The Meme-ing of Democracy!" Dec. 21, 2020, https://www.storybasedstrategy.org/blog-full/2020/12/21/top
-memes-2020-the-meme-ing-of-democracy.

14. Sarah Freeman-Woolpert, "Meet the Activist Who Brought the Monopoly Man

Meme to Life," *Waging NonViolence*, Dec. 12, 2018, https://wagingnonviolence.org /2018/12/meet-the-activist-who-brought-the-monopoly-man-meme-to-life/.

15. Harrison Smith, "How an Elaborate Act of Protest Stole the Show on Capitol Hill," *Washington Post*, Jan. 11, 2019, https://www.washingtonpost.com/lifestyle /magazine/monopoly-man-how-an-elaborate-act-of-protest-stole-the-show-on-capitol -hill/2019/01/11/983e73be-0d40-11e9-84fc-d58c33d6c8c7_story.html.

16. Ian Madrigal's X account: https://x.com/iansmadrig.

17. Freeman-Woolpert, "Meet the Activist Who Brought the Monopoly Man Meme to Life."

18. TrashTag, "#TrashTag Starts with You: Over 100 Million Likes…and Counting," trashtag.org, accessed Oct. 8, 2024.

19. TrashTag, "Welcome to the TrashTag Program," nationalcleanupday.org /trashtag, accessed Oct. 8, 2024.

20. Tara Haelle, "Hand Washing Becomes Fun with the #20secondchallenge and #washyourlyrics," *Forbes*, Mar. 16, 2020, https://www.forbes.com/sites/tarahaelle/2020 /03/16/hand-washing-becomes-fun-with-the-20secondchallenge-and-washyourlyrics/.

21. Haelle, "Hand Washing Becomes Fun with the #20secondchallenge and #washyourlyrics."

22. Haelle, "Hand Washing Becomes Fun with the #20secondchallenge and #washyourlyrics."

23. Haelle, "Hand Washing Becomes Fun with the #20secondchallenge and #washyourlyrics."

24. M. J. Raddick, E. E. Prather, and C. S. Wallace, "Galaxy Zoo: Science Content Knowledge of Citizen Scientists," *Public Understanding of Science* 28, no. 6 (2019): 636–51, https://doi.org/10.1177/0963662519840222.

25. People's Contest Digital Archive, Zooniverse, https://www.zooniverse.org /projects/kmc35/peoples-contest-digital-archive/about/research, accessed Jan. 24, 2025.

26. Jessica Bryant, "Students Believe Supporting Social Justice Drives Change," *BestColleges*, Jan. 20, 2022, https://www.bestcolleges.com/research/students-believe -social-justice-drives-change/.

27. For a map of police-training facilities, see "Cop Cities, USA," Is Your Life Better? https://isyourlifebetter.net/cop-cities-usa/, accessed Nov. 19, 2024.

CHAPTER 14: GAMES FOR DEMOCRACY

1. Peter Hunt Szpytek, "2021's Excellent Boss Fights Are Indicators of What's to Come," *GameRant*, Dec. 30, 2021.

2. Simon Parkin, *Death by Video Game: Danger, Pleasure, and Obsession on the Virtual Frontier* (New York: Melville House, 2016).

3. Steven M. Schirra, "Playing for Impact: The Design of Civic Games for Community Engagement and Social Action," master's thesis, MIT, June 2013, available at

https://www.semanticscholar.org/paper/Playing-for-impact-%3A-the-design-of-civic-games-for-Schirra/00744dc9e39821da2735526044351a68534a3c16.

4. Michele Norris, "Online Game Peers into Life in Darfur Refugee Camp," *All Things Considered*, NPR, May 5, 2006, https://www.npr.org/2006/05/05/5386745/online-game-peers-into-life-in-darfur-refugee-camp.

5. Emily Sheepy, "Get Water! Exploring the Adult Player's Experience of a Mobile Game for Change," master's thesis, 2015, Concordia University, https://spectrum.library.concordia.ca/id/eprint/980066/.

6. Legal Design Lab, "Social Justice Game Jam Tickets in Seattle," Feb. 13, 2017, https://www.legaltechdesign.com/2017/02/social-justice-game-jam-tickets-in-seattle/.

7. Justin Tang, "Ten Organizations That Support Diversity in Tech," Candor, July 22, 2021, https://candor.co/articles/immigration-intel/ten-organizations-that-support-diversity-in-tech.

8. Hanna Ziady, "Alexandria Ocasio-Cortez Just Played a Video Game on Twitch to Encourage Voting," CNN Business, Oct. 21, 2020, https://www.cnn.com/2020/10/21/tech/aoc-twitch-account-voting/index.html.

9. Noah Smith, "The Gamer Vote: Democrats Lean into Video Games to Aid Biden Campaign," *Washington Post*, Oct. 22, 2020, https://www.washingtonpost.com/video-games/2020/10/22/video-games-2020-presidential-election-biden-trump/.

10. Author interview with Louisa Hackett, Apr. 2023.

11. Josh Lerner, *Making Democracy Fun: How Game Design Can Empower Citizens and Transform Politics* (Cambridge, MA: MIT Press, 2014).

12. Roblox, "Corporate Overview," https://tinyurl.com/RobloxCorporateOverview, accessed Oct. 8, 2024.

13. Purdue University's degree programs in game development and design, https://polytechnic.purdue.edu/degrees/game-development-and-design.

14. Bruce Gillespie, "Using Digital Storytelling and Game-Based Learning to Increase Student Engagement and Connect Theory with Practice," published in *Teaching & Learning Inquiry* 10 (Apr. 4, 2022), available at https://journalhosting.ucalgary.ca/index.php/TLI/article/view/72707.

15. Creative Child Award Winners, https://awards.creativechild.com/product/4472-the-american-democracy-game%C2%A0, accessed Jan. 24, 2025.

16. National Conference of State Legislatures, "New and Updated NCSL Resources," *The Canvass*, Sept. 2020, https://www.ncsl.org/newsletter/details/the-canvass-september-2020.

17. Nora McGreevy, "Notre Dame Community Creates Space for Play in 'Money Worries,'" *Notre Dame Observer*, Mar. 7, 2018, https://www.ndsmcobserver.com/article/2018/03/money-worries-snite-museum-of-art.

18. *The Social Justice Game*, https://thesocialjusticegame.org/.

19. *The Social Justice Game*.

20. Scott Meslow, "How The Dark Knight Perfected Viral Movie Marketing," Imag-

ine Games Network, July 31, 2020, https://www.ign.com/articles/the-dark-knight-why
-so-serious-viral-movie-marketing-arg.

21. Such websites include argn.com, despoiler.org, wikibruce.com, and unforum
.net. See Rob Lammle, "A Beginner's Guide to Alternate Reality Games," *Mental Floss*,
Jan. 9, 2009, https://www.mentalfloss.com/article/20569/beginners-guide-alternate
-reality-games.

22. Patrick Jagoda's website, Terrarium (alternate reality game), 2019, http://www
.patrickjagoda.com/projects/terrarium.

23. Ellen Wiese, "Alternate Reality Game: A Labyrinth Offers a Model for
New Media in a Distanced Age," June 24, 2020, *U Chicago Arts Blog*, https://www
.uchicagoartsblog.art/archive/2020/5/27/alternate-reality-game-a-labyrinth.

24. American University Project on Civil Discourse, "Activism, Discourse, and
Identity with Amanda Werner," Nov. 16, 2018, available at https://www.youtube.com
/watch?v=JkMT7wZ-nF8.

25. Benjamin Stokes, *Locally Played: Real World Games for Stronger Places and
Communities* (Cambridge, MA: MIT Press, 2020).

26. Jaclyn Greenberg, "This Nonprofit Proves Games' Power to Create Social
Change," *Wired*, Nov. 28, 2022, https://www.wired.com/story/games-for-change-google
-nonprofit-fun-games-social-good/.

27. Max Berry, "Nation States Turns 20," Nov. 12, 2022, https://maxbarry.com/2022
/11/12/news.html.

28. *The Bad News Game* is a social impact game developed in collaboration with
the Dutch media collective DROG and graphic design agency Gusmanson. See https://
www.sdmlab.psychol.cam.ac.uk/research/bad-news-game.

CONCLUSION

1. "Hackers Testifying at the United States Senate," May 19, 1998 (L0pht Heavy
Industries), available at https://www.youtube.com/watch?v=VVJldn_MmMY.

2. US Senate Committee on Commerce, Science and Transportation Sub-Committee
on Consumer Protection, Product Safety, and Data Security, "Statement of Frances
Haugen," Oct. 4, 2021, https://www.commerce.senate.gov/services/files/FC8A558E-824E
-4914-BEDB-3A7B1190BD49.

3. Detroit Community Technology Project, "Stepping into 2024 with Detroit Community Technology Project!" https://detroitcommunitytech.org/?q=content/stepping
-2024-detroit-community-technology-project.

4. Detroit Community Technology Projects, Digital Stewards Program, https://
detroitcommunitytech.org/eii/ds, accessed Oct. 8, 2024.

5. Electronic Frontier Foundation *2021 Annual Report*, https://annualreport.eff.org
/2021/.

6. Introduced by delegates Jared Solomon (D-18) and C. T. Wilson (D-26), along
with Maryland senators Benjamin Kramer (D-19) and Chris West (R-42), the Maryland

Kids Code unanimously passed out of General Assembly on April 6, 2024, and was signed into law by Governor Moore on May 9, 2024.

A USER'S GUIDE FOR THE DIGITAL AGE

1. University of Toronto, "Digital Tattoo: Your Identity Matters. Let's Discuss," https://digitaltattoo.ubc.ca/abouttheproject/, accessed Nov. 19, 2024.

2. Staff Writer, "Social Media Platforms Generate Billions in Annual Ad Revenue from U.S. Youth," Harvard T. H. Chan School of Public Health, Dec. 27, 2023, https://hsph.harvard.edu/news/social-media-platforms-generate-billions-in-annual-ad-revenue-from-u-s-youth/.

3. Rhiannon Williams and Melissa Heikkila, "You Need to Talk to Your Kid About AI. Here Are 6 Things You Should Say," *MIT Technology Review*, Sept. 5, 2023, https://www.technologyreview.com/2023/09/05/1079009/you-need-to-talk-to-your-kid-about-ai-here-are-6-things-you-should-say/.

4. Fake News, Facts, and Alternative Facts Teachout, overview, University of Michigan Online, https://online.umich.edu/teach-outs/fake-news-facts-and-alternative-facts-teach-out/, accessed Jan. 24, 2025.

INDEX

accelerationism, 67

Access Now, 169, 227

ACLU (American Civil Liberties Union), 227

action civics, 159–61

Action Institute for the Study of Religion and Liberty, 54

Activision, 103

activism. *See* social justice activism

Ada Lovelace Institute, 165

Ad Council, 187–88

AdMeld, 81

AdMob, 81

advertising technology, online: ad-revenue sharing, 107; Cambridge Analytica, 87–90; cookies and, 148–49; development of, 79–81, 90–91; Google, 81–84; Interactive Advertising Bureau, 84–85; marketing government propaganda, 86–87

Age-Appropriate Design Code (Maryland), 213

The Age of Surveillance (Donner), 109

AI (artificial intelligence): chatbots, 95–96; commercialization of, 2; hallucinations, 26; hate-speech detection models, 68; interaction tips, 218–20; security and safety software, 117–18; watchdog organizations, 165–66

AI Now Institute, 166, 227

AJL (Algorithmic Justice League), 165–66, 227

Akamai Technologies, 134–35

Albright, Jonathan, 82–83

ALEC (American Legislative Exchange Council). *See* American Legislative Exchange Council (ALEC)

ALEC Attacks, 60

Algorithmic Justice League (AJL), 165–66, 227

algorithms, 5, 18, 82, 87, 92, 100, 102–3, 116, 163–64, 165–66; 177, 219

Allen, Danielle, 10

Alliance Defending Freedom, 60

Allison, Matthew, 67–68

Alphabet, 81–82, 99, 109

Alternate Reality Games (ARGs), 202–4

alternative facts, 20

alt-tech social media platforms, 75–76

Amaral, Peyton, 159, 160

Amazon, 93–94, 103, 113–14

American Civil Liberties Union (ACLU), 227

American Conservative Union, 52–53

American Democracy Game, 201

American Enterprise Institute, 49, 58

American Identity Movement, 75

American Institutions and Civic Knowledge curriculum, 13

American Legislative Exchange Council (ALEC), 50; activities, 57; *ALEC Attacks,* 60; Christian nationalism, 59–60; nationalist policy push of, 57–59; and State Policy Network, 60–61

American Renaissance (magazine), 55

Americans for Prosperity, 51

American Society of News Editors' Canons of Journalism, 28

American Swastika: Inside the White Power Movement's Hidden Spaces of Hate (Simi), 66

America's PAC, 77

Andreesen, Marc, 126

Anonymous Image Board (Anon IB), 167

antiabortion movement, 65, 119–20

anti-plagiarism software, 116

anti-Semitism, 67

Anton, Michael, 53

Apache web server, 125

appeal to authority, 25

Appeal to Heaven flag, 72

Apple: addictive qualities of innovation, 94–95; evolution of, 96–99; monopolistic practices, 93, 103, 105–7; Safari browser, 127, 131; Screen Time, 168; transnational corporate structure, 101

ARGs (Alternate Reality Games), 202–204

Atlas Network, 50, 56–57

authentication and passwords, 152, 183, 223

authoritarianism, 53–54

autocracy, 11, 77–78

autonomy, human, 1

Bad News (game), 205
Banning the Surveillance Advertising Act, 84–85
Bannon, Steve, 88
Baptist Joint Committee, 70
Bark, 117, 118–19
Barry, Max, 205
Be Internet Awesome (Google), 173–74
Beirich, Heidi, 68
Benet, Juan, 133–34
Berger, J. M., 63–64
Bernays, Edward, 20
Berners-Lee, Tim, 130, 134
Betancourt, Gabriel, 154–55
Bezos, Jeff, 138
Biblical Basis for War, 59
Big Tech: accountability, 166–67; addictive
    properties of, 168, 177; AI watchdog orga-
    nizations, 165–66; antitrust actions against,
    103, 105–6; Apple's ecosystem development,
    96–99; autonomy from, and digital literacy,
    102–3; avoiding government oversight and
    regulation, 100–2; bots, 92–93; content
    moderation and fact-checking, 163–65; and
    democracy, 99; digital bill of rights, 107–8;
    Epic Games lawsuits and, 104–5; and GDPR,
    99, 102, 138–40; and law enforcement,
    98–99; monopolistic practices, 211–12;
    normalized surveillance and entertainment,
    114–15; online tracking by, 4; as overlords,
    92; propaganda, 100; social justice activism
    and, 190–92; surveillance activities of, 111;
    user addiction, 93–96; and World Wide Web
    Consortium (W3C), 130–32
biometrics, 145, 178–79
Biometrics Information Privacy Act (BIPA),
    178–79
BIPOC communities, and ALEC-supported
    legislation, 59
Bitchute, 75
Bitcoin, 132
Black, Don, 70
Black, J. Derek, 70
Blackbaud, 177
Black Girls Code, 227
Black Mirror (TV show), 114
Black Sun imagery, 77
Blee, Kathleen, 67
blockchain technologies, 125, 132–33
Bonn, Scott, 86–87
book bans, 186–87
Booker, Cory, 85
"boss battles," 196

bots, 22, 23, 92–93, 95–96, 100, 218–19
Brennan Center for Justice, 50, 55, 227
Brill, Steven, 28–29
Brin, Sergey, 81
browser safety, 221
browser wars, 125–28
Buolamwini, Joy, 165

California Consumer Privacy Act (CCPA),
    141, 148, 157, 213
Call of Duty: Warzone, 73–74
Cambridge Analytica/Facebook scandal,
    87–90, 127
The Camp of the Saints (Raspail), 63
campus activism, 194–95
Capturing the Classroom (Tech Transparency
    Project), 115
Carson v. Makin, 65
Carthage Foundation, 57–58
C/C++, 38
CCA (Citizens' Councils of America), 55–56
CCPA (California Consumer Privacy Act),
    141, 148, 157, 213
CCR (Center for Constitutional Rights), 57, 60
CDN (content delivery networks), 134–35
CDT (Center for Democracy and Technology),
    169, 227–28
Center for American Progress, 50
Center for Applied Special Technology, 227
Center for Civic Education, 227
Center for Constitutional Rights (CCR), 57, 60
Center for Cyber Safety and Education, 227
Center for Democracy and Technology (CDT),
    169, 227–28
Center for Digital Democracy, 228
Center for Humane Technology, 107, 228
Center for Media and Democracy, 60, 228
Center for Media Literacy, 228
Center for News Literacy, 158, 228
Center for Story-Based Strategy, 190
Century Foundation, 50
CFPB (Consumer Financial Protection Bu-
    reau), 121, 228
Charles Martel Society, 77
chatbots, 95–96
Chaum, David, 132
Checkology (News Literacy Project), 156
child-terrorist socialization theory, 69
Chopra, Rohit, 121
Christian nationalism, 59–60. *See also* white
    Christian nationalism
Chromebook (Google), 115–16

church-state separation, 65
circular knowledge economy, 83
Citizen Lab, 228
Citizens' Councils of America (CCA), 55–56
citizenship test requirement, high school, 11
civic engagement: action civics, 159–61; in
    digital age, 226; internet and, 3, 4; tips for,
    226; voter turnout, US, 2, 12–13
civics and civics education: American Institu-
    tions and Civic Knowledge curriculum,
    13; college-level programs, 12–13; *Cook
    v. McKee*, 16–17; current state of, 9–10,
    12–13; Estonia, 154–55; Finland, 17–19;
    global assessment of, 13–14; history of,
    10–11; iCivics, 161–62; importance of, 2,
    6; military "citizenship programs," 14–16;
    misconceptions about, 153–54; NAEP civics
    proficiency results, 9, 13, 14; project-based
    focus, 159–61
Civics Jeopardy, 199–200
Civics Secures Democracy Act, 162
Claremont Institute, 53, 55
classrooms, mass surveillance and, 115–17
Clean Trails, 192
climate change legislation, 59
Clinton, Bill, 58
Close Up Foundation, 228
cloud computing, 93, 99, 135–36
COBOL, 41
Cochling, Eric, 56
Code.org, 172, 228
Cohen, David, 85
college campuses, 75, 77, 194–95
Collett, Mark, 74
Colonacosta, Gino, 112
Common Sense Media, 171, 228
"communists," 72
Community Votes, 199
Confronting Tech Power (AI Now Institute), 166
conservative mega think tanks: American Leg-
    islative Exchange Council (ALEC), 57–61;
    antidemocratic online presence, 54–55; de-
    velopment of, 49–51; language and rhetoric
    of, 55–56; nonprofit status, 61–62; propa-
    ganda of, 52–54; tax status of, 51–52
Conservative Political Action Conference
    (CPAC), 52–53, 77
Consortium News, 29, 168
Consortium of Cybersecurity Clinics, 43, 173
conspiracy theories, 3, 5, 24–26, 53, 67, 72, 74,
    76; prevalence on internet, 3; rhetoric of,
    25–26

consumer culture, 90–91
Consumer Data Protection Act (Virginia),
    213
Consumer Financial Protection Bureau
    (CFPB), 121, 228
Consumer Privacy Act (California) (CCPA),
    141, 148, 152, 157, 213
content delivery networks (CDN), 134–35
Conway, Kellyanne, 20
Cook, Aleita, 16–17
Cook, Tim, 138
cookies, 80, 102, 146–49, 221
Cook v. McKee, 16–17
Copeland, David, 64
Corin, Jaclyn, 24
corporate interests and legislation, 59
corporate sector digital hygiene, 37–40
Çoruh, Cankız, 154–55
Costales, Yvonne, 35–36
CoTech, 212
Council for Secular Humanism, 50
Council of Conservative Citizens (CofCC),
    55–56
Coursera, 156
Court Quest (iCivics), 162
CPAC (Conservative Political Action Confer-
    ence), 52–53, 77
critical race theory, 67
critical thinking skills, 4, 10, 11–12, 18, 30, 153,
    158, 182, 202, 204, 224–25, 228
Crossroads GPS, 51
Crovitz, Gordon, 28–29
crowdsourcing, 193–94
CrowdStrike, 38
Crypto Anarchist Manifesto (May), 5
cryptography technologies, 5–6
"crypto parties," 223
CSS, 130
culture wars, 71
CustomView, 79
cyberattacks, 2
cyber hygiene, 2, 6, 169; authentication and
    passwords, 152, 183, 223; basic practices,
    182–84; citizens' roles and responsibilities,
    181–82; cybersecurity clinics, 172–74; data
    protection, 183; device protection, 182–83;
    education initiatives, 171–72, 181–82; E-
    Rate program, 170; federal regulatory agen-
    cies, 179–81; legal action regarding, 177–79;
    librarians' role, 170–71; secure connections,
    183; sharing information, 183–84; whistle-
    blowers, 174–77

Cybersecurity and Infrastructure Security Agency (CISA), 43,179–80
cybersecurity clinics, 172–74
Cybersecurity Clinics Grant Program Act, 173
cybersecurity hygiene. *See* digital hygiene
Cypherpunks, 5

The Daily Stormer, 67
Darby, Seyward, 63
Darfur is Dying (game), 197–98
dark money, 51–52
data analytics, 4
data-breach 32–33, 38–39, 43–44, 88, 133, 138–39, 143–45, 178–79, 181, 191
data-broker industry, 121
data protection, 2, 99, 183
Data Protection Directive (1994) (EU), 139
data-protection impact assessments (DPIAs), 145–46
data smog, 4–5
Data & Society, 228
data storage, 133–35
Davenport, David, 160
Dawkins, Richard, 189–90
DCTC (Detroit Community Technology Company), 211–12, 229
Death by Video Game: Danger, Pleasure, and Obsession on the Virtual Frontline (Parkin), 196–97
Decker, Matthew, 176–77
deepfakes, 26–27, 162–64
DEEPFAKES Accountability Act (2018), 27
demagogues, 20
democracy: antidemocratic online entities, 54–55; antidemocratic rhetoric and propaganda, 53; attitudes toward, 11; Big Tech and, 99; Cambridge Analytica's threat to, 87–90; conservative think tanks and attacks on, 49–54; cyber citizenship to save, 2; democracy games, 199–202; white supremacy groups and, 53
demonization of opponents, 25
Department of Defense, 29, 41, 99, 129, 156, 179, 180
Department of Homeland Security, 39, 112
Detroit Community Technology Company (DCTC), 211–12, 229
device protection, 182–83
DigiCash, 132–33
digital bill of rights, 107
Digital Citizenship Curriculum (Common Sense), 171

digital creativity, 225
digital hygiene, 2, 6; corporate sector, 37–40; defined, 34; digital nativity myth, 44–45; elder scamming, 36–37; government agencies, 40–42; identity theft and fraud, 34–35; importance of, 32–33; Microsoft and government IT systems, 42–43; school districts, 43–44
digital inclusion, 128, 225
digital literacy: autonomy from Big Tech, 102–3; case study (2020 election), 22–23; case study (mass school shootings), 23–24; corporate-based media literacy movements, 156; defined, 21; detecting white hate groups and rhetoric, 76–78; education, 29–31, 158–59, 212–14; Estonia's example, 154–55; group-led movements, 211–12; hallucinating and deepfakes, 26–27; importance of, 2, 4–5, 6, 20; and mass surveillance, 120–22; media literacy education in schools, 158–59; modern Paul Reveres, 209–11; need for, 21–22; news media and, 28–29; and rebranded hate speech, 70–71; regulation revolution, 213–14; rhetoric of conspiracies, 25–26; source research, 167–68; in the US, 155–57; white nationalistic ideologies and, 52. *See also* User's Guide for Digital Age
digital nativity myth, 44–45
Digital Public Library of America, 229
Digital Responsibility, 229
digital rights management (DRM), 96–97
"Digital Tattoo," 215–16
Discord, 67, 74
discrimination, software biases and, 116–17
disinformation campaigns, 18, 164–65; 2020 election, 22–23
diversity, 14, 16, 53, 60, 71,78, 187–88, 199
Dobbs v. Jackson Women's Health Organization, 65
"dog whistles," 56, 66
Donner, Frank, 109
dopamine, 5
DoubleClick, 80, 81
Dovi, Suzanne, 13
DPIAs (data-protection impact assessments), 145–46
DRM (digital rights management), 96–97
Duke, David, 64

Economic Policy Institute, 50
edge computing, 134–36

education, civics. *See* civics and civics education

education, digital literacy, 29–31, 158–59, 212–13, 224

EFF (Electronic Frontier Foundation), 169, 212, 229

elder scamming, 36–37

e-learning software, 116–17

election interference (2020), 22–23

Electronic Frontier Foundation (EFF), 169, 212, 229

Elementary and Secondary Education Act (1965), 10

encryption, 183, 221–22

end-to-end encryption (E2EE), 150

Enemy of the State (film), 114

Enspiral, 212

entertainment media, mass surveillance in, 114–15

Epic Games, 102, 104–5, 107

Equifax breach, 39

Equitable Internet Initiative, 212

E-Rate program, 170

e-residency, 154–55

Erspamer, Daniel, 56

Estonia, 154–55, 213

European Union General Data Protection Regulation (GDPR), 99, 102, 138–40, 142, 144, 146–47, 149–50, 213

EU-US Data Privacy Framework, 144

evangelical Christian activism, 57–58

Evangelicals for Democracy, 64

exaggeration, 25

Experian breach, 39

Exploring Legal Mechanisms for Data Stewardship (Ada Lovelace Institute), 165

extremism. *See* white Christian nationalism

Facebook, 75, 151; and Cambridge Analytica scandal, 89–90; surveillance activities, 111

"face-swapped pornography," 27

facial recognition technologies, 143, 165–66

fact-checking, 19, 163–65

FairPlay, 96–97, 229

fake news, 4–5, 18–19, 24, 44, 72, 168, 224

Faktabaari (Fact Bar), 19

family activities, in digital age, 217–18

Family Research Council, 60

Fandom Forward, 185–87

fandoms, 185–87

far-right extremism. *See* white Christian nationalism

fear and paranoia, 25

Federal Information Security Management Act (2002), 140

federal regulation, cyber hygiene, 179–81

Federal Trade Commission (FTC), 180–81

Feinberg, Ashley, 67

Feuerkrieg Division, 74

Fight for the Future, 113, 229

Fight to Freedom (game), 204

Finchem, Mark, 57

Finland civics and civics education, 17–19, 213

Firefox, 127–28, 148

"The Flight 93 Election" (Anton), 53

FLOSS (Free and Open Source Software), 222

Fortran, 41

4chan, 63, 66, 73

Fourth Amendment, US Constitution, 112, 178

Free and Open Source Software (FLOSS), 222

"free" apps and games, 222

Freedom Forward, 229

Freedom Worldwide with Tom G. Palmer: Helping Americans Free Themselves from Welfare (video), 56

free-market ideology, 56–57

FTC (Federal Trade Commission), 37, 43, 89, 103, 180–81

Future of Privacy Forum, 229

Gab, 75, 76

Gaggle, 117–18

Galaxy Zoo, 193–94

Games for Change (G4C), 204–5, 207, 229

gaming, 196–97; Alternate Reality Games, 202–4; casual games, 197–99; creating a family game, 205–6; democracy games, 199–202; game design, 200–201; Games for Change, 204–5, 207; hate on platforms, 73–75; surveillance and, 114–15

Gateway Pundit, 24

"Gender Shades" project, 165

Gendron, Peyton, 74

General Data Protection Regulation (GDPR) (EU), 99, 102, 138–40, 142, 144, 146–47, 149–50, 213

Generation Citizen, 159–60, 229

Geneva Center for Security Policy, 69

"geofence" data, 120–22

Georgetown Law School, Center for Privacy and Technology, 229–30

Georgia Center for Opportunity, 56

Germany, 212, 213
Get Water! (game), 198
Gill, Nicole, 85
Gilster, Phil, 4–5
Girls Who Code, 172, 230
Global Privacy Control (GPC), 141–43
Global Project Against Hate and Extremism, 68
Gnosis IQ, 117
GoGuardian, 117
Goldberg, Carrie, 166–67
Goldwater Institute, 56, 61
Gonigam, William, 178–79
Gonzalez, Emma, 24
Google, 81–84, 93; antitrust issues, 103, 104–5; and Apple collusion, 106–7; Be Internet Awesome program, 173–74; Chrome, 127, 131, 148; Classroom, 115–16, 117; Digital Wellbeing, 168; lobbying, 101–2; privacy issues and surveillance, 120; Privacy Sandbox, 148; Project Dragonfly, 191–92; surveillance activities, 111

Goyim Defense League, 55
GPC (Global Privacy Control), 141–43
Gramm-Leach-Bliley Act (1999), 140
Grand Theft Auto V (video game), 114–15
grooming, online, 69–70
Gupta, Edha, 187

Hackett, Louisa, 199–200
hallucinations (AI), 26
Harris, Tristan, 107
Harrison, Randal, 202
Harrison, Shane, 24
hate group tactics and symbology, 220
hate speech, 55, 67; alt-tech social media platforms, 75–76; conspiracy theories, 72–73; on gaming platforms, 73–75; Google's role, 82–83; hyperbole, 72; rebranding, 70–71; repackaging racism, 76–78; tech companies monitoring, 68–70; victimization and "the other," 71–72; violence justification, 73. *See also* white Christian nationalism
Haugen, Frances, 211
healthcare applications, 136
Health Insurance Portability and Accountability Act (HIPAA) (1999), 140
Heritage Foundation, 49, 55, 57, 58
HIPAA (Health Insurance Portability and Accountability Act) (1999), 140
Hoffman, Jake, 54
Hogg, David, 24

Hoover Institute, 160
Horgan, John, 69
HTML (hypertext markup language), 130
HTTP (hypertext transfer protocol), 131
Humber, Dallas, 67–68
Hussain, Ahmed Hafeez, 162–63
hyperbole, 67, 72

IAB (Interactive Advertising Bureau), 84–85
ICBM missile systems, 40–41, 43
ICCE (International Civic and Citizenship Education) study, 13–14
iCivics, 161–62, 230
Identity Evropa, 75
identity theft, 1, 27, 34–35, 178, 181, 184
iKeepSafe, 230
Illinois Policy Institute, 61
inclusion, 53
information literacy, 18–19, 20, 30, 156–57; teenagers and, 44. *See also* digital literacy
information overload, 4–5, 20
Information Technology and Innovation Foundation (ITIF), 144
InfoWars, 24
Instagram, 18, 44, 54, 94, 118, 151, 163, 177, 183, 188–89
Interactive Advertising Bureau (IAB), 84–85
Interland, 174
internally caused security incidents, 32–33
International Association of Privacy Professionals, 230
International Civic and Citizenship Education (ICCE) study, 13–14
International Fact-Checking Network, 164
internet: corporate entertainment platforms, 4; as mechanism for mass control, 3–4; media literacy education and, 158–59; conspiracy theories on, 3
Internet Explorer (IE), 127
Internet of Things, 134, 135; digital hygiene and, 34; vulnerability of, 33
Internet Research Agency (IRA), 22–23
Internet Society, 230
InterPlanetary File System (IPFS), 133–34
An Introduction to Global Awareness (textbook), 15
Invite Media, 81
IPFS (InterPlanetary File System), 133–34
iPhone, 3, 85–6, 93, 96–99, 106, 210. *See also* smartphones
IRA (Internet Research Agency), 22–23
Iraq War marketing and propaganda, 86–87

Isaacson, Walter, 136
Islamophobia, 109
Itch.io, 198
ITIF (Information Technology and Innovation
Foundation), 144
iTunes Music Store, 96–97

Jahnkow, Rick, 15, 16
January 6, 2021 US Capitol insurrection, 23,
53, 57, 63
Janus v. AFSCME, 61
JavaScript, 130
JEDI (Joint Enterprise Defense Infrastructure)
cloud-computing project, 99
Jenkins, Daryle Lamont, 76–77
Jennings, Arielle, 159–60
Jewett, Steve, 192
Jim Crow laws, 60
Joe Foss Institute, 11, 15
"joggers," 74
Joint Enterprise Defense Infrastructure (JEDI)
cloud-computing project, 99
Jones, Alex, 24
journalism standards, 28–29
JROTC (Junior Reserve Officer Training
Corps) programs, 14–16
Junior Reserve Officer Training Corps
(JROTC) programs, 14–16

Kasky, Cameron, 24
Kelly, Benjamin, 24
Kennedy, Brian, 53
Kennicott, Philip, 110
Kern, Anthony, 57
Kesler, Charles, 53
Kid's Stormfront, 70
KindaFunnyGames, 199
Kivinen, Kari, 18
Koch, Charles, 57
Kohlenberg, Andrea, 178–79
Kotch, Alex, 77
Krebs, Chris, 33

L0pht, 175, 210–11
Landlord Game, 202
Law and Disorder (radio show), 6
law enforcement, Big Tech and, 98–99, 119–20
"Leaderless Resistance," 65
*Leadership and Ethics Naval Science 4 Selected
Readings for NJROTC students* (textbook),
15–16
Leadership Education and Training (textbook), 15

Leadership Institute, 77
Lerner, Josh A., 200
LFP (Library Freedom Project), 171, 230
liberal rhetoric, 71
liberal think tanks, 50
libertarian rhetoric, 71
Liberty Justice Center, 61
librarians, and cyber hygiene, 170–71
Library Freedom Project (LFP), 171, 230
lifelong technology learning and practice, 224–25
Lightspeed, 117
Limbaugh, Rush, 53
Linux operating system, 125, 128–29
litigation, and cyber hygiene, 177–79
Little, Mike, 129–30
lobbying, 58, 84–85, 101
*Locally Played: Real World Games for Stronger
Places and Communities* (Stokes), 204
location data, 120–22
Love Has No Labels campaign, 188
Lumen app, 121

Mackey, Douglas, 87–88
Macrina, Alison, 171
Madrigal, Ian, 191–92
Make America Great Again, 52–53
*Making Democracy Fun: How Game Design
Can Empower Citizens and Transform Politics* (Lerner), 200
Making Sense of the News (Coursera), 156
*Mandate for Leadership: Policy Management
in a Conservative Administration* (Heritage
Foundation), 49
mandatory minimum sentencing laws, 59
Marjory Stoneman Douglas High School
shooting, 24
marketing: access to youth audiences, 216–17;
advent and transformation of online, 79–80,
96–97; ARGs used for, 202–3; cookies, 80,
102, 146–49, 221; government oversight and
regulation, 100–2; of government propaganda, 86–87, 100; Interactive Advertising
Bureau and lobbying, 85; Turning Point
USA, 54; user addiction and, 93–96; viral
marketing strategies, 187–88. *See also* advertising technology, online
Markey, Ed, 113, 117
Maryland, 213
mass surveillance, 3, 109; digital illiteracy and,
120–22; neighborhood watch, 112–14; 9/11
Museum & Memorial and implementation
of, 109–12; normalization in classrooms,

115–17; normalization in entertainment, 114–15; security and safety claims, 117–19; targeting women, 119–20. *See also* privacy
Mastodon, 151–52
May, Tim, 5
McAndrew, Chuck, 171
McVeigh, Timothy, 63–64
media: news media legitimacy, 28–29; partisan media and think tanks, 49–50
The Media and Me, 155–56
The Media and Me (Roth), 155–56
Media Education Lab, 230
Media Justice, 113
media literacy, 30; corporate-based movements, 156; educating students and teaches, 158–59; source research, 167–68; states legislative efforts, 156–57. *See also* digital literacy
Media Literacy Now, 156–57, 230
mega churches, 50–52, 54
memes, 189–92
memes, extremist, 68–70
memory-related security flaws, 38
Mercer, Robert, 88
Meta, 94, 103, 177; and Cambridge Analytica scandal, 89–90
Metzger, Tom, 66
MeWe, 76
Microsoft, 94, 99, 103; browser wars, 126–28; W3C standards, 131
Microsoft and government IT systems, 42–43
Mikva Challenge, 159, 230
military "citizenship programs," 14–16
Miller, Cassie, 63
Minecraft, 201, 204
Minow, Martha, 17
Morales, Soraida, 35
Moral Majority PAC, 57
Mortenson, Sarah, 185–86
Mosaic, 126
Motherboard, 113
Mozilla Firefox, 127–28
Mozilla Foundation, 230
Mullenweg, Matt, 129–30
Murthy, Vivek, 30
My AI (Snapchat), 95

Nadella, Satya, 138
NAR (New Apostolic Reformation), 72
National Assessment of Educational Progress civics proficiency results, 9, 13, 14

National Association of Media Literacy Educators, 157
National Association of Scholars, 160
National Center of Academic Excellence in Information Assurance/Cybersecurity, 172
National CleanUp Day, 192–93
nationalism, 11; ALEC's policy push, 57–59; Christian nationalism, 59–60. *See also* white Christian nationalism
National Policy Institute (NPI), 51–52, 77
National Right to Work Legal Defense Foundation, 61
National Security Alliance Initiative, 231
NationStates (game), 205
neighborhood watch, 112–14
Neighbors app, 112–13
Nelson, Lisa, 57
neoliberal ideology, 56–57
Nest (Google), 113
net neutrality, 211
Netscape Communications Corporation, 126–28
New America's Open Technology Institute (OTI), 230–31
New Apostolic Reformation (NAR), 72
New Century Foundation, 55
Newell, Gabe, 74
New Jersey, 156–57
NewsGuard, 28–29, 168
News Literacy Project, 156
news media legitimacy, 28–29
New York, 167
New Zealand, 212
Nguyen, Terry, 189
9/11 attacks, 2–3
9/11 Memorial & Museum, 109–10
Nobel Peace Center, 204
Nobody's Victim: Fighting Psychos, Stalkers, Pervs, and Trolls (Goldberg), 167
No Child Left Behind (2001), 10
#NoMoreExcuses, 195
nonprofit tax status, think tanks, 51–52, 61–62
notifications, 5
NPI (National Policy Institute), 51–52, 77
Nuffield Foundation, 165

Obama, Barack, 10, 22, 41, 39, 64
obedience to authority, 12
Ocasio-Cortez, Alexandria, 199
O'Connor, Linda, 30
O'Connor, Sandra Day, 161–62

Odysee, 75
Office for Targeted Violence and Terrorism Prevention (DHS), 74–75
Ogletree, Aaron, 178
Oldsmar water treatment incident, 32–33
Omidyar, Pierre, 212
Omidyar Network, 212
One People's Project, 76–77
Open Source Initiative (OSI), 128–29
open-source, 125, 128–31, 136, 150, 200, 225, 230–31
opinion silos, 5
opinion *versus* fact, 21
OptMeowt, 142
OSI (Open Source Initiative), 128–29
"The Other," 71–72
OTI (New America's Open Technology Institute), 230–31
Ozkale, Samet, 154–55

Page, Larry, 81
Palmer, Tom G., 56
Parkin, Simon, 196–97
Parkland school shooting, 24, 118–19
Parler, 75, 76
password-manager tools, 152, 217, 223
passwords, 32, 34–35, 37, 39, 152, 183, 222–23, 172, 174, 179, 181–82
Patel, Purvi, 120
Patriot Front, 74, 77
Patriotic Alternative, 74
Patriotism: symbols, 100, teaching, 11, 12–15, 3, 10, 29, 55, 61, 72–73
Pelican Institute for Public Policy, 56
Pelosi, Nancy, 27
Penn State Applied Research Lab, 176–77
People's Contest, 194
"Pepe the Frog" meme, 69
Perens, Bruce, 128
"persecution," 71
personal information sharing, 183–84
Phelps-Roper, Megan, 70
Picciolini, Christian, 69–70
Pichai, Sundar, 138, 190
Pigliucci, Massimo, 55
plagiarism detection software, 116
Plessy v. Ferguson, 60
political parties, 2, 16
PolitiFact.com, 164
"PowerPoint Activism," 189

The Power Worshippers: Inside the Dangerous Rise of Religious Nationalism (Stewart), 53
privacy: Apple's policy and ecosystem, 96–98; Big Tech and, 111, 138; biometrics data, 178–79; cookies, 80, 102, 146–49; cryptography technologies, 5–6; data-broker industry, 121; data-protection impact assessments, 145–46; EU-US Data Privacy Framework, 144; General Data Protection Regulation (GDPR) (EU), 99, 102, 138–40, 142, 144, 146–47, 149–50; Global Privacy Control, 141–43; Library Freedom Project (LFP), 171; online monitoring practices, 177–78; privacy-enhancing technologies (PETs), 146; privacy-focused tools and apps, 222–23; smart devices and, 1; tools and strategy adoption, 152; trust tokens, 149; US legislation and policy, 140–41, 144; women targeted for surveillance, 119–20. *See also* mass surveillance
Privacy Act (1974), 140
Privacy Act (Colorado), 213
Privacy International, 231
proctoring tools, 116
ProctorU, 178–79
Project Censored, 155–56, 168, 231
Project on Youth and Non-Military Opportunities (Project YANO), 15
propaganda: 15, 18, 21–22, 28–29, 52, 68, 75, 82, 86–87, 100, 110, 114, 209
prosperity theology, 50–51
Proud Boys, 64
PSAs (public service announcements), 179,187–88
pseudoscientific jargon, 25
Public Knowledge, 231
public relations, 20
public service announcements (PSAs), 187–88
public Wi-Fi networks, 183

racism, 10, 67–70, 76–78, 188
radical white extremism. *See* white Christian nationalism
Raising Them Right: The Untold Story of America's Ultraconservative Youth Movement and Its Plot for Power (Spencer), 54
Raymond, Eric S., 128
Rebell, Michael, 17
Reconstructing After Natural Disasters (game), 205
regimentation of thought, 14–16

regulatory capture, 101
religious nationalism, 53
remote-access software, 32
Renfrey, Dominic, 57, 58
Respondus, 116, 179
revenge porn, 18, 26–27, 167
Revere, Paul, 209–10
Rhode Island, 16, 17, 159–60, 230
Right Moves: The Conservative Think Tank in American Political Culture Since 1945 (Stahl), 49
Ring (Amazon), 112–13
Ring Nation (TV show), 113–14
RINOs, 71
Robinson, Ron, 77
Roblox, 73–74, 200
Rochko, Eugen, 151
Roth, Andy Lee, 155–56, 168
Rothenberg, Randall, 85
Ruiz, Susan, 197–98
Rumble, 76
Russian election interference, 22–23

sabotage, 32
Safari, 127, 148
Sandefur, Christina, 56
Sandy Hook Elementary School shooting, 24
Sarah Scaife Foundation, 58
Satoshi Nakamoto, 132
Scaife, Richard, 57–58
schools: curricula, 10; DPIAs in, 145–46; mass surveillance normalization in, 115–17; school districts digital hygiene, 43–44
Schools and Libraries Program of the Universal Service Fund, 170
Schwedelson, Jay, 80
Scott, Tony, 41
search engine bundling, 106–7
Secure by Design (CISA), 180
secure connections, 183
Securly, 117, 118
segregation, 60
selective evidence, 25
sensationalism, 25
September 11, 2001 attacks, 2–3, 109–12
Seraw, Mulugeta, 66
Sesay, Musah Mohammed, 16–17
Shea, Matt, 59–60
"sheeple," 71
Sheets, Dutch, 72
Signal Foundation, 231
Signal messaging app, 150–51

Simi, Pete, 66–67
Sisters in Hate (Darby), 63
Slack, Andrew, 186
Slayton, Savannah, 160
Slow Factory, 189
smart grids, 136
smartphones: addiction issues, 95, 97, 107–8; digital hygiene and, 34, 179, 223; digital nativity and, 44–45; information overload and, 4; integrated with Big Tech product lines, 93, 106; Linux and, 129; location data, 120; privacy issues, 98–99, 120–21, 133, 147, 150–51; surveillance and, 3, 110. *See also* iPhone
Snapchat, 18, 44, 95
Snopes, 163–64
Snowden, Edward, 111, 150, 181, 210–11
"snowflakes," 71
Social Catfish, 36
social control and containment, 109
social justice activism: Ad Council, 187–88; campus activism, 194–95; crowdsourcing, 193–94; Fandom Forward, 185–87; gaming, 197–205; Instagram and TikTok, 188–89; memes, 189–92; social media campaigns, 189–93
Social Justice Game, 202
Social justice games, 229
Social Justice Game Jam, 198–99
social media: alt-tech platforms, 75–76; campus activism, 194–95; disinformation and election interference, 22–23; far-right extremism on, 67–68; impact on youth and mental health, 30; media literacy education and, 158–59; misinformation and disinformation, 4, 18–19; social justice activism on, 188–93; tech companies hate speech monitoring, 68–70; teenager nativity, 44
Solar Winds, 42
Soltani, Ashkan, 141
Sons of Liberty, 209–10
source research, 167–68
Southern Poverty Law Center, 55, 60, 63
Spencer, Kyle, 54
Spencer, Richard, 51–52, 77
Stahl, Jason, 49
standardized testing as social control, 11–12
Standing Rock protests, 59
"Stand Your Ground" laws, 59
State and Local Cybersecurity Improvement Act, 172
state-level lobbying and legislation, 58–59

State Policy Network (SPN), 50, 60–61
Stay Safe Online, 231
Steam, 74
STEM education, 10, 12
Stewart, Katherine, 53
Stillman College cyberattack, 43
Stokes, Benjamin, 204
StopBullying.gov, 231
#StopCopCity, 195
Stop the Steal, 75, 76
"Stop the Steal" rhetoric, 55, 57
Stormfront, 63, 66, 70
Students Allied for Freedom, 195
subversive exposure, 66
Super Chats (YouTube), 69
surveillance. See mass surveillance
Surveillance Technology Oversight Project, 231

Taylor, James B., 77
Taylor, Jared, 55
TechGirlz, 231
Technogiestiftung, 212
Telegram, 63, 67–68, 75, 151
Terrarium (game), 203
Terrorgram Collective, 67–68
Texas Public Policy Forum, 160
Thakkar, Rutvik, 178–79
think tanks, conservative mega: American Legislative Exchange Council (ALEC), 57–61; antidemocratic online presence, 54–55; development of, 49–51; language and rhetoric of, 55–56; nonprofit status, 61–62; propaganda of, 52–54; tax status of, 51–52
Thin Thread (NSA counterterrorism program), 111
third-party cookies, 148–49
"three strikes" laws, 59
"Tiger Leap" program (Estonia), 154–55
TikTok, 44, 54, 75, 164, 189
Time Well Spent movement, 107
Tor browser, 171, 223
Torvalds, Linus, 129
Trailblazer (NSA counterterrorism program), 111
#TrashTag, 192–93
troll farms, 22–23
Trump, Donald, 23, 52, 53–54, 72, 76, 88, 99, 191, 211
trust tokens, 149
truth decay, 20

The Turner Diaries (Pierce), 63–64
Turning Point USA, 22, 54, 57, 75, 77
TurnItIn (software), 116
Twitter. See X (formerly Twitter)

Twitter bots, 23
Tyler, Amanda, 70

Underground Railroad: Journey to Freedom (game), 204
UNICEF, 173, 181
United Kingdom, 212
United Nations Office of Counter-Terrorism, 74
Unite the Right rally (Charlottesville), 66–67
University of South Florida, 172
Unlawful Dissemination or Publication of an Intimate Image law (New York), 167
USA PATRIOT Act, 3, 111–12
US Cyber Defense Agency, 129
User's Guide for Digital Age: AI interaction tips, 218–20; browser safety, 221; civic participation, 226; cookies, 221; critical-thinking skills, 225; "crypto parties," 223; digital creativity, 225; digital inclusion, 225; digital literacy education and improvement, 224; "Digital Tattoo," 215–16; encryption, 221–22; family activities, 217–18; FLOSS (Free and Open Source Software), 222; "free" apps and games, 222; hate group tactics and symbology, 220; lifelong technology learning and practice, 224–25; marketing issues, 216–17; passwords, 223; privacy-focused tools and apps, 222–23; resources, 216; support and aid seeking, 225
us vs. them mentality, 26

Vakian, Michael, 115–17
Valve Corporation, 74
Vaughn, Ricky, 88
Veasey, Mark, 173
vendor lock, 42–43
Veterans Inspiring Patriotism program (Joe Foss Institute), 11, 15
victimization and "the other," 71–72
video games. See gaming
violence justification, 73
violent extremism. See white Christian nationalism
VK, 75
Voat, 75
Voatz app, 133
voting: ICCE study and, 14; restrictive voting

laws, 55; US voter turnout, 2, 12–13; voter-ID bills, 59

War on Terror, 86, 109
Warren, Elizabeth, 117
Warren AFB, 40
Wash Your Lyrics, 193
Watch Dogs (video game), 115
WebConnect, 79, 80
web forms, 5
Weinstein, Mark, 76
Werner, Amanda, 191–92
Westboro Baptist Church, 70
We the People: The Citizen and the Constitution, 231
Weyrich, Paul, 57
WhatsApp, 18, 94, 150–51
whistleblowers, 25, 88, 111, 122, 169, 174–77, 210–11
White Aryan Resistance, 66
white Christian nationalism: alt-tech social media platforms, 75–76; books and influence, 63–64; on college campuses, 75; hate speech on gaming platforms, 73–75; hyperbole, conspiracy theories, and violence justification, 72–73; ideology of, 64–65; legal and political impact of, 65; normalization and mainstream adoption, 66–68; rebranding hate, 70–71, 76–78; recruiting online through memes and games, 68–70; repackaging racism, 76–78; resilience and adaptability of, 65–66; technological acceleration of spread, 66; think tanks and organizations, 51–61; victimization themes, 71–72

Widner, Bryon, 76
Wikipedia, 30
Willoughby, Bill, 192
"woke," 22, 71,
women, targeting, mass surveillance, 119–20
WordPress, 129–30
World Wide Web Consortium (W3C), 125, 130–32, 231
Wyden, Ron, 120
Wylie, Christopher, 88

X (formerly Twitter): anti-democratic campaigns on, 54, 87–88; disinformation campaigns on, 3, 164–65; extremist recruiting via, 70; national security threats posed by, 174–75, 210; propaganda campaigns on, 52–53; racist rhetoric on, 67

Yahn, Zachary, 162–63
Young America's Foundation (YAF), 77

YouTube, 82; algorithmic targeting on, 18, 219; antidemocratic campaigns on, 54; cookies and, 148; deepfake detection on, 163; disinformation and fact-checking, 164; extremist advertising on, 82–83; Super Chats, 69; youth audience targeting, 216

Zatko, Peiter "Mudge," 174–76, 210–11
Zimmeck, Sebastian, 141–42
Zooniverse, 193–94
Zuckerberg, Mark, 138